the
hurt business

oliver mayer's early works

[+] PLUS

a portfolio of plays,
essays, interviews,
souvenirs, ephemera,
and photography

hyperbole books

edited by
William Anthony Nericcio

San Diego Laredo Calexico Tlön London Partanna Uqbar Macondo

The Hurt Business: Oliver Mayer's Early Works [+] Plus is published by Hyperbole Books, an imprint of San Diego State University Press.

Cover Design by Guillermo Nericcio García, Lorenzo Antonio Nericcio & Sophia Alessandra Nericcio; front cover includes photography by Oliver Mayer ("Balder, Beloved Bull Terrier and Friend") and HiMY SYeD ("Everlast Boxing Glove on Magic Carpet" [http://photopia.TYO.ca]).

ISBN: 1-879691-84-1 (pbk.)

Book design by Guillermo Nericcio García
memogr@phics designcasa

San Diego State University Press

San Diego State University Press and Hyperbole Books publications may be purchased for educational, business, or sales promotional use. For information write SDSU Press Next Generation Publishing Initiative (NGPI), San Diego, California 92182-6020

FIRST EDITION PRINTED IN THE UNITED STATES OF AMERICA

A person is a person through
other persons.
Archbishop Desmond Tutu

You're just licking the skin
of the watermelon.
Korean saying

dedicated to
mi Amor,
la perla
mas rara;
mi Mama;
and always,
to the dog

Table of Contents

Oliver Mayer: An Appreciation

Howard Stein

Professor Emeritus, Columbia University
Retired Chair, Hammerstein Theater Studies

Oliver Mayer is not a "message" playwright. One cannot remove sound bytes or one-liners such as "Life should not be written in dollar bills," or "When you talk about this...and you will...be kind," or "Attention must be paid!" and hope to capture the essence of the play or playwright. Mayer is an *experiential* writer, offering his audience a quality experience in the lines of his dramatic population as these people experience the process of growing into the existence of a *human* life.

A *human* life is not an easy accomplishment. It results from a substantial battle (Mayer's most resonant words are fighting and fucking) that exists for all members of the race. To be accomplished is an endless struggle, a fight, moving from one period of development to the next (child, youth, adult, human), through a succession of conflicts, skirmishes, and even battles. The journey is not neat, civil, or pleasant, but instead is very, very messy. The trip, which is embarked upon by *everyone,* is not by any means accomplished by *everybody.*

The human condition: one's self interest in conflict with the interest of another's—parents, siblings, mates, teachers, government, schools or churches—rages from the moment we arise in the morning until we finally lie down in bed at night, and does not subside except in sleep.

The plays in the volume contain experiences of the characters in the playscript that move from childhood (*Young Valiant*) into youthhood (*Bananas and Peachfuzz*) into adulthood *Joy of the Desolate*) and finally into manhood on the way into humanhood (*Blade to the Heat*). Mayer's population is steeped in Latino and Chicano culture, but he does not allow the audience the convenient experience of sentimentalizing or concentrating on the particular dynamics of that specific culture. Instead, that culture—that Hispanic background—permits him to allow his characters to deal with the *human* dilemma rather than simply a cultural one. Mantequilla and Pedro are forced to confront a human problem as well as one that derives from their background. Don Carlos must confront Dan and Holly and HRMF (as well as *Bach!*) despite their cultural differences. Similarly, the tension and the discomfort (as well as pain that emanate from the difference in the parts of Dad, Mama, *and* Boy) in *Young Valiant* conflict with their cultural heritage, but gender and heritage play no greater role in their conflict than do their specific cultural differences.

The passage from child to youth to adult to human is not simply a matter of rites of passage. Latino, an adult, must deal with Latina, a child, just as Mama, an adult, must deal with Boy, who is hurtling into youthland. The crucial condition for Mayer is that neither group of people can ignore the human demands, the human yearnings that erupt into conflict. Mayer honors the conflict (the fight) that emerges in the spirit of the body. But fighting is not just a metaphor in the boxing ring, or in the marriage bed. The reality is that Mayer dramatizes the problem, not the solution. The child and the youth confound the adult with bewilderment, with a body that separates them from their minds, with feelings that are not just emotions but passions. Mayer permits his characters their passion.

Now passion is not the same as emotion. Passion is primitive, animal, with no valence (neither good nor bad), an unrelenting, unyielding force or drive that justifies the cliché, "A stiff prick has no conscience," or as the epigraph to *Portnoy's Complaint* says (in translation), "When the prick is erect, common sense lies buried in the ground." Emotion, on the other hand, is passion filtered through a prudent will, a human talent which permits us to function in our daily lives. One might use both terms, but must know that they are *not* the same.

Latino, Boy, Don Carlos, Pedro, Sarita, Manequilla, Vinal—all the chapters in Mayer's plays—function as if they were shot with Aphrodite's arrow. As tempting as it might be to reduce them to conventional children, boys, girls, men, and women, they transcend the conventional emotional characters that populate most dramas that we read or see today. As for the "fighting" image that pervades Mayer's plays, we are encouraged to associate the root of the word "fuck" with the Latin word *fugare*, to fight—that which causes fighting, that which battles within the adult is real and ever-present and necessary if manhood is to evolve into humanhood.

Mayer's Hispanic population is a great asset for his writing and provides for him the opportunity to put the human dilemma in the minds, bodies, and spirits of an Hispanic culture. Mayer takes muscle, and spirit, and courage from his Latino /Chicano culture, a gift which informs the action of his dramas but which allows his dramaturgy to be closest to contemporary playwrights Sam Shepard and Edward Albee. His characters have a music in their blood that comes from their playwriting creator. Culturally, Mayer is connected to Maria Irene Fornes and Eduardo Machado, but dramatically he is connected to Albee and Shepard, writers who possess an astonishing courage, boldness, and freedom to invent plays that wildly deal with people's passions, animal powers, characters mad with sanity. This population offers the audience not only a reflection of the reality they recognize, but goes beyond the conventional reality—that offering is not just in magical realism or surrealism; it is in the unrelenting passion of the characters, whether a child or an adult, a passion that is primitive, untamed, and unyielding. In today's world of mechanical and technological sophistication, little if any room is available for the animal, the primitive aspect of the human being.

The human battle in these plays is also the struggle to discover one's own voice. In *Blade to the Heat*, Garnet describes the experience of locating his own voice only to have the Boss stomp on it and silence it:

> When I sang that song, the Boss said, "What the fuck is that? Who the hell to you think you are? Josephine Baker? Some piece of French toast? You think we want to hear you? See you? Singing in French? Singing in your own sorry-ass voice? What the fuck is that?" And he fired me!!

Garnet has been an imitator, an imitation, and has leapt to his own manhood with the discovery of his own voice, a leap not sanctioned by the force with whom he is in conflict.

On the other hand, in *Joy of the Desolate*, Holly says to Don Carlos, he who is desperately seeking his own voice:

> Listen Don Carlos. To really sing, let go. I'm not talking wine or sex. I mean inside. Let it out. The reason why you sing. The animal in all its beauty, all its shame.

And by the end of the play, Don Carlos has discovered his voice and explodes with the discovery.

A person's voice is not the same as one's fingerprint. Each fingerprint, like each person's individual voice, is different; in fact, the government claims that one's fingerprint cannot by imitated. One cannot reproduce another's print! One can consider this condition as the uniqueness of each and every human being on the earth. In a similar sense, one's individual voice is equally unique. But the voice differs from the print. The print is imposed upon us, stamped in at birth as our identifying feature. The individual's voice has to be discovered, revealed; it is an expression, an expression of a unique spirit, individual, private print. That discovery is not so easily available (as Don Carlos discovers) as one's fingerprint. The characters in the Mayer canon walk and run that journey to discover their own identity. That discovery comes with a journey, and requires the strength to put aside hiding, to confront the conflicts. From the battles will emerge the voice with which Don Carlos is suddenly blessed. To be blessed like that by a playwright demands a playwright who is *brutally* honest—not cruel but brutal.

Mayer's population is written in the language of the sun. A group of people have been created who confront the most forbidden subjects and actions because their nature propels them to battle. The battle is indeed a fight, a fight to evolve into a genuine human being, a *human* life rather than simply a life.

Mayer is writing at a time of dehumanization and technological sophistication, but his people won't let him off the hook. That population is rooted in human traffic provided by the playwright. His brutal honesty disappoints neither the characters nor the audience.

Oliver Mayer is one of the rare birds writing plays these days about the fierce beauty and truth of the human life, a life that is being smothered and bombarded into oblivion daily, every minute by the society in which Mayer writes. His strength as a playwright is a wonder to behold, and we in his company can return and return to his plays (beginning with *Joe Louis Blues!*) in order to experience the mystery and luxury of being human.

Los Angeles Theater Project Presents

YOUNG VALIANT
a new play by Oliver Mayer

Directed by Jack Rowe
Produced by Calysta Ruth Watson

CAST
Boy, 12 – Chastity Dotson
Dad, 55 – Hansford Prince
Mama, 39 – Marlene Forte

CREW
Production Stage Manager: Jake Epstine
Stage Manager: Joaquin Flores
Set & Lighting Design: Mia Torres
Box Office Coordinator: Oscar Basulto

Program from the L.A. Casa 0101
production of *Young Valiant*.

YOUNG VALIANT

World Premiere performed at
INTAR Hispanic Arts Center, NYC, 2002

Directed by Michael John Garces

DAD	Donald Silva
MAMA	Romi Dias
BOY	Alain Rivas

West Coast Premiere performed at
CASA 0101, Los Angeles, 2005

Directed by Jack Rowe

DAD	Hansford Prince
MAMA	Marlene Forte
BOY	Chastity Dotson

Sergei
Prokofiev
y familia

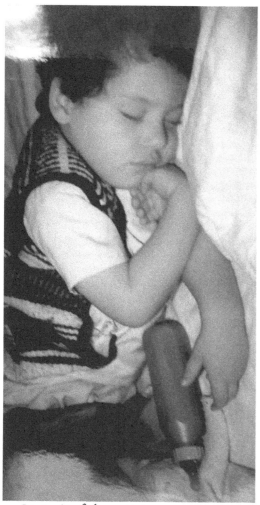

Portrait of the artist as a young man—
Oliver Mayer, age 2.

" . . . the crazy child of parents too
difficult to forget . . . "

anonymous

ACT ONE: SCENE 1

The house in darkness. There is a single light on, a night light on which a painted circus scene revolves. BOY sleeps in the bed by the light. MAMA and DAD are upstairs in bed. Very soft, almost subliminal, we hear the end chords from the Balcony Scene of Prokofiev's Romeo and Juliet. The upstairs bed begins to creak. MAMA laughs. BOY awakens. He sits up listening. Rises. Then the bed creaks again as DAD rises. The sound of his bare feet as he goes downstairs, perhaps his silhouette. DAD opens the refrigerator door. Drone of awakening machinery as the inner light comes on, illuminating DAD naked, his hairy ringletted chest prominent. DAD opens the door part way and removes a bottle from which he drinks. Liquid runs down his chest. BOY approaches cautiously. He wears only an undershirt.

BOY: Dad? (*DAD swings open the refrigerator door, illuminating his face that grins. The liquid grapejuice continues to run down his chest; he makes no attempt to wipe it away.*)

DAD: Boy. (*swigs from the bottle*)

BOY: (*laughing*) Geez! You made a mess!

DAD: Sssh. Mama's sleeping. And don't tell her either. She says use a glass.

BOY: Boy, if she saw you now, she'd give you a good one!

DAD: You know it. (*DAD takes another swig.*)

BOY: You must be thirsty.

DAD: Go back to bed. It's late.

BOY: Then how come you're up?

DAD: Oh . . . the fight's on TV. Them Mexicans are tough sons of guns. (*DAD forages in the refrigerator, finds a stick of pepperoni*)

BOY: Guess it made you hungry, too.

DAD: What did?

BOY: Can I have some?

DAD: Yeah, but only up to here . . . (*measures a portion with his finger*) . . . then bed. You hear me?

BOY: Mmmn. Good.

DAD: That's the truth. (*leans against the refrigerator*) Tell you, Boy—Mama's a beautiful woman.

BOY: Yeah.

DAD: Not a more beautiful woman in the world.

BOY: I know.

DAD: Then don't you forget it. You'll be lucky to find yourself a woman half as beautiful.

BOY: Yeah?

DAD: Damn right.

BOY: Will she laugh, too?

DAD: Who?

BOY: The one that's half as beautiful.

DAD: How do you mean?

BOY: Like what woke me up.

DAD: What did?

BOY: Laughing. Mama, she was laughing—

DAD: Laughing?

BOY: Yeah.

DAD: You were dreaming.

BOY: Nuh-uh. You woke me up.

DAD: Sorry.

BOY: No, I'm glad. (*pause, while DAD eats*)

BOY: Were you making a baby?

DAD: Go to bed.

BOY: Were you?

DAD: What's it to you?

BOY: I hope you were.

DAD: I certainly hope we didn't. Eat your pepperoni and go to bed.

BOY: Bet you did.

DAD: Look, Boy. What the hell would your mother and me want with another boy?

BOY: I don't know.

DAD: Listen, you're a sweet boy, but I'm in love with your mother. We were married six years before we even decided to have a baby, which is you. 'Cause I married her, see? I married your mother so we could be together. I don't want too many people around. Now we got you, and that's good, too. 'Cause you're our boy. But believe me, one boy is enough. (*DAD gives BOY the juice*) Here. Don't worry about it. Don't spill.

BOY: I never spill. Mmmn.

DAD: Good. Now bed. (*he kisses BOY*)

BOY: You oughta wipe yourself.

DAD: I know. I'm gonna get it this time, aren't I?

BOY: You will, unless you wipe yourself.

DAD: Good thinking. (*DAD uses a hand towel to wipe himself*) Thanks, Boy. Now goodnight. (*BOY just stands there*) What?

BOY: Can I sleep with you tonight?

DAD: With me?

BOY: And Mama. Can I?

DAD: What's wrong with your room? Your bed's good, in't it?

BOY: Sure, but—

DAD: No buts. (BOY stands there) But what?

BOY: But I wanna sleep with you.

DAD: How come?

BOY: But it's a lot warmer up there.

DAD: But you take up the bed you're getting so damn big—

BOY: I'll be real skinny.

DAD: And I snore.

BOY: That's okay, I can hear you down here.

DAD: I don't know.

BOY: But . . . what if something happened?

DAD: Like what?

BOY: Something bad. Then I could come up—

DAD: (a little strong) Hey, there's off limits, you know that, Boy. You want me, you yell. That goes for Mama, too. (slight pause) Unless it's something really bad . . .

BOY: Then I could. Right?

DAD: What's the idear, anyway? Spit it out. (slight pause)

BOY: Are you gonna laugh some more tonight?

DAD: She's sleeping.

BOY: Yeah, but are you gonna wake her up?

DAD: Why?

BOY: 'Cause if you are, I wanna see.

DAD: See wha—? (puts it together) Wait, now look here—

BOY: 'Cause I wanna know. You tell me kiss the girls, but they don't laugh, not like Mama. I don't know why, maybe I don't do it right. You told me to call Flory Aguilar my little mamacita. She told everybody and then they started making fun . . .

DAD: Fun of you?

BOY: 'Cause they know what it means . . . and I don't. It's not bad, is it?

DAD: Nah . . .

BOY: Flory acted like it was, and that's when her brother wanted to fight me—

DAD: Oh, yeah? So what'd you do?

BOY: I ran back to the classroom. I waited till he went home.

DAD: That's no good. Next time I don't want you running anywhere.

BOY: But he knows how to fight—

DAD: He a Mexican?

BOY: (glum) Tough son of a gun.

DAD: Your mama's Mexican.

BOY: I know it. Do you call her your little mamacita.

DAD: I think that'd make her angry.

BOY: That's what I figured.

DAD: Anybody makes fun of you, you make 'em pay. You hear me?

BOY: How? (DAD makes a fist)

DAD: Right in the nose. Their eyes get all watery so they can't see straight. And make sure you hit 'em first, too. As hard as you can. No boy of mine is gonna take any stuff, get me? (*BOY nods*) But if it gets bad, go ahead and run.

BOY: But I want to know what it means.

DAD: It?

BOY: 'Cause everybody seems to know. Everybody knows but me. So maybe if I come up you can show me, how you make her laugh at night, or like you do Sunday mornings. Sunday mornings you laugh a lot, both of you, well, sort of.

DAD: How long you know about all this?

BOY: I been afraid to ask you. Till tonight.

DAD: What's so special about tonight?

BOY: Tonight?

DAD: Yeah, tonight. (*BOY smiles to himself*)

BOY: Tonight I think I can. (*pause*)

DAD: I get the feeling you can, too. But don't rush. You'll get it right.

BOY: How 'bout I just look?

DAD: Go to bed. Your own bed, hear me?

BOY: Can I just—?

DAD: Sssh. Here. (*They share a final bite of pepperoni*)

BOY: Mmmn. Dad?

DAD: What?

BOY: When am I gonna be like you?

DAD: Don't be like me. I'm always fighting. Soon as I leave this house, I got to fight. Every day I got to prove myself.

BOY: Do you hit people?

DAD: Sometimes. But you can't hit every-body.

BOY: Is it gonna be like that for me?

DAD: Maybe you'll have it easier. Thank God you got your mama.

BOY: But I want to do what you do . . .

DAD: I hope you do it better.

BOY: Then teach me, Dad. (*slight pause*)

DAD: Teach you . . . what?

BOY: Teach me how to fight.

DAD: We'll see what your Mama says. Now get some sleep.

BOY: Goodnight.

DAD: Goodnight, Boy.

BOY: I won't tell Mama about the grape juice.

DAD: Good.

BOY: Wake me up in the morning.

DAD: Okay, Sweet Boy. (*BOY starts back to bed*) Little advice before you go. Them Mexicans . . .

BOY: Yeah?

DAD: It's worth the fight. If it's love, it's worth it.

BOY: I love Flory.

DAD: Then don't worry.

BOY: Sleep tight, don't let the bedbugs bite—

DAD: If they bite, bite 'em back.

BOY lies back in bed. DAD returns to the refrigerator, a bit tentatively. Closes the door. Darkness. Sound of DAD's heavy tramping. DAD stops as he nears BOY. Then he continues up to bed. *Creaking of the bed as he lies in it. DAD ponders, MAMA sleeping beside him. Then he puts an arm around her, whispering . . .*

DAD: *Mama . . . Mamacita . . . ?*

MAMA: (*in her sleep*) Nuhmm-mmmn . . . (*she fends him off*)

DAD snorts, but doesn't force the issue. Within seconds, both are breathing regularly, in sync. Barely audible, we hear the end chords of Romeo & Juliet.

BOY sits up, listening, transfixed.

Then he lies back and sleeps.

SCENE 2

As the music ends, early morning overtakes the house. Props are kept to a minimum. There is one wall visible, dividing the dining space from the kitchen.

Upstairs, the alarm rings. MAMA and DAD lie entangled beneath a large handmade quilt, and it is with effort that MAMA gets an arm free to shut the alarm off. DAD, who has been snoring, now awakens.

DAD: (*a bit violently*) Time to get up!

MAMA: (*calm*) Relax.

DAD: Show the fuckers.

MAMA: Show them Monday. (*DAD growls as he stretches*)

DAD: What d'you mean?

MAMA: It's Saturday.

DAD: But the clock—

MAMA: Forgot to turn it off last night.

DAD: Yeah, well, we had other things to do. (*slight pause as he relaxes*) I don't got to go to work.

MAMA: I'll put you to work. (*DAD hooks a meaty forearm around MAMA*)

DAD: Fine by me.

MAMA: I could use a bit more sleep.

DAD: Ah, you can sleep anytime.

MAMA: Can't we make love anytime?

DAD: Yeah, sure . . . I could quit work . . .

MAMA: Then we'd never sleep.

DAD: We'd sleep in snatches. (*rubs an unshaven cheek*) Didn't you sleep good?

MAMA: The little I had? (*she stretches*) Yesss. I slept like a stone at the bottom of the sea.

DAD: (*a little anxiously*) Come on, before the boy wakes up . . . (*they kiss*)

MAMA: Your breath.

DAD: My breath? Your breath!

MAMA: Its breath. (*They kiss again. DAD gropes beneath the sheets. MAMA fends him off*) Nope.

DAD: Why not?

MAMA: Aren't you hungry?

DAD: I certainly am.

MAMA: I'll go make some breakfast—

DAD: Later.

MAMA: But we're up.

DAD: Ain't that the truth. (*DAD pulls MAMA on top of him*)

MAMA: You're forgetting something.

DAD: What, the boy? Let him sleep.

MAMA: Not the boy.

DAD: All right, then. Come on, Mama, make me young.

MAMA: It's time to get to work.

DAD: WORK? You just told me it's Saturday—

MAMA: The studios don't pay you weekends. I do.

DAD: Then pay up.

MAMA: First you get to work. (*MAMA takes DAD's face in her hands and strokes his wild hair*) You promised. Knock down that wall in the kitchen, like you said you would. Then you can reach down into my pocket . . . gladly . . . and take as much as you want . . . (*She kisses him lightly*)

DAD: (*petulant*) Geez! How'd you get to be the boss?

MAMA: Nobody says you're not the boss. (*she gets off him*) You've just got some things to do. (*She rises*)

DAD: You know, I may not be around here too much longer—

MAMA: Don't be like that—

DAD: And then you'll be sorry—

MAMA: Don't be like that.

DAD: Like what? Old? Too late, it's me.

MAMA: Do you feel old?

DAD: I can still fuck your brains out, if that's what you mean.

MAMA: That's not what I mean. (*slight pause*) Do you feel old?

DAD: I'm getting there. Especially the weekdays.

MAMA: Well, it's a long way till Monday.

DAD: It's not like I'm planning on going anywhere . . . I mean, I'm not worried . . . (*MAMA gets on top of DAD again*)

MAMA: How old do you feel now?

DAD: You trying to give me a coronary?

MAMA: Just keeping you young.

DAD: Well, you gonna get it.

MAMA: I'm gonna give it . . . later. (*MAMA throws off the covers. Neither is seen completely naked—MAMA has on, or will soon have on, an attractive but plain housedress. DAD should have on BVDs and a dirty white tanktop*) Get up, Big Boy.

DAD: Thanks, Boss.

MAMA: I'll hold the tools for you. I'll be your apprentice. How's that?

DAD: No, I'll get the boy. You learn by doing. (*slight pause*) You gonna make some breakfast at least?

MAMA: I said I would—

DAD: Or do you think I'll work better on an empty stomach?

MAMA: You can lie there if you want to.

DAD: Oh, don't pull that on me—

MAMA: We agreed. Either we work on the house, or we find something bigger.

DAD: We don't have the money to move.

MAMA: Then let's start working. (*She watches him, perplexed, then tries a smile*) How's this. *Chorizo con huevos.*

DAD: (brightening) Yeah?

MAMA: Whatever you want. (as she goes)

DAD: Do you still love me?

MAMA: What?

DAD: I asked you if you loved me anymore?

MAMA: If you have to ask—

DAD: 'Cause I do. Like crazy. Do ya?

MAMA: "Always the beautiful answer who asks the more beautiful question."

DAD: Huh?

MAMA: You're ma husband. (pause) I'll start breakfast. (She starts downstairs)

DAD: Boy wants to learn how to make love.

MAMA: What?

DAD: He told me.

MAMA: You must have misunderstood.

DAD: It was pretty plain.

MAMA: He's too young. Making love? I doubt he even knows what it means.

DAD: He doesn't. That's why he wants to find out.

MAMA: From whom? You, or me?

DAD: Well, he asked me.

MAMA: I bet it was at school. I bet the kids teased him—

DAD: Kids do that—

MAMA: But he shouldn't learn like that. Bunch of snot-nosed ten-year-olds after school. Not like that. He's liable to get it ass-backwards.

DAD: Forget school. He says he hears us at night.

MAMA: He hears us? Doing what—? Think he knows . . . ?

DAD: Pretty smart boy. Like you said, we need a bigger house.

MAMA: Well, wait a minute, let's think about this. What'd you tell him?

DAD: I told him to mind his own business.

MAMA: I don't agree.

DAD: What are you talking about?

MAMA: There's things he can learn now. (slight pause)

DAD: Oh, yeah?

MAMA: Most definitely.

DAD: You wanna teach him?

MAMA: I want to steer him in the right direction.

DAD: But I thought—

MAMA: If he wants to know, let's make the most of it.

DAD: The most of what?

MAMA: His curiosity. And his talent.

DAD: Now he's talented? I thought he was an innocent.

MAMA: He's already picked some things up. He's a natural.

DAD: A natural what?

MAMA: Lover. He's sensitive. He's pretty. It's good experience. And maybe, with a little guidance, maybe he won't make the mistakes the rest of us make.

DAD: I'm supposed to teach him this?

MAMA: It's up to him to pick it up, from both of us. But I think I can help.

DAD: Thank God he's got you. That's what I told him. (*pause, as the cloud of unease returns*) What mistakes?

MAMA: What?

DAD: Mistakes. You said mistakes.

MAMA: So?

DAD: Did you make any?

MAMA: You tell me.

DAD: No, I'm asking. I'm talking about you and me.

MAMA: I know what you're talking about.

DAD: Then answer me, dammit.

MAMA: What are you getting upset about?

DAD: I'm NOT upset. I JUST want an ANSWER.

MAMA: Then you've got NOTHING to worry about.

DAD: Can't you just say yes or no, and put my mind to rest, for godsakes?

MAMA: Yes or no to what? And why should I put your mind at rest? You're having far too much FUN stepping on your own tits!

DAD: Look, I got a right to be jealous!

MAMA: You have NO reason. You think I'm fooling around?—I don't have TIME!—I'm too busy taking care of YOU—!

DAD: You implicated that we—

MAMA: Implied.

DAD: IMPLICATED that we made mistakes down the line, or am I completely out of my head. Help me out. Did we?

MAMA: Down the line?

DAD: Yeah, mistakes.

MAMA: No. (*He relaxes*) We haven't made any big mistakes, since we've been together—

DAD: (*flaring*) SINCE we've been together?!!

MAMA: I can't help it if I had a previous life before you. We BOTH had previous lives—

DAD: What the hell is this?

MAMA: Well, you were married before.

DAD: THAT was a mistake. You got nothing to be jealous about—

MAMA: NEITHER DO YOU!!

DAD: Look, if I wanna hear about your previous life, any other GUYS, goddammit—

MAMA: I didn't—

DAD: —then I'll tell you! Understand? I don't wanna HEAR about it!

MAMA: You're out of your mind.

DAD: I'm your man. I don't want any other guys around. Why you gotta do that?

MAMA: Do what?!!

DAD: Make me so goddamn JEALOUS!!!

MAMA: QUIT YELLING! You're gonna wake up the whole neighborhood. (*About now, BOY actually does wake up. He stays in bed, listening*) And I didn't MAKE you do anything!

DAD: Then don't bring it up, for chrissakes!!!

MAMA: QUIT SWEARING!!!

DAD: All I'm trying to say is, you're with me. I don't need any of this other stuff. If you're with me, then stick with me—

MAMA: STICK WITH YOU?!! You don't think I stick with you? You just try going it alone—

DAD: Don't threaten me—!

MAMA: And as for mistakes—! (*She completely loses patience*) Oh, forget it. (*pause. BOY edges quietly out of bed*)

DAD: (*softer*) Maybe I'm blind, but I don't see we made any mistakes. At least I haven't, I mean, choosing you—(*slight pause*) But see, I get crazy. Too many other men.

MAMA: I thought you like men looking at me.

DAD: That's different. They can look all they want. But I don't wanna hear about you and anybody else—

MAMA: But I didn't say—

DAD: I shouldn't worry. I know I got no reason. But I do, and it hurts. It hurts me here. (*They are close together*) But you know I don't wanna hurt you, Tweetheart . . . (*BOY has moved to the edge of the stair*)

MAMA: Then why the HELL do you have to swear so much—? (*She laughs despite herself*) See what you did? You even got me talking like you . . .

DAD: I'm sorry.

MAMA: What's got into you?

DAD: How the hell should I know.

MAMA: Why in the world would you think there'd be another man . . . ?

DAD: I can smell it.

MAMA: What?

DAD: (*with disgust*) Men. (*MAMA tries to laugh*) Men stink. They don't all smell good like me. (*He proudly smells his own armpit*).

MAMA: Well, there's only one man around here.

DAD: There'd better be.

MAMA: You big baby . . . (*She strokes his face. In one deft move, DAD gets his arm around her waist and manuevers her onto the bed*) Hey . . .

DAD: Now tell me one more time about breakfast—

MAMA: Hey wait a—(*Now DAD is on top of MAMA, and her resistance is token*)

BOY: (*after a silence*) Dad . . . ?(*slight pause*) Mama . . . ?

MAMA: (*to DAD*) What's that?

DAD: It can wait.

MAMA: No, it can't. (*MAMA pushes DAD off enough to get her head up to listen*) Is that you, Boy?

BOY: Can I come up?

DAD: No.

MAMA: (*to BOY*) What's the matter? (*BOY takes this as a "yes" and bounds up the stairs. He stops to find them in pretty much the same position, DAD refusing to get off MAMA, somewhat dead weight, both of them craning their heads to look at him*) You're up early.

BOY: Yeah.

MAMA: What's wrong?

DAD: Yeah, what do you want?

BOY: (*backing away*) Nothing . . .

MAMA: Where you going? Come here. (*slight pause*) Come on . . . Let me up a little, will you, honey? (*DAD lets her up, somewhat, with a sour demeanor*) Say something to him.

DAD: What the hell you want me to say?

MAMA: Come on, then. Get in the bed. (*BOY jumps, lands in their midst*) That's a good boy. (*BOY gets between DAD and MAMA. She kisses BOY. DAD halfheartedly puts an arm around him.*) You sleep okay?

BOY: I had a dream. (*BOY wedges himself securely between them. DAD removes his arm and BOY's head falls back against the pillow.*)

MAMA: What'd you dream?

BOY: I forgot.

MAMA: Already?

DAD: Come on, time to get up. (*He sits up, but BOY and MAMA remain.*)

MAMA: Talk to me.

BOY: Last night Dad was telling me . . .

MAMA: When last night?

BOY: You were sleeping.

MAMA: What was he up to this time?

DAD: Careful, Boy.

BOY: He was telling me— (*slight pause*). He said he'd teach me how to fight.

MAMA: Fight?

BOY: Dad's gonna show me how.

MAMA: (*to DAD*) You and your fights!

DAD: I didn't bring it up!

BOY: You were watching them on TV.

MAMA: That's all you ever look at.

DAD: Hey, the boy needs to know how to handle himself.

MAMA: There's other ways than punching somebody in the nose.

DAD: None better.

MAMA: I'll never get away from it. First my father, then my husband, now I guess my son is next. Can't get enough of the fights. Just can't wait to get your nose broken.

DAD: I like my nose.

MAMA: I do, too. But on you, not my little boy.

DAD: He's only watching it on TV, for chrissakes!

MAMA: STOP SWEARING.

DAD: I'll just show him a few pointers, a little self-defense, just for his own good. It's something all men gotta learn sooner of later. This'll put the boy ahead of the game.

MAMA: Whose game?

DAD: Oh, come on—you get into boxing too. I've seen you cheering.

MAMA: I've got nothing against it. But there's other things than fighting. There's dance, and music, and the arts . . .

DAD: Sure, I'm all for it.

MAMA: Don't you think you might want to teach him some of that? Isn't that something all men gotta learn?

DAD: Well, yeah . . .

BOY: But I wanna know how to fight. (*pause*) Can I?

DAD: Listen, Mama. There's a great fight on today, a championship—

MAMA: There just happens to be a ballet on the public station today!

DAD: But Tweetheart, it's that Mexican guy—the one that looks like your grandfather—the tall skinny guy, Zarate—

MAMA: And it happens to be *Romeo and Juliet*. (*slight pause*)

DAD: Prokofiev?

MAMA: I'm surprised you remembered.

DAD: How could I forget?

MAMA: I thought maybe you took too many punches. Come on, Boy. Let's go downstairs. I'll make breakfast.

DAD: Well, hold on here, let's think about this . . . (*But MAMA and BOY are already on their way downstairs to the kitchen. DAD reaches for his favorite pair of pants, inexpensive, dark-brown, pockets full of jingling change. Then he picks up a worn Mexican vest, and puts it on. It is immediately comical, but it suits him. Last he reaches for his black-rimmed prescription glasses, which in no way make him look any less imposing. This done, DAD checks his appearance in the mirror.*) Not bad . . . (*fingers the chin, then the nose*) Rather aristocratic . . . (*Then his expression clouds, hardens. He slaps himself, hard*).

SCENE 3

The kitchen.

MAMA and BOY. MAMA is making breakfast. She takes from the refrigerator scallions, eggs, and a string of chorizo sausages arranged in bolitas. She will use these as she needs to. She also has a trusty old Mexican skillet to cook with.

MAMA: Hungry? (*slight pause*) So then, what'd you dream?

BOY: Nothing.

MAMA: Talk to me. It's just us. (*slight pause*) You afraid?

BOY: No. (*MAMA gets the grape juice and notices that the contents are all but empty, just a bit at the bottom.*)

MAMA: The least he could do is finish the damn thing off. (*MAMA pours the remnants for BOY, chucks the bottle.*) Sometimes, being with your father is just like taking care of a big baby.

BOY: Yeah?

MAMA: (*BOY and MAMA look at each other*) How come you look at me like that?

BOY: Like what?

MAMA: Giving me those big eyes.

BOY: No, I'm not.

MAMA: How come you're so funny today?

BOY: It's not funny.

MAMA: What? Listen, you can dream. There's nothing bad about that. It's just something you have to do.

BOY: I have to?

MAMA: It just happens. (*slight pause*) I had a dream last night.

BOY: Were you afraid?

MAMA: Yeah, I guess I was.

BOY: Maybe it was the same dream.

MAMA: Maybe. I haven't dreamed like that since I was . . . your age.

BOY: What was it?

MAMA: You tell me.

BOY: No, you say it.

MAMA: It wasn't a bad dream. Was it?

BOY: I don't know.

MAMA: The scary thing was . . . Well, it was like this. I was sleeping. But it didn't really look like me. My hair was long, and blonde, and my skin was at least a couple shades lighter. And my eyes were blue. It was just the way I wanted myself to look when I was your age. And the funny thing was, I was your age. And then this music started playing . . . And then (*stops cooking*) then this man came in the picture. Well, not a man. Sort of a boy-man. He sort of looked like me—not the blonde me, but the way I really look. I mean, he was dark, and he had this smile . . .

BOY: Did he have a moustache?

MAMA: No, I don't think so. He was young. He came in, and you know what it was like? It was sort of like the Sunday comic strip I used to read when I was a girl. Prince Valiant. It was my absolute favorite. It was so beautiful. And there we were—I was Aleta, and he was Valiant, and we were dancing, and that's when the alarm woke me up. (*slight pause*) But the last thing I remember was his face. Such a pretty face, it didn't really look like me anymore. A little, but it had changed. And that's when I got scared. Because the face, well . . . It looked like you. (*pause*) Isn't that strange.

BOY: How come you got scared?

MAMA: Scared? I don't know. I wasn't really scared.

BOY: Where was Dad?

MAMA: In bed next to me.

BOY: No, in the dream.

MAMA: He wasn't in it. He woke me up . . . Why?

BOY: He's angry.

MAMA: No, he's not.

BOY: Then he's gonna be.

MAMA: Just don't make him angry. Okay? Hey, but this isn't fair.

BOY: What's no fair?

MAMA: I told you my dream, but you didn't tell me yours.

BOY: I can't.

MAMA: I'm your mother.

BOY: I didn't dream. (*slight pause*)

MAMA: You'd feel a lot better if you told me.

BOY: Am I handsome?

MAMA: What? (*slight pause*) You're pretty. (*This is not what BOY wanted to hear.*) Not like that. Like a little man. (*BOY smiles*) So what's all this about fighting?

BOY: A man's gotta fight.

MAMA: That what Dad told you?

BOY: It's the truth.

MAMA: But you're a boy.

BOY: That's why I gotta learn.

MAMA: Men aren't the only ones who know how to fight.

BOY: Yeah?

MAMA: A woman can tear you apart. We got weapons you never even seen, and we don't fight by the rules. So take my advice, Boy—be nice.

BOY: I'll be nice. (*pause*) What's it like to be a woman?

MAMA: What?

BOY: And go to bed . . . And go to sleep with . . . somebody?

MAMA: It depends on the somebody.

BOY: If you were a girl, and somebody came up to you and called you his little *mamacita*, would you want to go to sleep? I mean, with that . . . somebody? Or would you punch him in the nose?

MAMA: Why would anybody call me his little *mamacita* . . . ? (*then she smiles to herself*)

BOY: 'Cause he loved you. 'Cause you're worth fighting for.

MAMA: Am I? Now I wonder who told you all this?

BOY: Nobody told me anything. It's true. I do love . . . somebody.

MAMA: Well, then, Step Number One, drop the little *mamacita* bit. I can assure you, that will get you nowhere. (*shaking her head*) Your dad—

BOY: No. Me.

MAMA: Then you're the guilty party. I guess you are in love. So tell me about the girl.

BOY: She's Mexican.

MAMA: Really? Well, in that case you've really got to be a lover. Mexican girls don't go around kissing and holding hands that easy. Don't expect quick results. I was scared to death of boys when I was your age, but that only made me hungrier to know more . . . about boys . . .

BOY: What do boys mean to you?

MAMA: What boys? I'm married to your father.

BOY: Does he make you hungry?

MAMA: Yeah. But he's a man. He's my man. (*BOY smiles*)

BOY: He's a baby. (*MAMA laughs*) He's a big baby. (*MAMA laughs again*) You see, I can make you laugh, too!

MAMA: What?

BOY: I knew it. I knew I can.

MAMA: Can what?

BOY: We both can. Dad's just bigger.

MAMA: What are you talking about?

BOY: I don't want a woman half as beautiful. I don't want Flory.

MAMA: Who's Flory? Is she—

BOY: I don't want her anymore.

MAMA: But you just dreamed—(*Before she knows what is happening, BOY has her face in his hands. He kisses her on the mouth. BOY's whole countenance has darkened and intensi-*

fied; he acts and thinks as a lover. MAMA pulls back in confusion.)

BOY: I dreamed about you.

MAMA: But that's not right—

BOY: And you dreamed about me. (*They stare at each other.*)

(*Then DAD enters down the stairs.*)

DAD: Where's breakfast? (*MAMA jumps, startled. BOY freezes.*)

MAMA: The *chorizo*!!! (*She runs to the skillet to stir the chorizo, which is burning.*)

(*DAD and BOY look at each other.*)

DAD: Boy. (*slight pause*) Keeping Mama company?

MAMA: (*struggling*) Be ready in a minute.

DAD: (*to BOY*) Why don't you put some pants on? (*BOY goes to the bedroom, and DAD tossles his hair, but with a sense of halfheartedness. BOY exits. DAD watches MAMA grapple with the skillet.*) Listen, we can go out for breakfast . . .

MAMA: I said, in a minute.

DAD: Don't raise your voice to me. I didn't burn the *chorizo*.

MAMA: Then shoot me!

DAD: Hey, I like burnt food—

MAMA: Then BURN IT YOURSELF!!! (*She abandons the skillet.*)

DAD: Where you going? Aren't we gonna eat?

MAMA: (*on the move*) That's ALL you ever think about!

DAD: Mama! What'd I do?!! (*exit MAMA upstairs and off*) Aren't you gonna feed your boy?

MAMA: (*off*) NO!!!

(*DAD stands there for a moment, then goes to the chorizo, begins picking at it, tastes a bit with his finger.*)

DAD: It's not that bad, Mama! (*slight pause*) Mama! (*reenter BOY, with pants on. They stare at each other*) Do you know what's going on here? (*slight pause*) Why you look at me like that? Did I miss something? (*slight pause*) I swear, a man could get lost around here between the two of you. So did you do something bad, or what?

BOY: I did it.

DAD: What? (*He grunts, throws up his hands.*) I had about enough of all this crazy stuff. Let's get to work. Go get the tools. (*BOY is slow to move.*) You hear me? (*BOY responds to the threat. Goes to where the tools are kept, and returns with a mallet, a maul, a crowbar, and a couple of heavy chisels. DAD stands in front of the lone wall. If there is furniture, etc., then DAD moves it away from the work space.*)

(*pause*)

BOY: Dad?

DAD: You got something to say?

BOY: What are you gonna do to me?

DAD: Do to you? What'd you think—I'm gonna do something to you?! (*slight pause*)

BOY: Then what are you gonna do?

DAD: Well, it looks like I'm gonna break down this wall, kid. Unless you wanna help me out a little. Here, pick that up. (*BOY picks up the mallet.*) Now you're gonna hit the wall with that.

BOY: I'll knock the house down.

DAD: You're not gonna knock the house down, Boy.

BOY: What if I did?

DAD: It's a strong house. But the wall's gotta go. Now watch. (*DAD takes a hammer. Reenter MAMA in street clothes, with makeup, purse in hand. She looks stylish, beautiful, and mad as hell. She strides past them for the front door.*)

DAD: Mama—?

(*DAD watches her go. BOY looks at him strangely, raises the mallet. DAD turns back to see BOY.*)

DAD: Not me—It. (*BOY lowers the mallet.*) Geez. I wouldn't like to meet you on a country road.

BOY: When are we gonna fight?

DAD: We'll do this first. I'll teach you later.

BOY: I want you to know, Dad.

DAD: What?

BOY: I'm ready.

DAD: Good, give it a shot. (*BOY takes aim.*) What were you and Mama doing anyway?

BOY: I made her laugh. (*Slight pause. Then BOY swings.*)

end ACT I

ACT TWO: SCENE 1

Ninety minutes later. The wall is down, wood and nails everywhere.

DAD is alone on the floor, still wearing the Mexican vest, removing nails with the crowbar. Sawdust clings to the air around him, not unlike a halo. With his wild hair he looks a bit like Lear or the Mad Professor, but the madness in him is mostly frustration, the residue of hard work.

DAD's throat is dry. He looks up sweating, scanning the room.

DAD: Boy . . . (*After no response, he rises. Full of phlegm, he tries hackingly to clear his throat as he goes to the refrigerator. He takes out a bottle of Mexican beer and takes a long pull. From the upstairs bed, BOY becomes visible. He has been there for some time. He is holding MAMA's discarded housedress.*) Boy . . . ! (*Neither moves. Then DAD puts down the bottle and starts upstairs, while at the same moment BOY springs out of bed downstairs. They meet somewhere halfway.*) What the hell are you doing?

BOY: I thought we were done.

DAD: Who told you?

BOY: We knocked it down.

DAD: That means you can walk away?

BOY: No—

DAD: Play, sleep, whatever the hell you were doing—?

BOY: No—

DAD: Let the old sonofabitch downstairs clean up-

BOY: NO!

DAD: Go back to sleep, kid. (*DAD goes back to work. BOY takes a moment, then follows.*)

BOY: I wasn't sleeping.

DAD: You weren't working, either.

BOY: I was thinking.

DAD: Why don't you think about picking some of this crap off the floor. (*BOY begins to pick up nails, scraps.*)

BOY: Are we gonna knock down any more walls?

DAD: One's enough.

BOY: Why'd we knock it down, anyway?

DAD: More space.

BOY: More space?

DAD: Yeah, thought we'd open up the dining space a bit.

BOY: It's the same space.

DAD: But it feels bigger.

BOY: I don't feel it.

DAD: You will. Anyway, I like to watch your mama cook.

BOY: I don't get it.

DAD: What?

BOY: You want more space, why dontcha build another room?

DAD: Well, that takes a bit of cash—

BOY: You want more space, why dontcha knock down all the walls—

DAD: You can't just—

BOY: One big room fulla space—

DAD: Boy—

BOY: You want more space, why dontcha—

DAD: Stop already. There's only so many walls you can knock down, all right? This is an interior wall. It's cosmetic. It's not really holding anything up. It just separates things. So we knocked it down. We joined two rooms. Nothing fancy. Why you give me such a hard time? (*slight pause*) Look. You're getting bigger every day, you take up space in the house. We're in the same room. I can feel you growing. You probably don't even know it, but I feel it. Everything about you is getting bigger, and louder and stronger, and one day you're gonna be bigger than me. We won't be able to fit in the same little room. And that's the day you'll leave this house, my word on it. But till then it's got to fit the two of us, even though every day it's shrinking—

BOY: Shrinking?

DAD: Every day.

BOY: Can we move?

DAD: You got the money? Look, it's our house. You never lived nowhere else. I figure the least we can do is try to make it fit us better.

BOY: Does Mama fit?

DAD: It's her house. I bought it for her.

BOY: Then how come she left?

DAD: She had to go buy something.

BOY: When's she coming home?

DAD: I don't know when she's coming home.

BOY: Was she's upset?

DAD: She'll get over it. Here, hold this. (*BOY gets on the floor to help DAD. For a moment they work together.*) Good boy. One day you'll do this to your own house. Maybe even with your own son.

BOY: I don't think so.

DAD: Bend those nails down so they don't stab nobody . . . (*watches BOY fumble with the hammer*) Let the hammer do the work. Like this. (*demonstrates*) Don't make it harder than it already is.

BOY: It is hard.

DAD: Nothing comes easy.

BOY: How old is Mama?

DAD: I dunno.

BOY: I bet she's young.

DAD: Yeah, she looks it.

BOY: How old are you?

DAD: What's it to you? (*slight pause*) Fifty-five.

BOY: That's old!

DAD: Go do something with that trashcan, huh?

BOY: How come you're so much older?

DAD: Look, it's not that much older.

BOY: But why didn't you marry somebody your own age? And why didn't she marry somebody young?

DAD: I guess we loved each other, all right?

BOY: But can't she love somebody young, too?

DAD: Ask her, huh? Quit bothering me. (*slight pause*) Geez! What the hell's on your mind anyway?!!

BOY: I was thinking . . . if you marry who you're supposed to. Or can you make a mistake.

DAD: You can always make a mistake.

BOY: Did you?

DAD: (*stops working*) Oh, yeah . . . (*catches himself*) Not your mother, I-I mean before . . .

BOY: Before?

DAD: Well, it was a mistake.

BOY: What mistake?

DAD: Well, I got married too early. I was young at the time.

BOY: Who was the girl?

DAD: The wrong one. Everybody makes mistakes. Mine was not admitting it. Not till it was too late.

BOY: What do you mean?

DAD: The time it took me to get divorced, I wasn't young anymore. You know, I don't remember being young. I know it must have happened, but I never got the chance to enjoy it. I was always working. (*slight pause*) Pick that up, wouldya?

BOY: Then I was right.

DAD: About what?

BOY: Mistakes.

DAD: You never know. I met your mother. It was something I hadn't planned on. But my whole life just fell into place.

BOY: What about Mama?

DAD: What about her?

BOY: Did her whole life fall into place?

DAD: I dunno—

BOY: Maybe it didn't.

DAD: Of course it did.

BOY: You ask her?

DAD: What's to ask? We've been married God knows how long.

BOY: You didn't ask her.

DAD: What the hell am I supposed to say?

BOY: Maybe you made a mistake. (pause)

DAD: Mistake, huh? Did Mama mention a mistake to you . . . ?!!

BOY: To me?

DAD: Did she?!!

BOY: No.

DAD: All right, then. No mistake. (tense pause).

BOY: Was Mama married before?

DAD: Why?

BOY: Just wondered.

DAD: No.

BOY: Then you're the first.

DAD: Yes, I'm her first and we're very happy. All right, Boy? (slight pause) I gotta get going, anyway.

BOY: For what? For what?!! The fights?

DAD: (proudly) Carlos Zarate. Ah, man, he's the best! Left hook to the ribs. I've seen a lot of fighters in my time. The best is this guy Zarate. Brave as they come. Clean, but with a temper. Geez, kid, in his prime—

BOY: When?

DAD: Before you started watching. Mama and me, we used to watch him Saturday nights. She loved him. I mean, she used to holler and scream when he won, though she'll deny it. Those were great days. But then they took his title away—

BOY: Who did?

DAD: Las Vegas judges. They fucked him.

BOY: What for?

DAD: They wanted somebody new, somebody young . . . who knows? He retired that night.

BOY: Why'd he do that?

DAD: Look, Boy, when you're a man . . . I mean, when you're proud, when you've worked so damn hard . . . and you get disrespected, you get passed by . . . well, that's when a man's got to take a stand. Or get out of the game. (slight pause) They think you got no feelings. You're in it for the money, whatever. It never occurs it's your manhood on the line. Well, I looked in the sports page the other day and I couldn't believe his name was there. Zarate's back! (slight pause) I gotta tell you, I'm a little worried.

BOY: Why?

DAD: He's not a young man anymore. It's a young man's game.

BOY: But he'll win, won't he?

DAD: That's what I'm hoping. Maybe he can hold out against it.

BOY: What?

DAD: Youth. (*slight pause*) Shit, what am I saying? He'll win. Anyway, I'll be there.

BOY: Me, too.

DAD: Nuh-uh.

BOY: Why not?

DAD: You stay with your mother.

BOY: But she's not here—

DAD: She'll be back.

BOY: How do you know?

DAD: She'll be back for you. She wants you to see the Prokofiev.

BOY: The what?

DAD: The Prokofiev.

BOY: I wanna see the fight.

DAD: Well, you're gonna see the ballet.

BOY: It's a ballet?!

DAD: The genius who wrote it, his name was Prokofiev.

BOY: What happened to him?

DAD: He's dead. But the music, Boy. I think you're old enough to appreciate it. Anyway, your Mama wants you to see it on TV.

BOY: If it's so good, why aren't you gonna watch it with us?

DAD: I already know it. I can play the whole thing in my head.

BOY: How come?

DAD: Well, it was the music your mother and I first made love to. I didn't have too many records. But this one, I used to turn out the lights and sit in bed listening. Then I met your mother. As soon as I saw her, I heard Prokofiev. She and the music sorta came together in my mind. (*slight pause*) I don't think she expected me to play it. We just sat in bed and listened to the whole damn thing together. Her face was . . . I don't know, transported . . . and then she was crying. I don't know exactly when. (*slight pause*) That music was all the art I ever wanted to do and never made time for, all the youth that got sucked outa me over time or that I gave away to all the wrong people. Here. (*DAD retrieves a single album. The cover is old*) This is the stuff.

BOY: Can I play it?

DAD: Watch it with your mother.

BOY: But there's only one TV. How are you gonna—?

DAD: I'm going to the bar down the corner.

BOY: But they don't watch the Mexican station—

DAD: I'll ask 'em real nice.

BOY: But—

DAD: No buts. Why dontcha get me another beer. (*BOY gets another beer*)

BOY: Who's he fighting?

DAD: Some young guy, I don't know.

BOY: I want the young guy.

DAD: To Win?!! Why?!!

BOY: 'Cause he's young. He could win.

DAD: Just 'cause he's young he's gonna win?

BOY: He could. (pause)

DAD: You wanna bet?

BOY: I think Zarate's too old.

DAD: How much you wanna bet? (BOY shrugs) All right. Gentleman's bet. (They shake, serious.) I hope he beats the shit outa that fucking kid.

BOY: I bet the young guy's better. I bet he's better looking.

DAD: What the hell's that got to do with anything?

BOY: I betcha.

DAD: Zarate's a handsome man. Ask your mother.

BOY: But I bet she likes young men better.

DAD: Oh yeah?

BOY: 'Cause old men don't got the punch. That's why there're old. Young men got the punch. It's better to be young.

DAD: It that so?

BOY: Young men are pretty. Mama said so.

DAD: Yeah? Well, pretty don't last.

BOY: I know. After pretty, boys get handsome. Young and handsome.

DAD: Not quite.

BOY: Mama said so—

DAD: Then Mama made a mistake. How old are you?

BOY: You know how old—

DAD: Then you don't got long.

BOY: Till what? (DAD grins and kills the beer) Till what?

DAD: Till all hell breaks loose.

BOY: Hell?

DAD: No one's ever gonna call you pretty again. Least of all yourself. You think you're safe? Think you're always gonna be a prettyboy?

BOY: I'm gonna be a man.

DAD: Then lemme show you how you get to be a man. Feel. (grabs BOY's hand and puts it to his face) It's not soft. The hairs on my chin are sharp. They stick out. I shave 'em off every morning and before dinner they're back. You're gonna get 'em. Just like you're gonna get a permanent hard-on. And pimples.

BOY: I don't want 'em!

DAD: You think you have a choice? You'll wake up one morning with your hand on your dick, and bumps on your face, and suddenly no one's gonna want to kiss that ugly swollen mug of yours. But you on the other hand are gonna want to make every girl, woman, and grandma you lay your eyes on. And you'll wonder what ever happened to that little boy everybody said was so cute, so pretty. 'Cause you'll look in the mirror and see a slack-jawed horse-face, half-man, half boy. And so help me, you'll want out so bad you'll wish you were old. (slight pause) Does that scare you? You still think it's better to be young?

BOY: I don't know.

DAD: (*dead serious*) Then listen to me. I'm your father. I know how old I am, kid. I know how beautiful your mother is. But goddamn it, I'm the BOSS—(*slight pause*) I don't know what I'd do . . . I'm just telling you so you know.

BOY: I know.

DAD: Then you're gonna stop? Making us both crazy?

BOY: No.

DAD: Why?!!

BOY: 'Cause Mama loves me—

DAD: Of course, but—

BOY: More than you. (*pause*)

DAD: Yeah, well, you're her boy . . . women are like that . . .

BOY: Not women. Mama.

DAD: How the hell do you know?

BOY: I just know.

DAD: I think you're wrong. Yeah, I do. How would you know?

BOY: I never made a mistake. (*pause*)

DAD: Okay. So what're you gonna do about it?

BOY: I'm gonna ask her.

DAD: Oh, yeah?

BOY: How to fight.

DAD: I'm teaching you how to fight.

BOY: I want Mama to teach me.

DAD: She fights different.

BOY: That's how I wanna fight.

DAD: You wanna fight like a woman? I thought you wanted to be a man.

BOY: I just wanna win.

DAD: You don't think I'm gonna win?

BOY: I know Mama's gonna win.

DAD: But Mama's not here.

BOY: I'll wait.

DAD: Yeah, but I got some things to teach you—

BOY: Teach me later.

DAD: I'm gonna teach you now.

BOY: No!

DAD: Come here. Do you hear me? (*BOY stands before his DAD.*) All right, kid. Take a shot.

BOY: What?

DAD: Come on. Hit me. Give me your best shot.

BOY: No.

DAD: You want to, dontcha? Come on. Knock me over. I'm asking for it. Let's see you throw that left hook to the ribs.

BOY: I don't want to.

DAD: Come on. I'll get down on my knees. (*He does so.*) Here's my chin. Now let me have it. You don't like it? Go for the nose. Break the fucker.

BOY: Dad—!

DAD: Whatsa matter? It's the shot of a lifetime. Go on. Beat the shit outa me. Lemme show you. (*DAD, still on his knees, takes BOY's arms and forces him into a boxing stance.*) Like this. Keep your eyes open. I want you to see what you're doing. One shot's not gonna do it. I'm a big man. You're gonna have to hit me with both hands. There. See what you're doing? Now you're ready. This is your chance, prettyboy! Come on, you little half-Mexican sonofabitch. Throw the fucking blow!!!! (*BOY closes his eyes and swings as hard as he can. DAD avoids the blow, then grabs BOY by the shoulders.*) Nuh-uh. You got to look me in the eye. (*slight pause*) Do it again. (*Sound of a car coming to a stop.*) *BOY looks up, wide-eyed. DAD waits for him to throw the blow.*

Then the sound of the front gate.

MAMA: (*off*) Honey?!!

DAD: You shoulda hit me, Boy. That's the last chance you'll ever get.

MAMA: (*off*) There's groceries!!

DAD: Go help your mother. (*BOY runs off. DAD is alone.*)

A moment later MAMA and BOY enter with groceries. She also has a bouquet of fresh-cut flowers and a dress-bag from a Spanish-language store. She cuts a figure of abundance. MAMA and DAD look at each other.

MAMA: I bought food, too. (*seeing the work*) Oh the wall . . . Wow . . . (*then looking from DAD to BOY*) What?

DAD: I'm going.

MAMA: Where?

DAD: I'll leave you with the boy.

MAMA: What happened?

DAD: I'm going to watch the fight. That's all. TV's yours.

MAMA: I don't give a damn about the TV. Now what happened?

DAD: We did a little home improvement.

MAMA: I'm getting sick of all this—

DAD: Well, you're not as sick as me. (*DAD starts off*)

MAMA: (*to BOY*) What's going on here? How come your face is all red?

BOY: We had a fight . . .

MAMA: (*to DAD*) Did you hit him?!!!

DAD: No. You think I'm a bully?

MAMA: Yes, I do.

DAD: Well, thank you very much. Your little prince tried to hit me.

MAMA: What did you do to deserve it?

DAD: Goddamn it, why do you pick on me?!!

MAMA: Why don't you go watch your fight. (*MAMA turns away from DAD and hugs BOY.*)

DAD's expression dissolves into that of a child.

DAD: Why do you do that? Why do you hurt me? I didn't do anything—

MAMA: You want to fight? Well, then, go somewhere and fight. Go on. Just keep it out of my house.

DAD: Your house?

MAMA: You heard me.

DAD: You think I got no feelings. You think all I do is eat, and shit, and fuck, and work.

MAMA: That's not true—!

DAD: Well, I love you!

MAMA: I love you, too! But something's wrong.

DAD: Let me fix it—

MAMA: Leave it alone. For now. We'll fix it later.

DAD: Tweetheart—

MAMA: Go. Go and watch your fight. (*Pause. DAD is about to respond, but nothing comes out. He half-smiles, then exits. MAMA and BOY are alone. Pause*) Are you hungry? (*BOY nods "yes."*) Why don't you put this stuff away? I'll make us something fresh. I'm hungry, too. (*slight pause*)

MAMA: You did a lot of work. You helped him, didn't you?

BOY: I knocked it down.

MAMA: All by yourself?

BOY: I broke it first. Then later I cleaned it up.

MAMA: That's good. Dad's a good worker. He can teach you things.

BOY: How come you were gone?

MAMA: I bought a dress.

BOY: Can I see it?

MAMA: When Dad gets home.

BOY: How much did it cost?

MAMA: Enough. (*puts flowers in a vase*) Did you make your bed?

BOY: No.

MAMA: You should do that in the morning. You shouldn't wait for me to do it for you.

BOY: But you always—

MAMA: Not today. Not tomorrow, either. And you should get your dirty clothes together. I'm going to do a wash.

BOY: You were gone a long time. (*BOY finds a large cube of corn* masa, *which looks a bit like modelling clay*) What is this?

MAMA: *Masa*.

BOY: *Masa*?

MAMA: It's fresh. I'm going to make *tortillas*.

BOY: Fresh *tortillas*?

MAMA: It's all fresh. I had to drive a long way. Back to where I used to live as a kid. I went to the *mercado*. That neighborhood sure has changed. I could hardly recognize the old streets. Made me kinda sad... (*BOY continues to remove fresh peppers, tomatoes, and leafy spices from the bags.*) But the *mercado*, now that's just like it used to be. You find all sorts of things you can't buy out here. There were even some local *mariachis* singing the old songs. And the people, whole Mexican families shopping together, real old-world. I should have taken you with me . . . It's funny . . . you forget. . .

BOY: What?

MAMA: I don't know . . . Where you come from. What it smells like. How it feels. (*She takes the* masa *from him.*) I bought a mango on a stick and ate it sitting on the sidewalk. Just like I used to, jeez, thirty years ago. That really started me thinking back, remembering when your grandma and grandaddy used to take me out to the *mercado* with them. I sat there with mango juice dripping down my arms, like a child . . . And for the life of me I could not remember ever kissing my father the way you kissed me. (*slight pause*) I probably wanted to, but I sure as hell never did. I don't think I knew how. Where'd you learn that? At school? I doubt it. Did your father teach you? (*BOY turns away, cold and angry.*) Hey, don't be angry. What are you angry about? (*no response*) Listen, you! You kissed me. I didn't know what you were doing. I hadn't even had a cup of coffee, and you kissed me. You put yourself dead square in the middle of my day, and you expect me to just let it happen, smile, shrug it off and make breakfast?!! You gotta be kidding! I'm the one who should be angry.

BOY: You were.

MAMA: You're damned right I was. But I got over it.

BOY: I'll never do it again.

MAMA: What? Kiss me? You better kiss me. But not like that. Nobody kisses me like that. Nobody but my husband. (*slight pause*) So whatever Dad told you—

BOY: Not Dad. Me.

MAMA: All right, you. Whoever. It's got to stop. It's not right. Boy, you've got to stop.

BOY: It's not just me. (*This stops her.*)

MAMA: I know. But that's no excuse.

BOY: But you love me.

MAMA: I love you more than anything, but you're not a man to me. And even if you were, you wouldn't be my man. You're a boy.

BOY: But you're my girl.

MAMA: I'm not anybody's girl. I am your mother. And you better listen to me. (*pause*) I'm sorry. I'm flattered—confused—but flattered. Now let's forget about it.

BOY: I CAN'T!!

MAMA: You must.

BOY: But I'm the one who made you laugh! He made you laugh before, but that's because I never tried! I didn't know. I was too young.

MAMA: And now you're suddenly old and wise?

BOY: You laughed. I saw you. You laughed for me.

MAMA: But that's not making love—

BOY: That's how I make love. Dad told me you gotta make 'em laugh. I never could before. But now I can. Now I can do it better than him.

MAMA: Then make somebody else laugh.

BOY: But I want you.

MAMA: Well, you can't have me. And if you keep trying, then one of us, either Daddy or me, is gonna get angry. And I don't think you're gonna like that.

BOY: Didn't you ever love somebody else than him?

MAMA: Of course, but . . . no. Nobody like him.

BOY: Do you think maybe you ever will?

MAMA: I don't think so. There's only one man for me. (*pause*) Don't you love your father?

BOY: I wish he was dead. (*A moment, then MAMA strikes him. The blow is hard, glancing, tousling his hair and sending his head spinning. MAMA's eyes are aglow.*)

MAMA: Don't you say that. Don't you ever say that. Your father loves you. He'd give his life for you. You'll never know what he sacrificed for you. For you!

BOY: But he loves you more.

MAMA: So you wanna kill him?

BOY: I hear him shouting. I hear you cry sometimes—

MAMA: You want him dead for that?

BOY: I wouldn't make you cry.

MAMA: That's your father . . .

BOY: I wish he'd go away.

MAMA: You'd miss him.

BOY: But I'd have you.

MAMA: But you'll miss him. (*slight pause*) Believe me, you will miss him. (*Then BOY very quietly starts to cry.*)

BOY: I know.

MAMA: No, you don't. You'll know when he's dead. (*BOY looks up in pain.*) But of course it's too late by then . . . (*BOY continues to cry alone. MAMA finally takes him in her arms, but without quite forgiving him. Her face is fierce, but calm deep-down.*) That's your daddy. And he loves you. And you are so lucky. One day you'll know that, but you'll wish you knew it sooner. (*slight pause*) Your father and me had you together. We made you. It was in the morning—a hot August morning. Dad brought a cante-loupe and a little bottle of champagne up to bed. We toasted your health. We talked about you. We wondered if you'd be an artist. I thought you might be a dancer. We figured you'd be good looking, but we wondered how—what kind of eyes, how big and tall you'd be. We even threw a few names around. I chose your name that morning. I knew you'd be a boy. And then we made love. We made love as good as we could make it. And then we went to sleep. Because we thought maybe we'd dream of you. At least we could try. We didn't really expect anything. We just wanted you to know.

BOY: What?

MAMA: I don't know. Your father and I, well, we've always wanted to do something. I mean, really do something. And we've done things. But the two of us, the two of us together could really do something. We could make a work of art. But it takes so much work. And then of course the real work's up to you. (*slight pause*) I want you to apologize to your father. But you've got to do more than that. I'm not totally sure what you have to do. He's not that old. The problem is, he thinks he is. And that's bad. Because then that wish of yours is not that far away.

BOY: But I don't wish it anymore—

MAMA: You said it already.

BOY: But—

MAMA: It'll happen one day. To me. To you. And we'll miss each other. (*slight pause*) Come on. It's time to eat.

BOY: Mama . . .

MAMA: I'm right here.

BOY: Then gimme a kiss.

MAMA: You give me one first. (*She seems ready to withstand anything, but when he kisses her on the lips, again, it's still a musky kiss. MAMA, a little dazed, breaks it off.*) Okay. (*shakes her head clear*) What am I gonna have to do . . . ? (*They look at each other. Then she sees the* masa.) Come here.

BOY: What?

MAMA: I'm going to teach you how to make *tortillas*. (*regaining her composure*) This is *masa*. It's corn. You have to grind it down. We're cheating a little 'cause I bought it ready-made.

BOY: *Tortillas* are flat.

MAMA: Yes they are. You know how they get that way? (*BOY shakes his head "no."*) You have to knead it. Then you pat it in your hand. See? Pat, pat, pat, back and forth in your hand, from one hand to the other. You shape it that way.

BOY: Like this?

MAMA: You're getting there. You gotta put your hands in it.

BOY: It's fun.

MAMA: It's work. But it makes for good eating. (*They work together for a moment.*)

BOY: Mama?

MAMA: Yeah?

BOY: When is Dad coming back?

MAMA: When he stops fighting.

BOY: How come you married him? (*slight pause*)

MAMA: How come? Because he made me laugh. (*slight pause*) Keep kneading it. I want to try on my dress. (*starts for her bedroom*) And you could set the table, too . . . (*She goes upstairs and gets undressed quickly to her underwear, which is simple but sexy. The dress is white, very Mexican, with embroidered flowers, and beautiful earthy colors. She will remain barefoot. She looks in the mirror, likes what she sees.*)

Downstairs, BOY continues to work the masa. *DAD appears in the doorway. He just stands there, vest in hand.*

BOY hesitates, then runs straight for DAD and hugs him. He holds DAD about the waist. DAD tries to remove him, but BOY holds on.

DAD: Hi. What're you up to? (*absentmindedly tossing BOY's hair*)

BOY: I missed you, Dad.

DAD: Yeah, how come?

BOY: We're making *tortillas*.

DAD: I can see. What's the occasion?

BOY: I missed you—

DAD: Yeah, you already said that.

BOY: I'm sorry.

DAD: Don't be sorry. You won the bet. (*MAMA, hearing DAD, has gotten into the dress. DAD is on his way upstairs when she appears.*) That's a beautiful dress.

MAMA: It is, isn't it.

DAD: You mad at me?

MAMA: Why should I be mad? I got a new dress.

DAD: Is that all you got?

MAMA: It's enough.

DAD: I like it.

MAMA: I'll start lunch. (*They stand there.*)

DAD: Who's stopping you?

MAMA: You are, unless you step aside. (*He does so.*) Thank you.

DAD: (*as they are close together*) You sorta busted my ego.

MAMA: I'm sure it'll swell back up to size.

DAD: I still love you.

MAMA: I should hope so. (*slight pause*) You look sad.

DAD: Why should I be sad.

MAMA: Food'll be ready soon. (*She thinks about kissing DAD. Instead, she returns to the masa. DAD sits at the table.*)

DAD: (*to BOY*) What's the matter with you?

BOY: I don't feel so good.

DAD: Siddown. (*BOY goes to sit on this lap; DAD motions him off.*) No, gimme some room. (*DAD begins to bite his thumbnail, not overtly nervous, more a casual gnawing. MAMA listens as she makes tortillas.*) You know, that's not a bad bar. Nice big TV. I had a good time. I was thinking about dying. (*slight pause*) And I was wondering— what would be the worst way to go? You know, if I was to beat an exit . . . Figured I'd go over the possibilities. 'Cause some ways are a helluva lot worse than others . . .

MAMA: Sweetheart—?

DAD: I'm talking to the boy. (*slight pause*) Think about it. Heart? Lungs? Nah. Cancer's the worst. Don't kid yourself. But what kind? I haven't smoked in years. Now the spine, that would be bad. Then you couldn't get around. But you know what the very worst would be?

BOY: No.

DAD: Stomach. Then you couldn't eat. And I can't eat, I might as well be dead. Right? You see what I mean?

BOY: I guess.

MAMA: Why are you talking—?

DAD: Lemme finish. (*slight pause*) 'Cause then I really started thinking. That was about the time Zarate started getting beat . . . So I figured, what the hell, what's the best way? If I gotta go, I might as well go in style. Wouldn't you say? (*slight pause*) I'm asking you a question . . .

BOY: I don't know—

DAD: Don't you? And then I saw it right in front of my eyes. How 'bout a swift double left hook, one to the kidneys and one to the chin—?

MAMA: He didn't—?!! My god is he dead—?

DAD: Nah, Zarate's all right. He just lost. That's all. (*slight pause*) Nah, I wouldn't really wanna get hit. Not like that. Less pain the better. Maybe in your sleep . . . But I wanna know when I go. I don't just wanna go. That's not a man's death. Sounds stupid, but it's not a man's death.

(*slight pause*) Maybe it'd be all right if I was with your mother, maybe on a Sunday morning, maybe in bed—(*He stops*) No. Too traumatic for all concerned. (*slight pause*) But then it hit me. The best way for me to go would be . . . eating. While I was eating. Quick heart attack and a face fulla chicken *mole*—

MAMA: Stop it!

DAD: I'm sorry. Guess I got a little carried away. (*slight pause*) You know, Boy—if you wanna kill me off, why don't you be nice and do it over dinner? Remember your dad's last wish . . .

MAMA: I TOLD you to STOP IT.

DAD: (*to BOY*) I don't mean to make her angry. I'm just thinking. That's what old men do.

BOY: You're not old. You're young.

DAD: Oh, now I'm young.

BOY: You're not old.

DAD: Zarate's old . . . He looks the same. Handsomer, I'd say. And he's still got that something when he gets in the ring. But the timing, Boy, the timing is gone. When it goes, it's gone for good. He always seemed to come up a little short. It went like that for a while, four, five rounds—and then the young guy started to figure him out, started taking chances. And that's when Zarate started getting hit. A couple of 'em were knockout blows. I'm telling you, he shoulda gone down . . . but Carlos . . . (*he starts crying*) I'm not crying for Car-los. He doesn't need me crying for him. He's a brave and strong man . . . there's nothing to be ashamed of. I'm crying for the time. The lost time. It's not the mistakes you make. The mistake is the time you lose. Not even realizing. Until suddenly it counts, and you come up short. I shoulda met you sooner, Mama. (*he tries to laugh*) And we shoulda had this boy sooner. 'Cause then I'd see him grow. Get stronger, bigger, stinkier, until he was a man. And we'd both be men. And I still wouldn't have gotten old. (*slight pause*) I guess we did the best we could. (*Pause. Then MAMA walks slowly to the table. She stands in front of him. Then she kneels. She looks him in the eye and gives him a big wet kiss, a long one.*) That's even better than fresh *tortillas*. (*Mama now looks at BOY.*)

MAMA: Give your Daddy a kiss. (*BOY, awkwardly, goes to kiss him.*) Nuh-uh. Like you kissed me. (*BOY and DAD kiss each other on the lips. It is a pretty damn good kiss.*)

DAD: Who the hell taught you to kiss like that?

MAMA: Must be hereditary. (*BOY looks around the room.*)

BOY: I think I feel it.

DAD: What?

BOY: More space.

DAD: That's 'cause it works. (*They all look at each other, each about to express doubts. Instead, they are silent. MAMA returns to the tortillas. BOY looks from one to the other. Then he quietly goes to the stereo.*) Boy, I'm hungry.

MAMA: Won't be long.

DAD: You know what I'd really like . . . ?

(*Before he can say, BOY has turned on the stereo. The Prokofiev music plays. Everybody stops. The music washes over them. DAD begins to cry, then stops. All face out, listening, till it ends.*)

fin

Young Valiant
entremeses | *intermezzo* | inter-acts

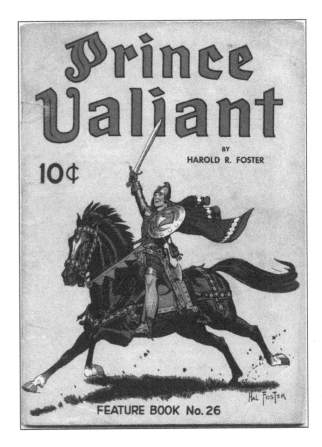

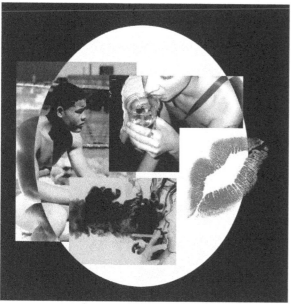

Original cover-design digital collage for *The Hurt Business* by Guillermo Nericcio García.

Algunos pensamientos sobre Young Valiant and Oliver Mayer

Jorge Huerta

I first met Oliver during the "Hispanic Playwrights Project" hosted by the South Coast Repertory Theatre in Orange County, California in 1989. We were by the hotel swimming pool, and Oliver and the director of his play, the late José Guadalupe Saucedo, were sunning themselves, looking for all the world like a couple of carefree bourgeoisie. Saucedo was very enthusiastic about Oliver's play and told me that this young playwright was somebody worth watching. So here we were, poolside, the dark-skinned Saucedo, tanning by the minute, and this tall, light-skinned Chicano, looking like your prototypical lifeguard. I was immediately taken by Oliver's youthful exuberance, an exuberance and idealism he maintains to this day. With his M.F.A. in Playwriting from Columbia, Oliver was one of the first members of his generation of Chicano/a playwrights with an advanced degree in this field. Further, he was working in the literary department of the prestigious Center Theatre Group of Los Angeles, so Oliver was one of the few playwrights of the period to be "gainfully employed," working for the theatre company that had produced

Zoot Suit, a production that had changed his life.

Oliver captivated me with his wonderfully engaging smile and an enthusiasm for the theatre in general and Chicano/Latino theatre in particular. Although he had studied on the East Coast and at Oxford University in England, Oliver had done his homework and could talk about Chicano theatre with intelligence and the critical eye necessary to achieve his dramaturgical vision.

I wondered what Oliver might know about the "Chicano experience" but as we talked I began to understand that he had chosen not to "pass," instead engaging his bicultural background with pride and an openness that was and is disarming. "Passing" is a common trope in studies of race and ethnicity relative to African-Americans and was a common theme in the literature and dramas of early America. Early plays such as Dion Boucicault's *The Octoroon* (1859) exposed the racism that separated someone from the white majority if he or she had one-eighth "Negro" blood.

In the evolution of Chicano theatre passing has not been a common theme, nor has anybody (to my knowledge) questioned whether a Chicana or Chicano playwright was passing to gain agency in the hegemonic structure. Ironically, Mayer could easily have distanced himself from his Chicano roots with his father's last name. He did not abandon his name or his heritage(s) in this play nor in any subsequent play.

Oliver Mayer with Bill Nericcio along with Marianne Sadowski, circa 1988, Ted's Pub, Storrs, Connecticut.

I love the interview that Bill Nericcio has with Oliver in this volume because it speaks volumes—about the playwright, about Nericcio. Each one is looking at life after 15-odd years of having been classmates at Cornell.[1] Classmates in a class by themselves as two of the few Chicanos at

[1] "Freud, Prokofiev, Desire, Art and the Naked Asylum of the Theater: A Conversation with Oliver Mayer and William A. Nericcio."

that prestigious Ivy League college; but more importantly two young students who were not ashamed of being Mexican. They were Chicanos who were conscious of the indignities their people were being subjected to on a daily basis in this country and all over Latin America.

Back to the conversation by the swimming pool, I did not yet know this play, but as I would discover, the ever-evolving Chicano drama had entered a new phase with a play by a bicultural playwright, half Anglo, half Chicano. He had a vision of what the Chicano family looked like, a vision that defied all previous expectations of what a Chicano play should look like.[2] When I watched and heard the staged reading of this play, I understood what Mr. Saucedo was talking about. Here was a play of such maturity one might assume it had been written by a much older playwright. The three characters were real people, not stereotypes, fascinating in their contradictions and captivating in their distinct desires. No previous Chicana or Chicano playwright had created a character like "Dad," an Anglo married to a Chicana whom he loves and respects. Heretofore the Anglo characters that Chicana and Chi-

cano playwrights had created were mostly evil stereotypes, cardboard figures to be laughed at. But not this representation, an endearing, respectful portrayal of a loving, troubled husband and father.

Like most playwrights early plays, this one has autobiographical influences. As Mayer states in this volume, "I don't hide the substantial similarities between my own family and the three people I write about." Oliver's father was Anglo, his mother a Chicana. When Oliver was 17 years old his father died at the early age of 63. By the time Oliver reached his 21st year, he began this play, an homage, really, to his hard-working father and his loving mother. Dad in the play is 55 and feels the indignity of old age rapidly approaching. He can still make love to his younger beautiful wife with what seems like the stamina of a 20-year-old, but he also fears that he might lose this young woman to a younger man. He discusses how he wants to die, a common theme among people who have come to accept their own mortality. His final choice, to die while eating—"Quick heart attack and my face full of chicken *mole*"—is a classic image.

This play was originally titled "Food and Evil," an image that is far from what we see and feel in this play. There is food, yes, with the majority of the action taking place in the kitchen and including the cooking of food from the first to the last scene. But I saw and see no "evil" in this play, only the

---

[2] Cherrie Moraga, our other bicultural playwright, had not yet written *Heroes and Saints*, premiered in 1992, and which also features a bicultural Chicano character, the activist priest, Father Juan Cunningham.

natural impulses of the preadolescent contrasted with those of the aging Dad. Forget Oedipus: in this play nobody really wants to kill anybody but Death and Sex still hover over the action. This is a play about space, sex, and desire, life and death, food, boxing and, most importantly, our own mortality.

As I sat in the audience of that first reading I could visualize the setting, the furniture, the costumes. And as I read the play today, I can still feel the emotions it elicited in me when I first heard it read so many years ago. Every time I read this play I cry for Dad and I cry for Boy as well as Mama, this archetypal trio all yearning for one another's love. Metaphors and symbols abound in this play, space being one of the central images. The family lives in a space that is getting too small, and walls, both real and metaphorical, must be torn down if they are to survive one another's growth. Other images are more stark, beginning with the opening scene in which the naked Dad drinks grape juice in front of the open refrigerator, the juice dripping down his hairy chest as his ten-year-old son looks on, dressed only in a tee shirt. The boy and the father, silhouetted in the light of the refrigerator, is a classic image, a wonderful way to begin a play about images.

Along with the visual imagery Mr. Mayer has created are the literary images. In this play of words, small conversations have larger-than-life implications. The dialogue is sometimes simple and direct, like child-speak; at other times the words pour out in monologues that rival any playwright's constructions of emotive language. Mayer has written some monologues that challenge any fine actor—moments of introspection or discovery that make for excellent audition pieces, actually. And these are not easy to find in Chicana/o drama! For example, Mama's shared memories of growing up in a barrio but wanting to be white; her cross-town return to her girlhood neighborhood where she is reminded of the smells, the tastes and the sounds of Mexico. Images of Mexican food and flowers, *mariachis*, and *masa* re-connect her to *her Mamá* and all the Mexican women before her who made their marks with their first hand-made *tortillas de maiz*.

What comes across most is the deep love the playwright feels for his characters. This atypical American household of younger mother and older father from different cultures, brought together by a wonderfully precocious young son, is really the family of today. This nameless *familia* is the future of *California*, where we find more and more mixed marriages with hybrid offspring and the culture clashes that come naturally with these transculturations. Where else do we find a Chicano play that opens and closes with the sound of Prokofiev's "Romeo and Juliet" while also paying homage to that very Mexican yet universal sport, *el boxeo*? Himself an amateur boxer in his youth, Oliver honors the Mexican boxers he watched with his own father. Like the classic Greek tragedies, the action of this play takes place on only one day, a day in the life. The family in *Young Valiant* survives this day with love and art, Prokofiev and chicken *mole*. What more can one ask for?

Jorge Huerta and Oliver Mayer
©2005 hyperbole books

Jorge Huerta and Oliver Mayer at a UCSD Theater Department event, 2005.

Freud, Prokofiev, Desire, Art and the Naked Asylum of the Theater: A Conversation with Oliver Mayer and William A. Nericcio[3]

William Nericcio: So I say the word "Naked" and what's the first thing that comes into your mind?

Oliver Mayer: Free. And cold. Liberty feels great. But it can be mighty cold outside. When you're naked there's not much sense hiding, and there is no real protection from the elements, nor from other people. But you yourself can feel elemental, as one with the elements around you. It's great if you don't have to stay that way, if you know you can get warm again soon.

WN: It is one of the clichés of criticism, but it's always interesting anyway, considering the line between fiction and autobiography—thinking about drama and fiction as coded or disguised self-portraits. Would such an approach be a help or a hindrance to a critique of Young Valiant?

---

[3] This conversation, between William Anthony Nericcio and Oliver Mayer, took place in the early 1990s, when Nericcio and Mayer collaborated quite often and Mayer was a regular feature in Nericcio's classes at San Diego State University. The title of the class *Young Valiant* appeared in was "The Naked Eye," hence the lurid line of questioning that opens the exchange.

OM: I don't hide the substantial similarities between my own family and the three people I wrote about. I even began the piece as a valentine to my mother, an intimate shared memory of my dad swigging grape juice in the middle of the night. But a funny thing happened along the way. I set out to right [sic, *nice Freudian slip, ed.*] a story about people I knew well, and found myself writing a myth. I was not overtly conscious about what was happening. But about halfway through the initial draft I realized the piece had gone beyond what I'd planned. It was bigger, and deeper than I intended. And I was pleasantly surprised. I think this may have happened because I did things in the play I only dreamed of doing in my life. And because of that, the play became an act of freedom, so get psychological and contextual as you please, but do so at your own risk—because this play lives in the land of dreams.

WN: *Speaking of dreams, can you share one of the most recent dreams you have had recently, and do you recall ever having a dream related to* Young Valiant?

OM: Dangerous question. My dreams tend to run mighty free . . . More than the particulars, from last night, I remember the general feeling, which was good. I like to think I'm getting visits from friends and lovers, past and future. A recurring dream is of my dad, who died seventeen years ago. He stays the same age in the dream, but I keep getting older—in the dreams, not to mention life. I tend to wake up glad but unsettled. I don't remember the last time I dreamed about Mom.

WN: *Here's one I think you might enjoy. What is the relationship between theater and boxing?*

OM: Well, when both are good you don't know what's going to happen next, or how it's going to end. Even if you feel the inevitability, even if you sense the end, there's still something incredibly alive about the experience. There's a question. Of course, in both theater and boxing, most of the time you're watching sub-par performances. I prefer boxing. More integrity. To me these days the most exciting thing is music. Whenever you hear music live, it comes to life and achieves a kind of death at its end. You're glad to hear it, but you feel sad, too. And you remember the last chords still ringing in your head. If it's good, you do. I want my plays to live in memory like that, even after a long time has passed.

WN: *Is that what Prokofiev's* Romeo and Juliet *is doing hanging out at the opening of* Young Valiant?

OM: Indeed. There's about a half-minute of Prokofiev's music that I simply cannot forget. When I was in Biology 101 at Cornell, they showed a movie about flowers and pollination, and using stop photography they showed the life and death of a single flower with that same half-minute of Prokofiev as background. And I cried and cried. My dad had just died, and it all just hit me, right in the middle of freshman biology. I don't intend for everybody to cry like I did, but I do think certain passages of music take you places. For me, that bit of Prokofiev is the key to the myth of the play.

WN: Moving on, could you say something about the relationship between insanity and the arts; I mean, after all, you've spent a good deal of your life in the theater, which is, for John and Jane Doe, a rather curious institution, or even an asylum of sorts.

OM: If it's madness to devote one's life to free artistic expression, then I am loony tunes. I mean, no one put a gun to my head and made me become a playwright. And believe me, aside from moments of sheer luck, there is no money to be made in the theater. Rather, it's somewhat of an irrational medium. I think plays should be more irrational, less normal, more wild. And I guess that is a little mad. My mom's best friend says I'm a playwright, accent on the "play" — and she's right. I like to play, whether it's word games or sex games or sheer hijinks. And whether I'm any good or not, I am what is called "an

artist." The best definition is that in the arts, non-artists talk about art while artists talk about money. And in essence, that's pretty crazy because there's precious little money in the arts for anybody but the chosen few. But don't cry for me. I'm having fun.

WN: One last question and then we can call it a day. If you didn't write, what would you be up to from sun-up to sun-down?

Oliver: Probably stewing in an office somewhere. I'd dig ditches, but I'm not so strong as I used to be. Before I caught the writing bug, I thought I'd be a little like you. Teach lit at a college, give tutorials to pretty girls, be some kind of *rockenrol* revolutionary academic Che Guevara. But we're all lucky that I found writing instead. It's the only thing I really know how to do anymore. Let's just hope it doesn't dry up for me. And it won't, as long as I don't dry up. I'm like that flower in Bio 101 — it'll happen, but we gotta play the music through first.

February 1999

Wild Child: In *Young Valiant*, a traditional ethnic story grows up

Erin Aubry Kaplan
Originally published in L.A. Weekly, August 25, 2005

An arts patron awaits the opening of Casa 0101 Theatre in September 2005.
photography by Guillermo Nericcio García

In the darkened Casa 0101 Theater at the western edge of Boyle Heights, the tableau onstage looks homey, a fair approximation of the community just outside the theater walls. A small, sparely furnished house is occupied by a family of color: the father is black and overworked, gruff and caring but not the most educated of men; the mother is a spirited Latina who tends to house and family; their nearly teenage son sports cornrows and a restless, taciturn air common to 12-year-old boys, especially boys of color growing up with modest means in a big city. But the familiar ends here in Oliver Mayer's *Young Valiant*, which is framed by race but hardly contained by it. The strains of Prokofiev's *Romeo and Juliet* that open the show hint at unlikely things to come, as unlikely as classical music enlivening a space that might otherwise be just another drab house in the hood, or the 'burbs.

Almost as soon as the notes fade away, the boy is awakened by the sounds of his parents making love in the room directly above him; he is troubled because he wants a girlfriend now, and the girl he wants is not his sixth-grade sweetheart—his would-be *mamacita*—but his own mother. Why not? She is lively and passionate, a pleasingly Rubenesque figure who still likes what she sees in the mirror and who loves the cultural pleasures of Prokofiev and ballet as much as cooking up *huevos* and *chorizo*.

The boy seethes, begins to hate his father, whom he admires for his boxing know-how but who he thinks is too old and unsophisticated to be real competition for him, and a competitor in the world. Toward the end of Act 1, at the height of the boy's agitation, he advances on his mother and kisses her long and squarely on the lips, like a lover; she gasps, as does the audience, but the chemistry between the two is unmistakable. As the lights go up for intermission, that chemistry hangs almost visibly in the air, and instead of feeling disconnected from the play for the next 15 minutes, I feel exposed by it. What would Eugene O'Neill say?

Mayer has always been good at delving into complex emotional issues within the framework of race (*Blade to the Heat, Joe Louis Blues*)—no easy task, since race tends to swallow any other subject matter in its path. In *Young Valiant* (which premiered in New York in 2002), race doesn't disappear and life doesn't become magically balanced; to the contrary, life feels terribly askew. But in the end, it's askew for reasons unique to the play rather than for reasons common to a whole demographic.

Sometimes both the play and its demographic resonate in a single powerful moment: as when the father (Hansford Prince) talks about having to work his whole life and missing the occasion of his youth, and his sorrow feels intimate, but also ancient. Mama (the aptly named Marlene Forte) tries to resolve her nameless ambition—partly expressed in the burning sexuality that so fascinates her son—with memories of Mexico, *mercado*, and home. As the boy, Chastity Dotson is a small miracle—a woman credibly playing a nascent man half her age, she is tough and ethereal, sullen yet wide open, the kid we've passed a million times on the street but never felt on this scale. Mayer's signature role reversals and gender-bending add to the complexity that is so often missing in stories about colored people, as does keeping the characters nameless and therefore emblematic; whatever happens, they are bigger than the circumscribed life that beats down on them and their forebears. But neither does anyone in *Young Valiant* come up with any answers; things do not get better so much as they evolve, incrementally, into something else. That's as good as life gets for most of us. Jack Rowe directs.

permalink:
http://www.laweekly.com/stage/theater/wild-child/333/

The cover of *Out of the Fringe,* a collection edited by Caridad Svich and Maria Teresa Marrero (New York: Theatre Communications Group, 1999)

U.S. Polyglot Latino Theatre and Its Link to the Americas[4]

Caridad Svich

Political upheaval and emigration are cornerstones of our experience. Our identities are constantly examined because we exist as "the other" in the US.[5]

In the U.S. the Latino population (which is comprised of Latinos, Latin Americans, immigrants, exiles, refugees, border peoples, and rafters) is the "largest 'minority,'" and yet many are working below the poverty level without health benefits, and often at great personal risk, especially in jobs that require hard labor. Latino/a voices are heard most consistently by and large under the cultural "radar," rather than above it, except for in the fields of

[4]A shorter version of this text was originally presented at the "Re-mapping Latino Theatre: American Playwrights on the Edge of the Edge" panel held at University of California, San Diego in February-March, 2005, moderated by Jorge Huerta and Caridad Svich. A later iteration was presented as the closing Routledge lecture in the Symposium on Cross-Cultural, Intercultural and Postcolonial Theatre at Royal Holloway, University of London, May, 2005. It appears in slightly different form in *Theatre Forum* 27 (Summer/Fall, 2005).

[5] Alejandro Morales, from a private interview with the author, 2003.

music, fiction, visual arts, and film, where the high-octane pop quotient of Latino work has become a veritable brand. The contemporary force field of the ruling culture, moreover, continues to determine the Latino as a racialized Other whose ethnicity is superficially marked by language, fashion and cuisine, and whose best use is toward the advancement of a market-driven economy. The unstable ontological space characterized by double-ness that is endemic of U.S. Latino/a movement and text-based work is glossed over in favor of surface readings of texts by audiences and producers habituated to presenting the work, if at all, within the confines of Otherness. Unequal control over the media and their disseminating systems of symbols, thus, perpetuates the problematic status of Latino writing for the theatre in particular, save for rare cases. Practitioners have little say as to how their work will be marketed for an audience, and ultimately how the work will be represented historically, regardless of whether it is deemed as belonging inside or outside the canon. If during the first height of Latino theatrical consciousness in the U.S., the era of Luis Valdez' *Zoot Suit* and Miguel Piñero's *Short Eyes*, the possibility of fair representation seemed within reach, today that possibility is elusive at best, despite accepted cultural signs that point to the contrary, for, in truth, U.S. Latino drama, which is every day not only more and more poly-ethnic

but polyglot in nature, is at a significant crossroads in its development, presentation and dissemination.

Although the second Latino cultural "boom" of the 1980s and early 1990s has ostensibly resurfaced in the new third "boom" predicted to occur after Nilo Cruz was awarded the Pulitzer Prize in 2003 for *Anna in the Tropics*, producers at arts venues across the U.S. have continued to exercise caution in their programming selections. U.S. stages do not represent the depth and scope of the work made by U.S. Latino theatre practitioners in spite of the fact that the work is remarkably diverse in form and content, geographic and regional specificity, and in its bodily embrace of sexuality and difference. Culturally dominant venues (and thus those covered most visibly by the mainstream press, and later codified by the academic press) slot a Latino play irregularly at best, and then often in the most patronizing circumstances. Thus, despite good intentions, Latino work is still viewed and received primarily as "alien." This has enabled many alternative theatre and performance practitioners to use the term "alien" (with its accrued cultural, political, psychological, spatial, and sexual definitions) to create work that is alternately playful and passionate in opposition to the delegation of their beings to either the Anglophone curio cabinet or a status of statelessness. Recuperating tropicalist stereotypes of the erotic Latin body, and marking their territory in rebellion to the power dynamics that designate what belongs in the center and what fits in the margin of global culture, alternative Latino theatre practitioners, particularly those who refuse to participate in the marketing of their work to fit a neatly pre-prescribed sociological agenda, are engaged in the active restructuring of not only the form and content of their work, but also its place in culture as a whole. Nevertheless, the troubling fact remains that to either be alien or alienated is still the politically operative choice for U.S. Latinos in theatre.

Much of this has to do with the changing map of Anglo to Latino consciousness in the United States and its growing disaffection generation to generation from its neighbors across the border and the Americas. The fact that we are living in one hemisphere is politically obscured by the harsh reality of immigration controls, the tightening of asylum requirements, and motions to now complete the border fence between California and Mexico. It is also enforced by a pervasive sense of divisiveness complicated by both the left and right's political machines, whose tormented co-dependent relationship ever since the Cold War has exacerbated the willful use of power north and south of the border. If the American voice (and by American I mean in this instance the U.S. voice) is a "mask" as sociologist Constance Rourke so eloquently remarked in her early landmark study of the U.S. national character *American Humour*, then it is a mask adept at hiding not only the local colors of its voice but also its face. This mask has served the U.S. for good and ill ever since pioneer days, and it has been instrumental in its march toward progress. In fact, part of the act of assimilation and its performance is attributed to how well the émigré adopts the U.S. "deadpan" mask. This poker face, which hides vengeance, violence, and greed, also hides warmth, tenderness, and compassion. The survivalist face, thus, is one that erases its emotive properties and can even in extreme circumstances erase its ethnicity.

Latino theatre practitioners and especially those in performance have used this mask, to use Rourke's phrase, as a "portable heirloom." Whether they are children or grandchildren of émigrés who evince strong cultural ties to Latin America, or are multiple-hybrid citizens moving freely among various cultures, the inheritance that is shared and commented upon in their work continually spins on the axis of how they have made use of this affective legacy. Unframing the discussion of their work from anthropological terms, these practitioners who are born into two if not three languages, and swear themselves as artists into another, find connections in the intermingling, in the creolization, of immediate, oral, idiomatic forms and centrist, impersonal, technocratic ones as well as the intermingling of bodies on stage and in their texts. Putting on the heirloom and taking it off is only one part of the act; the other is showing what's present behind the heirloom, and even how the heirloom has traveled and been adopted or discarded from country to country. But nationalist and more particularly nativist sentiments have interrupted this artistic passage. As international visa controls have become more strict, and a U.S. Latino culture has begun to shape itself along exceptional, unique lines in order to be heard midst the impossibility of a true democratic oasis, American-ness has been co-opted as a singularly U.S. term that excludes Canada, Mexico, and the rest of the Americas that stretch to the South Pole.

Cultural exchange has diminished, thus, especially over the last twenty years or so for myriad political, cultural, and economic reasons, making the U.S.' link to its neighbors and *compadres* in Central and South America more fragile than it should be. Ironically, however, the illegal, profit-making exchange of cocaine, for instance, the precious "white stuff" that trails across Latin America from the valleys of Peru to the poorest sections of Rio de Janeiro, has increased three-fold, causing significant environmental damage to our sister countries, who are ravaged by political instability and a mutually beneficial government-to-drug trader illegal economy fueled by a violent, rogue mentality. The

U.S.' demand for cocaine, and it is in the U.S. where the demand is the greatest according to studies released early in 2005, grows exponentially while the demand for listening to and witnessing the voices of native, displaced or hyphenated American artists from Latino and transnational neighborhoods across the U.S., Central, South America and the Caribbean grows less.

"Make sure your play has lots of magic, cause that's what a Latino play is," a theatre producer said to me not long ago. As writers born into our Latinidad or of Latino heritage, we all have inherited somehow the peculiar dilemma of having to answer to Gabriel García Márquez's magic realism. Instead of serving as imaginative models of liberation, Márquez's work and that of other master storytellers have been used to limit Latino writers in their range of expression. The devil of censorship is less markedly visible here than in our sister countries, but it does exist and indeed plays a role in not only the way U.S. Latino stories are perceived, but how they are written and revived.

As a 1950s-era type of conservatism takes hold of the sociopolitical climate in the U.S., and grass-roots, faith-based coalitions increasingly dictate liberties of speech, expression and lifestyle, the portrayals of Latino characters in the mainstream reflect the right-of-center/left-of-center bind in which Latinos find themselves. While there are more secondary and tertiary roles now for Latino actors in film, television and theatre than there were fifty years ago, the semi-plateaued careers of Jimmy Smits, Elizabeth Peña, Benjamin Bratt, and John Leguizamo (who has the distinction of being the only Latino writer who has filled a Broadway house to capacity with his solo shows) speak to the problematic nature of Latinos being fully accepted in leading roles, and economically entrusted with carrying the full weight and motion of stories. On U.S. television, for instance, few shows have centered on Latino characters or families, save for comedian George Lopez's recent, mildly received sitcom, and the short-lived PBS series "American Family." In film, the promise of Gael Garcia Bernal has yet to be realized in a mainstream, Hollywood-bankrolled feature, and Benicio del Toro, despite an Academy Award to his credit, cannot green-light a project with his participation alone. Salma Hayek, Penelope Cruz, and Paz Vega have been able to position themselves as variably potent commodities in the U.S. film market, but still cannot command the salaries or critical respect of leading actor counterparts Matt Damon, Adam Sandler, and Edward Norton. By contrast, U.S.-based Latino directors in mainstream and independent films have fared considerably better, criss-crossing languages, countries, and genres. Gregory Nava, Luis Mandoki, Alfonso Cuaron, and Robert Rodriguez all have established careers, if not household renown.

The box-office potential or success of Latino actors has depended on the branding of Latinidad itself. Jennifer Lopez is the most notorious example of an actor-singer performing an acceptably white-dominant, "homegirl"-camouflaged role of Latina beige-ness for the masses. But J.Lo's sustained public performance of Latina-ness in the fields of film, music, and television is arguably less problematic than another disturbing trend that has re-surfaced in recent years, which is the redoubtable return of the Maid or servant figure in mainstream film and theatre works. With an almost cavalier shrug, the put-upon, comic, foreign-born, usually-but-not-exclusively Latina maid has been seen in as disparately-lauded theatrical works as Lisa Loomer's *Living Out*, Sarah Ruhl's *The Clean House*, Paul Weitz's *Privilege*, and Rinne Groff's *Inky* as well as in James L. Brooks' film *Spanglish* and the J. Lo-starring vehicle *Maid in Manhattan*. In almost all these examples the retro-fit notion that the maid is present simply to serve the growth and maturation of non-Latino characters is exercised. Ostensibly politically correct and wrapped in well-intentioned pedigrees of progressiveness, these pieces, which are symptomatic of a creeping trend, reinforce the position of the Latina/o as whimsically Other. The roles, thus, for Latino actors by and large, despite protestations to the contrary, and save for a few singular exceptions (recent films *Frida* and *Maria Full of Grace*), remain the same as they ever were, with female and male whores, bombshells, gangsters, and comic sidekicks holding the most narrative sway.

In the last two years alone, notable U.S. programs devoted to the development and showcasing of the Latino/a theatrical voice have been cut: South Coast Repertory Theatre's Hispanic Playwrights Project, and Mark Taper Forum's Latino Theatre Initiative (as well as all its other programs of diversity. The Ricardo Montalban Theatre in Los Angeles, which was created with the sole purpose of presenting Latino work, has shut down. The long-standing theatre company INTAR in New York City is undergoing not only a change in leadership but also a significant financial crisis from which it may not recover. On television, news stories from Latin America and about U.S. Latinos are 14% of all coverage in both cable and network programming, even though population demographic figures released in May of 2005 assert that one in seven residents of the U.S. is Latino.

Budget cuts and increasing right-centered conservatism may be to blame for the lack of crucial support of Latino programming in the media at a level commensurate with the population growth and the rise in Spanish and Spanglish as second languages in the U.S., but an un-spoken restriction placed upon the content and form of Latino writing is more at issue here. The complex, neo-baroque nature of Latino work and playwriting specifically goes against the less pluralistic view of pictorial, emotional and verbal languages preferred in U.S. Anglophone narratives. The fusion of Iberian, African, and indigenous origins shared by tens of millions reflected in Latino theatre's transformative template is misunderstood and mis-labelled by U.S. critics and audiences. Latino writing, for example, is at its best African, Taino, Mayan, Mapache, Aztec, Guarani, Chinese, Portuguese, and Spanish, as well as Cuban, Mexican, Colombian, Puerto Rican, Nuyorican, and Aboriginal; yet in a country where Native American stories are treated as "foreign," how can Latino linguistic and political experiences north and south of the border as represented in the theatre and other genres be fully or partially recognized by those who witness them? If the US national character seeks the deadpan as its most idealized mask, its most American face, how can it accommodate the stories told through a necessarily syncretic lens, one that refuses the erasure at the heart of the making of such a character? Retrieval and recovery becomes the predominant methodology for Latino artists in the telling and shaping of their stories. Bricolage is the modus operandi on the page as well as in the structuring of the urban neighborhood, as artists and citizens use largely recycled materials from different sides of the borders to reclaim and proclaim their identity. Thus, local histories and performance traditions are recuperated midst polycultural and polylingual theatrical mash-ups, which speak directly to the ongoing project of what America means.

> Oye oye oye oye oye oye oye
> This is the voice
> The voice
> The voice . . .
> This is the voice of radio Dos Equis in
> the A, B, D and number four,
> you hear me?
> This is the electric boogaloo of the cowboy of the islands who seeks remedy,
> remedy and fast, for his ailing everything
> because everything is broken down
> down
> and way down
> in the triple crown
> of the Mayor and Governor
> and all the Powerful with
> the capital P.
> The microphone is defunct, you see?
> And everything has gone K-side,
> As in by the wayside
> waylaid
> and outside the official news.
>
> The Z doesn't work. For nothing. You hear me?
> The Z is absent, failing, stretched out
> limbless and waiting for X
> as in Dos Equis

as in as much as you can take.

> In which language do you want me to
> speak?
> There is no one language or haven't you
> heard del Babel in which we live?
> This is the new Babylonia and it is
> grand.
> So grand you can't even remember what
> you said after you've said it.
>
> We're in an inferno like Dante's. Remember him? Dante knew everything.
> He was prescient.
> He was one of those super-intellectuals
> who ate it and good. Because he told it
> how it was, is and will be, and we're just
> following.
> You hear me?
>
> In this language mangled and spit I
> speak to you
> Like two and two are six!
> And no one can stop me 'cause I still got
> my tongue.
> No one can stop me 'cause I still got my
> tongue.
> No one can stop me 'cause I still got my
> tongue.[6]

Un-mapping corners of the national psyche, Latino drama in the US insists upon portraying its citizens outside the comfort

---

[6] Caridad Svich, from *The Tropic of X*, an unpublished playscript, from 2004, now archived at alexanderstreetpress.com

of their own commonwealth, or at very least stranded in its limitations. Sometimes the stories move on a straight line and sometimes they zigzag and turn cartwheels in time and space. Comfortably plural in their disposition toward language, culture and identity, formally diverse writers such as Oliver Mayer, Naomi Iizuka, Jose Rivera and Alejandro Morales are engaged in a deep understanding and explication of the fact that Latinos love and perform in more than one language or nation. Latino dramatists have learned from Calderon de la Barca and Lope de Vega, as well as from Tennessee Williams, Arthur Miller, Eugene O'Neill, Sam Shepard, Miguel Piñero, Luis Valdez, and Maria Irene Fornes. There is no reducible essence to Latinidad....

Raised in L.A. and New York of Afro-Mexican-Irish extraction, Oliver Mayer came to attention as a Latino dramatist with his play *Blade to the Heat*, originally produced at the Public Theatre in New York under George Wolfe's direction. Set in the 1950s, the play centers on the world of boxing and the competitive relationship between Cuban-American Mantequilla Decima and another contender, Wilfred Vinal, who accuses Decima of being a homosexual. The *teatro* of the ring and how it affects the world outside the ring is the play's focus. Working with the heightened melodramatic structures of 1950s classic Actors Studio-era American films, Mayer

constructs an impassioned homoerotic dance of violence between the two men, pointing up the spectacle of their choreographed brutality and how an ingrained sense of *machismo* destroys them both. Mayer's plays are willful constructions that are indebted in form and content as much to the remembered residues of Mexican *carpa*, as to the American musical. The language in his plays, which include the Filipino-Mexican-African *mestizo* piece *Conjunto*, the boxing play *Joe Louis' Blues*, and the love story *Dias y Flores,* draws from jazz, vaudeville, minstrelsy, Mexican ballads, and hip-hop. In his cracked-antebellum epic *Ragged Time*, he creates an old-fashioned argot inspired in part by early American folk drama and comic books:

Sanctimonious: See, kid—it's just you. Now envision this scenario. No parents, no history. No history, no memory. No memory, clean slate. Think of that—a clean slate! That's what boss Hearst sent us out to look for! You! You and a million other yous coming into Ellis Island and wading across the Rio Grande and getting into the lovely tenements of the Lower East Side! Kid, you're the New American. ...You're gonna save your pennies, you're gonna make a buck or two here and there, and you're gonna spend them on the funnies, or whatever technological equivalent thought up by the mind of Hearst, and all the other Hearst to come. You, kid, may be the Lost Boy, but believe it—You Have Been Found.[7]

The sense of exuberance in Mayer's writing is part of a long-standing U.S. tradition of Yankee work that identifies and celebrates the post-colonial American spirit. It is on the whole open and direct, plainspoken and forthright. Although Mayer freely acknowledges the influence of William Saroyan on his work, he has a closer rapport on the page with early Eugene O'Neill, who was in turn greatly influenced by the theatre of his father's day. Captivated by the loose weave that is endemic to U.S. dramatic structure, Mayer spins tales of figures shaken but not destroyed by the promise of the American dream. His theatre is essentially one of optimism, an optimism tinged, however, with regret. In his work, there is always a streak of bluesy sadness that shows the cost that chasing the almighty dream of the dollar has had on his Latino and non-Latino characters....

The work by Latinos in the US continues to be written, if not recorded. Stories are unearthed from history's rubble and dramatists are rebuilding the who, where, and what of ruptured communities left behind in the name of progress. New stories are imagined that point to the vital intersection of classes and ethnicities that make up the social fabric of the U.S. and the Americas. The hip-hop phenomenon and spoken-word movements have emboldened Latino artists to discover new ways of presenting their work and speaking to the public, and have indeed encouraged new work to be written. A re-awakening of interest in the writers of the Spanish Golden Age, who are virtually unperformed in the U.S., is offering different career options for some in translation and adaptation. Moreover, the slow re-discovery of the writings of Valdez, Piñero and Fornes by untutored younger artists is allowing them to begin to connect the dots within the U.S. Latino tradition, and see that experimentation is actually the norm for a writer, and not a one-off act of folly.

We as Latinos are front and center in American writing. I was rereading NAUFRAGIOS of Cabeza de Vaca, circa 1542. This Spaniard began his odyssey in Tampa, shipwrecked in Galveston, and walked all the way to Baja California, over eight years of truly new experience. His writings predate all writing taught in most American lit classes, and in many ways we can draw a line from him to each of us. We, too, are walking—sometimes aimlessly, sometimes with purpose—through an America that is mysterious, changeable, full of magic, danger, and a million

---

[7] Oliver Mayer, *Ragged Time*, in *Out of the Fringe: Contemporary Latina/o Theatre & Performance*, eds. Maria Teresa Marrero and Caridad Svich (NY: TCG, 2000), p. 263-4.

fears. Yet we walk, and write, and hopefully we can come together as we do to meet and recount our odysseys on page and stage.[8]

U.S. Latino theatre is due for a major revival, one that will inform the younger generation of what came before so they will continue the evolution of the theatre. Where is the all-star revival of *Short Eyes*, for instance, now that there have been revivals of *A Raisin in the Sun*, *Twelve Angry Men*, and several recent re-stagings of *A Glass Menagerie*, *Long Day's Journey into Night*, and *A Streetcar Named Desire*? Where are the starry revivals of *Zoot Suit*, *Abingdon Square*, *Promenade*, and *Roosters*, for that matter, so we can better understand where Eduardo Machado, José Rivera, Oliver Mayer, Nilo Cruz, Migdalia Cruz, Octavio Solis, Anne Garcia-Romero, Bernardo Solano, Naomi Iizuka, Ricardo Bracho, Jorge Ignacio Cortiñas, Luis Alfaro, and Cherrie Moraga (to name only a few of many talented writers) come from? And whatever happened to the fusion experiment of *Capeman*, which for all it flaws, did bring to the Broadway stage the talents of Paul Simon, Mark Morris, Derek Walcott, and a pre-J.Lo Marc Anthony, Ruben Blades, and Ednita Nazario,

---

[8]Oliver Mayer, from unpublished cyber-transcript on "Re-Mapping Latino Theatre" panel, Feb.-Mar., 2005, University of California, San Diego Department of Theatre & Dance.

to a new audience? Is the Broadway staging of Oscar Hijuelo's *The Mambo Kings Play Songs of Love* the only answer in the seemingly never-ending trend toward replication: the constant turning of hit books into movies and then into musicals, and back again?

Latino playwrights are eternally on the border, straddling boundaries, and wondering if they fit in, if they want to fit in, and if so, why, and what can be gained by doing so beyond a little more significant cash in their pockets at the end of the day. Moreover, who is it that they are writing for? In effect, who is their audience?

This last question seems to be the most crucial if Latino theatre is to be truly re-mapped in the United States. For a long time, fellow practitioners have been the audience, not the secular folk out there who buy tickets. The other audience for Latino work has been primarily comprised of producers and funders, who graciously and patiently have viewed the works as eternally "in-progress" and/or as beautiful freaks that need to be watched over carefully lest they cause too much havoc. In between there has existed a floating audience of arts patrons, Anglo Latinophiles, academics, and curious spectators willing to gamble on Latino playwriting talent to see what will come of it. But now, even with multiple stagings of *Anna in the Tropics* at regional theatres across the U.S., Latino dramatists are still writers in search of an audience. And unless they move into the more precarious and potentially rewarding worlds of film, pop music, hip-hop, and/or *rock en español*, the subterranean culture of theatrical invisibility will continue.

Bridging the divide, if not eliminating the divide altogether, is the common goal. Yet no clear-cut strategies are in place to help the writers do so beyond the haven offered by the academy in terms of research and production, and the humble reward of the printed page where these voices have the possibility of living longer than on the U.S. or even the world stage. Two generations of dramatists have already spent years creating and producing work. In so doing, they have carved out an idiosyncratic place for it to live in the fractured and continually fractious U.S. landscape that is marked by a stubbornly binary public cultural discourse. These American dramatists have been poised time and again for mainstream glory with all the ostensible goodies such glory would afford. They have taken their work uptown and downtown and even back to the streets, while the climate of privatization has encroached upon the arts ever so steadily. As we look now at the magnificent map they have already made, it is time to realign and redraw the coordinates of their visions, so that their work is not taken out of their hands through censorship, the demands of living as part of the peasant class, or spirit-sucking enterprises that disable their ability to dream.

If as Latino theatre practitioners, as hemispheric artists, we take the step toward reconfiguring who we are now and who we want to be (and not who we want to be like), we will be able to fight the racism against dreaming that permeates U.S. culture, and offer the full measure of who we are as artists, thinkers, and citizens in this, our baby America.

The Redeeming Demon: Great Work Demands a Self Torn Open, Each Time Revealing a Hidden Truth, Illumination Woven from Darkness

Oliver Mayer

Special to *The Los Angeles Times*, August 14, 2005

WHAT is *duende*?

In Spanish, that storehouse of extreme feeling, it's one of many words that convey the spirit of deep soul. Lorca defined *duende* the best he could as "a momentary burst of inspiration, the blush of all that is truly alive, all that the performer is creating at a certain moment."

In song, the *duende* would appear not in a beautiful voice but when that voice tears, scorches, robs itself of the security of technique and opens into the unknown.

And onstage? *Duende* rises to edgy, inexplicable urges; it applauds impossible unions, sexual and otherwise. It resides in irrational fears, oversized desires and long-buried secrets.

According to Lorca, "All arts are capable of *duende*, but where it finds greatest range, naturally, is in music, dance and spoken poetry, for these arts require a living body to interpret them, being forms that are born, die, and open their contours against an exact present."

I like to think that *duende* lives deepest in the writing of plays.

But it does not repeat itself. When the writer strains for effect, it recedes or completely disappears. Then the work feels empty, didactic, aped. Sometimes others champion such writing as beautiful, revealing. But the writer knows deep inside his/her blood that it's weak, insincere—not worthy.

We feel it more than think it. When the *duende* is activated in a person, we all vibrate.

Lorca says it best: "The *duende* takes it upon himself to make us suffer by means of a drama of living forms."

But it's not all suffering. "The magical property of a poem is to remain possessed by *duende* that can baptize in dark water all who look at it." Just because the water is dark doesn't mean it can't be blessed. And a poem can also be a song, a play or a moment of exquisite performance.

Writing is a hurt business, akin to ballet, boxing, chess and other trials by fire. If you come out of it unscathed, you most likely haven't done very much. I have been wrestling with my personal *duende* for nearly 20 years of playwriting. This guarantees me neither award nor pension. But it grants me lived experience going after life, love, and death *on the page* and, hopefully, eventually *onstage.*

The things we rightly avoid in daily life we want and must have in our theater. I want to live happily and quietly, but in my plays I need to search for extremity, for boiling points, in each character as well as in the greater story.

This is how a dramatist can be revolutionary. I'm not simply talking politics. Rather, I mean actively unearthing taboos, transgressions, in order to unleash the real feelings beneath the surface of a character. This can be brutal business, because the unearthed revelations are often highly personal.

Undoubtedly, there are feelings, ideas, images and words that can be dangerous when exposed. But Lorca and I demand the strenuous use of the heart muscle. This means taking chances.

The dramatist *invents* opportunities for characters to reveal themselves. This is how we open up what's really going on inside a person—inside ourselves.

We trade in the unexplained when we write for actors; we hear voices, we channel experiences outside our daily grind. We summon thoughts, feelings—even the ghosts of the departed—in the drumbeat of our work. Playwriting is a bit of a black art, and we shouldn't be ashamed of that.

It's a solemn rite. We rouse the animal want inside each of us from its sleep. We give it voice; we add pain, increased awareness of death, and the mordant sense of humor and even joy that comes with it. Then we fling it into the wind.

That is what a play can be.

On main stages throughout the country and in the language, writers and audiences settle *for so much less.* Minus this level of investment and immediacy, plays and performers miss their ritual and spiritual aspects, and theater loses its elemental functions. With neither flow nor connection on an animal level, plays function according to type at surface levels, hardly dipping into the deep waters that are always there.

Ambition is the question. Not the ambition to win a Pulitzer or a movie deal but the appetite for investigation—first of oneself, then for the world—one person at a time.

Playwriting is a terrible business. Theater is indefensible on a spreadsheet. Numbers don't add up because it's not about the numbers. Of course we in the theater want hits, cash, adulation—but the joy of doing it is not about any of those things.

We're counterintuitive; we often do our best work for free, when we're hungry and tired, with only a few stragglers in the audience. Because we live in an age of rampant capitalism, we in our poverty can be made to feel that we've failed when compared to this week's blue-screen blockbuster's box office returns. But ours is another kind of currency.

When we're doing what we should onstage, we're battling to free our inner selves by using all the charm, beauty, ugliness, and rage we share at this moment, living on this planet together. We're diving into dark waters with no idea how deep down they go. We're tickling the universals, unsure whether we'll get a laugh or a sneeze in return. We're creating something new, and that's always the hardest of businesses, because it's not a business at all. It's a vocation, a calling.

Each of us has a particular path to destruction, individual as a thumbprint or a smile. Whether comedic or tragic, good writing provides a candle to enlighten at least our first few steps into this cave of ourselves. After that, each of us is on his/her own.

My desires, fears, and secrets are as particular to me as yours are particular to you. But we both have them.

We in the theater are miraculously beholden to no one but ourselves. We're outside the corporate mentality, the steady paycheck and the loyalty oath; and here in Hollywood, despite our shared talent pools, we're often separate from the movie industry. And this may just be a very good thing.

We have the chance, if we take it, to be free—even if it's only for a moment. Not irresponsible, or silly. But liberated to say what's sleeping in our blood, what's beyond language, what's outside reason and away from the dollar sign.

What is truly new. Truly now. And we

have the chance to do this together.

The way to begin is deceptively simple. Rather than reaching to Joycean literary extremes or subscribing to one faith-based politics or another, the foolproof way to awaken one's own revolutionary urges is to really ask—what do I want? What am I afraid of? What is my secret?

Once you really know those things (which by the way are quite changeable from day to day), and once you are willing to take the chance of revealing all, then you will feel amazingly free to give these desires, fears, and secrets to your characters, which in turn gives them life, specificity, and hopefully that blushing, scorching, vibrating immediacy we come to theater to see.

Lorca asks, "The *duende*... where is the *duende*?" He answers, "Through an empty arch comes a wind, a mental wind blowing relentlessly over the heads of the dead, in search of new landscapes and unknown accents... announcing the constant baptism of newly created things."

What new landscapes remain to be baptized? We'll never know till we know how to ask.

In my new play, "Young Valiant," one of the characters quotes e.e. cummings when she says, "Always the beautiful answer who asks the more beautiful question." The dramatist spends a career, or a lifetime, asking the unanswerable. The answer, if there is one, does not belong to us, or what we've written. If an answer comes at all, it will be in the blue streak of recognition we all feel—when we're very lucky—during a performance.

What blushing revelations are about to be unearthed? What exquisite *duende* can we tempt from the dark caves within us?

I'm asking.

Oliver Mayer is assistant professor of dramatic writing at the USC School of Theatre. His plays include "Blade to Heat," "Joe Louis Blues," "Ragged Time," and "Conjunto."

Copyright 2005 Los Angeles Times

Federico García Lorca, in a novelty shot with his friend, the director Luis Buñuel.

freud's bastard children

May 5, 2005

Oliver Mayer, in the house for Young Valiant, a play made for Freudian obsessional compulsives!

These images were created for a San Diego State University literature class where Oliver Mayer guest-lectured on *Young Valiant*, Spring 2005.

Digital graphics by Guillermo Nericcio García.

Young Valiant: Oliver Mayer's Curious Freudian Valentine

William A. Nericcio

i. City and Country

We are concerned here with the encounter of at least two realms: the psychological and the theatrical—the dark, fertile corridors of the unconscious and the dark, evocative aisles of the theater sharing more than one might think at first glance. The work of Los Angelino Oliver Jai'sen Mayer seems of particular interest in this regard.

Some background first: unlike other 60s and 70s-era Mexican-American writers, Oliver Mayer's narratives do not focus upon the rural, agricultural Latino experience. Mayer's father was an art director in Hollywood, his mother an administrative health professional for the city of Los Angeles. His obsessions, then, are not fields, ranches, and valleys but boxing, downtown chaos, broken love, and a past that is rapidly disappearing—in the city, rapid, concrete "progress" mutates the cultural and geographic landscapes of Chicano communities on a daily basis—think "Chavez Ravine" in Los Angeles, and "Chicano Park" under the Coronado overpass in San Diego, to name just two.[9]

Where Tomás Rivera (. . . *y no se lo tragó la tierra*) locates Chicano angst in the rolling trucks of the migrant caravan, Mayer finds it in the bedrooms and kitchens of the middle-class home. Both Rivera and Mayer's protagonists are confused young men, but the site where each encounters the crisis of adolescence could not be more different: Rivera's boy mad beyond belief suffering beneath a house; Mayer's Boy hornier than a goat, and suffering as a result, knocking down walls within a small home.

This is neither bad nor good—it merely shows the range of the Mexican American textual production, the range of classes within our community. As Bruce-Novoa suggests, the trend in Chicano narrative and in its criticism has been to favor the rural over the urban Chicano.[10] This is not the case with *Young Valiant*. Like Sandra Cisneros in *The House on Mango Street*, Mayer charts the rocky waters of adolescence, teaching his audience about late

twentieth-century Americana, even as he painfully delineates the culture of the urban home, where growing up always amounts to growing out of something (the walls Dad and Boy destroy) or of somebody (Boy's death wish for Dad).

ii. In Which is Told the Tale of the Play

Essentially, Mayer's autobiography-tinged *Young Valiant* tells the story of three characters: Dad, Mama, and Boy. Dad is in his "early fifties, physically powerful and gentle despite himself." Mama is in her "early thirties, Mexican-American, no perceptible accent, but dark, strong, and beautiful." Lastly, Boy is "eleven." The only description Mayer provides is that he is "his parents' child," though the epigraph to the play adds that BOY (or Mayer?) is "the crazy child of parents too difficult to forget."

Mayer's two-act drama traces the fractures of middle-class family life as each of the play's protagonists crosses the threshold of some dangerous and unavoidable borderline: Dad facing old age with rage, doubt, and fear; Mama contemplating a life without her older husband; and Boy confronting the terrors and desires of early manhood. To its credit, Mayer's *Young Valiant* reveals the passions of dual-ethnic discord even as it carefully maps the pathos of growing old. In a sense, he

---

[9] Hop on over to the following PBS website (http://www.pbs.org/independentlens/chavezravine) to see what I mean and check out David R. Diaz's *Barrio Urbanism: Chicanos, Planning, and American Cities* (London: Routledge, 2005) for more on these urban transmutations.

[10] Juan Bruce-Novoa, *Retrospace: Collected Essays on Chicano Literature, Theory and History* (Houston: Arte Publico, 1990).

targets two overlapping *fronteras*: that between cultures and that between generations. This is typical of his generation of contemporary Chicano writers and of the next, those whom I have burdened with my neologism *Xicanosmotic*.[11] Newly established in the creative establishment of the entertainment arts, *the entertainment industry*, they are more interested in documenting the pathos and banality of everyday life than recreating the mythos of some tragically squandered and/or stolen utopic past, even if it is called Aztlán (No worries, brown-beret sporting essentialists! Those crafty Mexica, however, still always find a way back in—it's our Chicana/o destiny).

iii. Young Valiant *Cliffs's Notes*

The "action" of the play takes place in one morning and afternoon. In the first act, Boy wakes up to the sound of his parents making love. Hearing Mama laugh, Boy wants to make his mother laugh like his father does, which leads to a conversation between the boy and his father about making love. The boy, now confused by the trials of love (who wouldn't be?), discovers erotic love through his mother, later

smacking her with a moist "musky" kiss. Confused, startled, and angry, Mama stalks out of the house to her old, largely Mexican American neighborhood where, offstage, she revels in the pain and pleasure of nostalgia—attempting to figure out the puzzle of her son's precocious, misdirected passion. Meanwhile, Boy and Dad stay home and knock down a wall so as to make the house feel more spacious (this, as was mentioned above, has larger psychological implications). Here they talk, argue, battle, insult and finally engage in a mock boxing match only to be interrupted by the return of Mama. Dad goes to a bar to watch a boxing match, while Mama and Boy finally talk—Boy confessing he wants his father dead. Mama slaps the boy (completing the boxing lesson introduced by Dad?). As the play comes to a close, Dad faces the terrors of personal obsolescence—this is especially evident when when we learn an older, Mexican boxer Dad adored (Zarate) has been beaten by a younger man in the ring. The play ends as it begins, with the music of Prokofiev's *Romeo and Juliet* framing characters no longer sure of where or who they really are.

This brief synopsis does not capture the many levels Mayer is able to sustain throughout his script. Even as this play melodramatically chronicles the pains of growing old, it also and at the same time reinscribes the site of the legendary Oedi-

---

11 William Nericcio, *Tex[t]-Mex: Seductive Hallucination of the "Mexican" in America* (Austin: The University of Texas Press, 2007).

pal struggle *estilo Chicano*, rethinks the ethos of boxing, explores anxieties intrinsic to mixed-generation marriages, and exposes the ties linking jealousy and fear, anger and self-doubt. The *Romeo and Juliet* angle also yields meaningful revelations with regard to love and taboo love—one never wants to underestimate the impact of Shakespeare on the mind of a contemporary playwright. That's a lot to roll into a *Bildungsroman* of a play that would give Oedipus, Sophocles, and Freud a lot to talk about—Jocasta might want to buy a ticket to the preview as well.

iv. Amor, Dolor, Escritor

It is with the character of Mama that Mayer chooses to explore the painful scars that cognizance of racial difference, of existential inferiority, inflicts upon individuals and, implicitly, on entire communities. You do not have to be a student of Freud, Lacan, or of Gloria Anzaldúa, Henry Louis Gates, or Luce Irigaray to glean the significance of the following dream sequence I cite below at length (readers of Toni Morrison's first novel *The Bluest Eye* will find Mayer's dramatic reveries familiar):

> Mama: I had a dream last night . . . The scary thing was . . . well, it was like this. I was sleeping. But it didn't really look like me. My hair was long, and blonde, and my skin was at least a couple shades lighter. And my eyes were blue, as blue as Dad's. It was just the way I wanted myself to look when I was your age. And the funny part was, I was your age. I couldn't have been more than 10 or 12. And then this music started playing . . . very romantic music, something from a lot later in my life . . . And then . . . (she stops cooking), then this man came in the picture. Well, not a man. Sort of a Boy-Man. He sort of looked like me—not the blonde me, but the way I really look. I mean, he was dark, and he had this smile . . . He came in, and that's when I opened my eyes, the blonde me that is . . . And then the music really started picking up, like a dance. And then I saw us come together, and you know what it was like? It was sort of like the Sunday comic strip I used to read when I was a girl, *Prince Valiant*, it was my absolute favorite, it was so beautiful. And there we were—I was Aleta, and he was Valiant, and we were dancing, and that's when the alarm woke me up. (slight pause) But the last thing I remember was his face. Such a pretty face, it didn't really look like me anymore. A little, but I had changed, And that's when I got scared, Because the face, well . . . it looked like you.

Misreading the dream, Boy (no doubt enchanted by new emotions and hormones wracking his system) gives his mother a passionate kiss. This particular scene, as sensitive to the influence Anglocentric *totems* in mass culture have on non-represented minorities (the brown-skinned, dark-haired Mama dreaming a "blonde me" via romance *Prince Valiant*-style) as to the dynamics of the Oedipal triangle (Boy desires Mama/Boy desires death of Dad), bothered early critics of the play. Mayer even considered changing it. As he ran the script through readings with his actors, though, Mayer saw how essential this domestic transgression (Boy's "musky" kiss of Mama) was to the spirit of his project. As he said to me in a recent interview, "I learned not to flinch from the intimacy."

v. Ethnic Studies and the Realm of the Aesthetic

I do not want to overemphasize Mayer's ethnicity at the expense of his artistry—both spice up the mix of his dramatic *sopa de gran pena*/heartbreak soup.[12] Even as he makes it more difficult for reader and spectator alike to generalize what constitutes *the* Mexican American experience, he is hard at work *doing the stuff* dramatists have always done for their audiences—creating stories that allow us to leave our world and enter others. The catch is that once we return we are never free again to see things as we once did. The "escape" Mayer's *entertainment* provides returns us to our own world changed.

After reading or witnessing *Young Valiant*, it will do us little good to romanticize the innocence and simplicity of childhood: that idealized hearth—the *home* which sheltered our lives as children—is the "uncanny" site of the same emotional and sexual tensions, the same overlapping alienations we usually associate with our adult living spaces.[13] It is to Mayer's credit that he has been willing—like John Rechy (*City of Night*), Sandra Cisneros (*The House on Mango Street*), Arturo Islas (*The Rain God*), Carla Trujillo (*What Night Brings*), and Tomás Riley (*Mahcic*)—to portray the sexual reality, *live in* the sexually problematic space of a 20th- and 21st-century *United-statesian* domestic scene with a distinctly West Coast *Chicano/a* flavor.

vi. The Parting Shot

In its prehistoric past *Young Valiant* was developed at the Columbia University graduate program for playwrights and had readings and stagings at INTAR in New York, at the South Coast Repertory Thea-

---

[12] Gilbert Hernandez, *Palomar: The Heartbreak Soup Stories/Love and Rockets* (Seattle: Fantagraphics Books, 2003).

[13] For more on "The Uncanny" see Freud's essay of the same name in the *Standard Edition of the Complete Psychological Works of Sigmund Freud*, trans. and ed. James Strachey, 24 vols. (London: Hogarth Press, 1953-74). For cool, slightly more recent takes on the same, see Jane Marie Todd's "The Veiled Woman in Freud's "Das Unheimliche" *Signs* 88:6 (1986), 519-28. Also priceless? Read *The Purloined Poe: Lacan, Derrida, and Psychoanalytic Reading*, John P. Muller and William J. Richardson, eds. (Baltimore: The Johns Hopkins University Press, 1987).

ter in Costa Mesa, California, and at the Shenandoah Playwright retreat in Staunton, Virginia—its last incarnation was at Casa 0101 in Los Angeles.

At Columbia University, Mayer's teacher, Albert F. Innaurato, called the first version of the play "a sorry piece of shit—an elusive, hiding poseur piece that was anything but good." Mayer's response was to write a second act and to stage readings in New York—Innaurato was sure no Nostradamus, thanks be to the gods.

We should be glad of Mayer's perseverance, what I have called elsewhere (probably while we were drinking tequila together on Ithaca's Buffalo Street hill in upstate New York) his wicked and electric, mule-channeling *stubbornness*.

For *Young Valiant* is a production to be reckoned with. It does not rest content merely to rehash the clichéd angst of white mid-American suburban culture. It goes much further, exploding the empty sham of the home as site of safe and comfortable *self* development. Mayer reminds us that the home is the site of personal growth *and*, necessarily, personal alienation.

The product of a dual ethnic upbringing, Oliver Mayer carefully walks the line between autobiographical excess and objective artistry reminding us of the incestuous ties that reveal the two as one.

Oliver Mayer with roommate James Guiry in the wild snows of Ithaca, 1986.

The classic shot of Sigmund Freud, 1920.

Oliver Mayer's Father, Alexander Mayer

Long ago and farther away each day, a distinctly Southern California family set to work on their Studio City home in the hope of making it fit them better. Sweat flew, walls came down, drywall dust clung to the air seemingly for days. That's Dad, in his Mexican vest, under the sink. Mama took the polaroid. Boy is probably up in his parents' bedroom, certainly avoiding as much labor as possible, most likely dreaming about his future victories and loves. The house changed along with the people in it. Eventually we three left the house—one way or the other—although the house will never leave us. That polaroided day lives on in some mythic extension of ourselves. Somewhere along the way, the photo took a direct hit from mop water and morphed into its present state. May it live forever (however short or long that may be) here now, with you.

Oliver Mayer

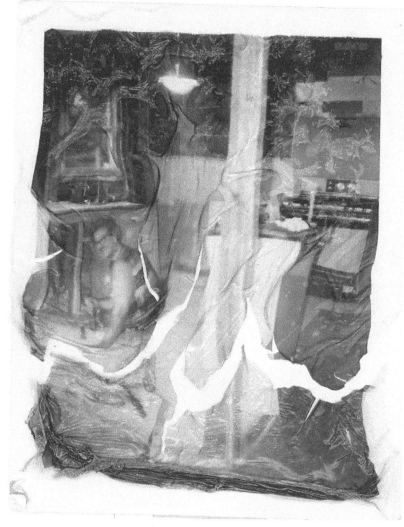

Oliver Mayer's Mother, Gloria Mayer, née Padilla

The program from the Public Theater production of *Blade to the Heat*, 1994.

BLADE TO THE HEAT
World Premiere 1994, performed
at the Joseph Papp Public Theater

directed by George C. Wolfe

PEDRO QUINN Kamar de los Reyes
MANTEQUILLA DECIMA Paul Calderon
WILFRED VINAL Nelson Vasquez
SARITA Maricela Ochoa
GARNET Carlton Wilborn
ALACRAN Jaime Tirelli
THREE FINGER JACK Chuck Patterson
REFEREE James Colby
CONGUEROS Ron McBee, Carlos Valdez

A revised version of the play premiered 1996,
performed at the Mark Taper Forum Mainstage

directed by Ron Link
PEDRO QUINN Ray Oriel
MANTEQUILLA DECIMA Dominic Hoffman
WILFRED VINAL Raymond Cruz
SARITA Justina Machado
GARNET Hassan El-Amin
ALACRAN Sal Lopez
THREE FINGER JACK Ellis E. Williams
REFEREE/REPORTER/ANNOUNCER Gerrit Graham
ENSEMBLE Wayne Brady, Cesar Hernandez, Maceo Hernandez, Michael Hernandez, Zilah Hill, Alfredo Ortiz, William Stephen Taylor, George Villas

And he swings
Oh swings: beyond complete
immortal now.

Robert Hayden

For the dog

Frontispiece from the infamous *Prensa de la Vanidad* edition of *Blade to the Heat*.

A bull terrier barking.

DRUMS. Then BELL rings. THE GYM, heavy bags, speed bags, ropes skipping, shoes squeaking. Sweat and cigar smoke. Men working out with each other and in front of mirrors. Then MUSIC, loud and strong. Garnet enters, the spitting image of Jackie Wilson. He sings an intense rhythm and blues number, which is strongly imitative of Jackie Wilson. As he sings he executes a tight one-leg shimmy to perfection. Lands a split, then pulls the mike close. As the song builds to climax, and he is about to land the backflip on the downbeat—BELL rings. Two FIGHTERS spar. THREE FINGER JACK and ALACRAN shout instructions.

JACK: (*to one*) The head!

ALACRAN: (*to the other*) *Tira!*

JACK: Punch him in the head!

ALACRAN: *El gancho al hígado! Al hígado!*

JACK: Punch a man in the head it mixes his mind.

ALACRAN: Work the body! Break him into little pieces! *Tira, coño!* (*His man goes down.*)

ALACRAN: They no listen.

JACK: Neither did we. We didn't listen to nobody.

ALACRAN: That's 'cause nobody listened to us!

JACK: You and me, we was the uncrowned champs!

ALACRAN: You mean chumps!

BELL rings. The fighters towel off, resting. Only

PEDRO, alone in a corner, continues to shadow-box.

JACK: Yeah, but there's still hope. The boy who wins nowadays got to have the heart, the fire, and he got to be a roman'ic.

ALACRAN: Ah, you always talking poetry.

Cameras flash. MANTEQUILLA DECIMA, the champ, enters with entourage. REPORTER approaches.

REPORTER: Hey Champ! Give us a good shot! Which hand you gonna knock him out with?

MANTEQUILLA: (*brandishing the right hand*) El Suzie Q.

REPORTER: Smart money's on you, as always. You beaten everybody else. So what's next? Retire? Run for president? What?

MANTEQUILLA: I was born to fight. To wear the belt. Is a beautiful sport. A mang can be a mang. You dance, you play, you get angry. But in the end it all come down to *corazón*. And this too. (*makes a fist*) My dream? I beat this guy—retire undefeated—then I go home to my country. My people, I love them very much. So after we get rid of this *como-se-llama* Castro, then *¿quién sabe?*

REPORTER: You got my vote!

MANTEQUILLA: Too bad you' not my people! (*BELL rings*)

ALACRAN: (*pointing at MANTEQUILLA*) ¡Qué chulada! That man is like a god. I useta fight just like that—*igualito*! Décima, he's a trainer's dream, if he gave me a chance, *híjole*—!

JACK: (*pointing at PEDRO*) Now that's beautiful. Most beautiful thing in the world, a boy working his little butt off. Pure gold, and you can bet he listens! (*to PEDRO, who is still boxing*) Don't burn yerself out now! Take it slow now, 'cause we want you to take that title! Yes we do. Take it on back for all us never got the chance! 'Cause you our boy!

ALACRAN: Ain't mine.

JACK: But he a Messican!

ALACRAN: With a name like Quinn?

JACK: Don't blame him. Blame his daddy!

ALACRAN: Mick-Jew-whoever the hell he was.

JACK: But to go agin yer own —

ALACRAN: Y tú, ¿qué sabes? You look in the mirror recently? Mantequilla ain't black and ugly like you, but he is black!

JACK: But that don't count. He' a Cuban!

ALACRAN: Talk trash at me . . . Support your own, *cabrón*!

JACK: Boy like that, you give him half a chance, he' dangerous. Like one of them pit bulls.

ALACRAN: That mutt?

BELL rings. Reporter approaches Pedro.

REPORTER: Got anything to say, Kid? No one expects too much. You going up against the best pound for pound and all that. What do you get for a fight like this? Besides a beating? Do you really think you can take him?

PEDRO: Me?

REPORTER: Yeah, you! Who else?

PEDRO: I'm just gonna do the best I can.

REPORTER: (exiting) He's dead!

Pedro exits the other way.

ALACRAN: (looking at MANTEQUILLA)
There's the man. *Todo hombre. ¡Como ésto!*
(raises his fist like an erection)

JACK: Is that what I think it is? I swear
sometimes you' queerer than Dick's hat
band.

ALACRAN: Who?

JACK: You who!

ALACRAN: *¡Tú!*

JACK: Tu-tu! Always knew there was something funny about you, sucka!

ALACRAN: Who you calling sucka, sucka?

*They slap-box for a few moments, both ending
up on the floor, winded.*

JACK: Damn!

ALACRAN: *¡Cabrón!*

JACK: Gonna be a great fight! Two fellas
washed in the blood. Just like we was. Two
young men with their whole lives ahead of
'em. Two mighty mighty men. Fighting for
us. And for that belt. That beautiful belt.
Them two —(DRUMS) They deserve every
damn thing they get.

*BELL rings. Cheers, jeers, catcalls. A growing
animal hum from an immense crowd. THE
RING. Mantequilla and Pedro come together in
ring center for the FIFTEENTH and FINAL
ROUND. The REFEREE makes them touch
gloves. They fight. DRUMS punctuate punches
landing or whizzing by. Pedro fights moving
forward, throwing punches constantly. Mantequilla retreats boxing beautifully and scoring
combinations. Each man scores well and heavily. There's an unintentional head-butt—
Referee checks for cuts. Pedro apologizes.*

REFEREE: Box!

*Mantequilla lies back, then throws the vaunted
SUZIE Q—a wide bolo punch, which corkscrews
up like a machete cutting sugarcane. It lands
like a shotgun blast on Pedro's chin. FREEZE on
what ought to be a knockout—you simply cannot throw a punch any better. Mantequilla
steps back, admiring his work. But Pedro ab-
sorbs the blow. His body shakes from the
impact but he won't fall. Then, inexplicably, he
SMILES. A mysterious, unsettling smile. Pedro
drives Mantequilla to the ropes and rains
blows. Mantequilla tries to hold, but Pedro
yanks himself free. BELL rings. The fight over,
they stagger apart. They embrace. Mantequilla
confidently does a victory lap around the ring,
while Pedro shrouds himself under a towel. The
microphone drops from the rafters.*

ANNOUNCER: After fifteen rounds . . .
(sound echoes in the stadium) We have a split
decision . . . The winnah, and NEW
CHAMPION OF THE WORLD . . . PEDRO
QUINN!!! QUINN!!! QUINN!!!

*Pandemonium. Cheers, boos. Pedro disbelieving
as his hand is raised and he receives the championship belt. Flashbulbs. Mantequilla alone in
defeat. MUSIC, very Perez Prado.*

DRESSING ROOM. *Mantequilla unwraps his*

hands. The right is hurt. SARITA, in a black turtleneck and pants, lights a cigarette.

MANTEQUILLA: ¡HIJO de la gran PUTA—!!!

SARITA: So you lost.

MANTEQUILLA: ¡Hijo de la gran PUTA!!! *(flexes the injured hand) Come mierda—(hits himself hard with it)* COME MIERDA!!!!

SARITA: Don't do that. You're still my champ. *(beat)* Well, you are, aren't you? You look good. Not a mark on you. That counts for something. And God knows you dressed better. You won that hands down—he had some very ugly accessories. And the tassels on his shoes. Please. Promise me, baby, don't ever wear tassels. Tassels went out a long time ago. Lampshades wear tassels, and they're so girly—when you get hit they make you shake like a good-time girl —

MANTEQUILLA: ¡Por FAVOR, chica!!

SARITA: So I'm nervous. I never seen you lose.

MANTEQUILLA: I never lose.

SARITA: Everybody loses, baby.

MANTEQUILLA: No' me. I beat them all. La Havana, Oriente, Ciudad Mexico, Miami Beach, Estockton, Las Vegas—*las gané todas—con ésto—(the left hook) con el Suzie Q—(the right bolo) y con ésto! (pounds his forehead)*

SARITA: Yeah, you got a pretty mean headbutt.

MANTEQUILLA: *¡No tonta! ¡Mi inteligensia! ´Mi imaginación!*

SARITA: Just a joke. Little joke—

MANTEQUILLA: *(not a compliment)* Chicanas.

SARITA: Don't say that word. I don't like it. Say Spanish.

MANTEQUILLA: *¡Chicanas!*

SARITA: I'm Spanish! I'm from El Lay, all right?

MANTEQUILLA: *¿Como Quinn?*

SARITA: Yeah. Like Quinn.

Pedro crosses the stage. He has a black eye. He looks like a kid. Inexpensive clothes and worn gym bag. Opens a door—camera FLASHES, screams, shouts of "PEYDRO"—he reacts as if caught in headlights. Door closes behind him. Meanwhile, Mantequilla strips naked and is about to enter the shower.

SARITA: Hurt?

MANTEQUILLA: *(gestures)* This hurty.

SARITA: I got a feeling it'll swell back up to size.

MANTEQUILLA: *(under the spout)* He no' even punch hard! I hit him goo' *pero* he no wanna go.

SARITA: Us Mexicans are pretty tough.

MANTEQUILLA: Alla time I hit him, he stang there in fronta me, just stang there, *con esa sonrisa, comemierda!*

SARITA: He was smiling?

MANTEQUILLA: *(still showering)* You no see it?!!!

SARITA: A smile?

MANTEQUILLA: He makey fun of me?!!!

SARITA: My pop always said when you see a guy smiling like you didn't hurt him—

you hurt him.

MANTEQUILLA: *¡Seguro! ¡Sin duda!* I hit him purty goo' *en la panza*—he gonna go hurty when he go pee-pee. He no feel too sexy now.

SARITA: He never did.

Mantequilla turns off the shower. Advances on her naked.

MANTEQUILLA: What you say?

SARITA: Dry off baby. We don't want you catching cold. (*throws him a towel*) Kinda sexy when you're mad.

MANTEQUILLA: *Oye.* I am always sexy. (*embraces her*) *¡Qué bien te ves, chica!*

SARITA: Just your basic black.

MANTEQUILLA: *Pero* I wish you' wear a dress, *coño!!*

SARITA: They're not beat.

MANTEQUILLA: *Pero* you look like a little boy.

SARITA: That's why you like me.

MANTEQUILLA: (*pushes her away*) No play like that! (*He dresses, clothes expensive and well-tailored.*)

SARITA: So touchy! Come on. Let's go listen to some jazz. Let's go uptown and dance! A little rum and coke, a lotta me . . . You sure you okay?

MANTEQUILLA: *Algo . . .*

SARITA: What?

MANTEQUILLA: That guy —

SARITA: Who?

MANTEQUILLA: Quinn!

SARITA: Forget him!

MANTEQUILLA: Too . . . *como se dice . . .* nice. I no like nice. We fighting in close, *así*—(*demonstrates on her*) and I hitting him in *el hígado*, in the liver, and he hit me with his head—BOOM! —and he say "Escuse me." Escuse me? What is that? He makey fun of me? I pop this guy—*tremendo golpe como cañonazo—y nada.* El Suzie Q—and he just kinda smile. You no see that smile? I gonna see that smile in my dreams! (*stares at himself in the mirror*) I gonna see it in my dreams.

SARITA: You hit him so hard I thought you killed him. Some people smile when they die. Maybe he died a little. (*as he dresses in silence*) You know, I got a pretty good smile, too! You ever dream about my smile?

MANTEQUILLA: Not like that.

SARITA: Well, I'm smiling. So forget about Petey Quinn.(*a moment, then*) Are you hungry?

MANTEQUILLA: *¡Espérate—!*

SARITA: Let's go get something to eat —

MANTEQUILLA: D'you say Petey? Petey Quinn?

SARITA: What do you mean?

MANTEQUILLA: D'you know this guy? This Petey Quinn?

SARITA: Of course I know him!

MANTEQUILLA: *¡CARAJO!!!*

SARITA: Don't do that.

MANTEQUILLA: D'you go with him?

SARITA: No I didn't go —

MANTEQUILLA: D'YOU WENT WITH HIM?

SARITA: Don't be jealous —

MANTEQUILLA: ¡COME MIERDA!!!

SARITA: I don't go out with *Chicanos.* Gimme a little credit here. And DON'T INTERROGATE ME. (*silence*) So he's cute. So shoot me.

MANTEQUILLA: CUTE?!!!

SARITA: I can't even talk about a guy —!!!

MANTEQUILLA: NO OTHER GUYS!!!

SARITA: YOU SEE!!!

MANTEQUILLA: I'm the only guy! I'm the mang!

SARITA: Not anymore. (*silence*)

MANTEQUILLA: Hmm. (*collects himself*) Maybe this time he win. *Pero* the next time —(*makes fist*) *me llamo martillo. El ponchador martillo.* I gonna dead him sure with my hammer.

SARITA: You gonna show him your hammer? I thought I was the only one gets to see it.

MANTEQUILLA: You joke alla time.

SARITA: Not all the time.

MANTEQUILLA: You no like me no more?

SARITA: I like you.

MANTEQUILLA: *Pero*, like that.

SARITA: Yeah, like that. (*They come together, reflected in the mirror.*) Do you ever think about me when you're in the ring? When you're in there, doing what you do, you ever see us making love? (*kisses his knuckles*)

MANTEQUILLA: You no make love in the ring.

SARITA: I wish you did. (*beat*) You look like a champ.

MANTEQUILLA: *Pero* I no champ no more. Chit. Chit chit chit.

SARITA: I love it when you talk dirty.

MANTEQUILLA: I win next time. I get back my belt. I work so hard for that belt!

SARITA: We both do. Let's get beat.

MANTEQUILLA: I no wanna get beat.

SARITA: Not "beat"—Beat. Red hot and cool.

MANTEQUILLA: Tha's my goo' bad girl. (*cracks his Sugar Ray Robinson grin*) I look okay?

SARITA: Baby, you're the champ.

MUSIC. Classic R&B as GARNET imitates Jackie Wilson and James Brown. THE GREEN ROOM. James Brown plays distantly. Garnet enters, sweating. Pedro is waiting there.

GARNET: No stuff! (*They slap five.*) I guess I can call ya Champ. (*grabs the belt*) Aw, man—I always wanted one of these! (*walks around with it*) Local Boy Done Good! (*resumes undressing*) I knew you could.

PEDRO: (*listens to the tune*) James Brown?

GARNET: The man sweats too much. Can't be healthy. Shouting and wheezing and slaver all over the place. (*beat*) Wish I coulda been there tonight —

PEDRO: Naw, you had a gig —

GARNET: Shoulda took the night off. But I

knew you'd win. (*drinks from flask*) Here's to the King. And long may he reign.

Pedro doesn't drink. He seems wound-up, ill at ease. Garnet picks up the championship belt.

GARNET: Fit?

PEDRO: Nope.

GARNET: Lemme see.

PEDRO: Didn't think it would be like this.

GARNET: Didn't figure you'd come here. Tonight of all nights. I mean, why aintcha out on the town? Must be a victory party or something —

PEDRO: I walked out on it.

GARNET: You what?

PEDRO: Didn't feel right.

GARNET: But it was for you!

PEDRO: I don't want a party. I don't deserve a party.

GARNET: But you're the Champ! You won—

PEDRO: It was just a decision. That's no way to beat a king.

GARNET: (*with the belt*) But it's yours —

PEDRO: But it doesn't fit.

GARNET: Don't they size these things?

PEDRO: Look. You beat the man who beat the man —

GARNET: Maybe you're supposed to wear it over one shoulder —

PEDRO: Like a line of kings. It's supposed to fit. Fit Mantequilla like a glove. He deserved it. He earned it. And now I got it and it just don't fit —

GARNET: (*showing him*) Little clasp on the back.

PEDRO: He's the Man.

GARNET: No, you the Man.

PEDRO: But —

GARNET: Don't matter what you think. You the Champ. You passed the test. You come out the other side.

A new song by Jackie—something raucous and gospelly.

GARNET: Here. Listen up, you damn sad sack. This'll set you right. This belt will protect you!

Suddenly Garnet is on his feet lip-syncing and dancing to the song, landing a leg-drop, then popping up to a one-leg shimmy. It's wild and sexy and fun.

PEDRO: Wow! You're great!

GARNET: Not me. Jackie is the king.

PEDRO: Jackie Wilson?

GARNET: He's an emperor. But Brown wants the crown.

PEDRO: They're both kings.

GARNET: But there's only one crown. (*beat*) I'd take Jackie any day. Better looking. James just don't look wholesome. Not exactly what you wanna take home to Mom and Pop. Yeah, well, neither of them. But see, that's the thing. Don't matter how you look. It's who you are. (*tosses PEDRO's hair*) You wanna know something? Listen up. James Brown was a boxer.

PEDRO: Naw!

GARNET: Yep. He boxed. And you know

what else? Jackie, too.

PEDRO: Jackie boxed? No way.

GARNET: Hey, I know some things about boxing too.

PEDRO: But—I mean, he's so cool—I mean, the moves—

GARNET: Those moves of his? Boxing moves. What he learned he learned in the ring. See, he always saved a ringside seat for his Ma. So this one time she doesn't show, and he keeps looking over at the empty seat. So they're grabbing and clutching and leaning on each other and alla sudden Jackie sees her and he can't help himself. He just says "Hi Ma!" and—(three punches) Wop. Bop. Mop. See, he learned the hard way. Don't be looking to nobody. Not even Mom. Get down to business. And watch yerself in them clinches. Don't wanna get hit any more than you have to. (touches PEDRO's eye)

PEDRO: Useta dream about it all the time. And then tonight. There I was. Getting smacked around by the Man himself. I had to smile. I was so happy to be there. It made me smile. Even when he really hit me. Weird, getting hit. You feel so alive. (beat) That's the thing.

GARNET: What?

PEDRO: It doesn't last.

GARNET: What doesn't last?

PEDRO: That feeling. That . . . thing.

GARNET: How's your eye?

PEDRO: I don't feel it.

GARNET: You got to feel something. I mean, you're the champ. You been working your whole life for this! You been dreaming about other guys all these years. Now people gonna start dreaming about you. (PEDRO reacts) They will. Probably are already.

PEDRO: But I'm not good enough.

GARNET: (clasps his shoulder) It's all right. You got what you wished for. It's hard to get what you wish for.

PEDRO: I wish I could be like you.

GARNET: You don't wanna be like me.

PEDRO: And do what you do onstage. And move like that —

GARNET: Like what?

PEDRO: Like that move. You know—the one, the one —

GARNET: It's a tough one. You gotta keep your concentration. I studied Jackie like a book, worked on it for days and days in fronta the mirror. You gotta look super-sharp, you gotta look the people in the eye, you gotta be able to top all the knee-drops and one-leg shimmies them other contenders be putting up, you gotta be right in the middle of the song when they're right in the palm of your hand, when it's all on the line, and you gotta (demonstrates) land that backflip on the downbeat, come right on back with a shooby-doo-wop, and your pompadour not even mussed! Yeah, I nailed it. (They slap five on the backhand side.)

PEDRO: I've spent my whole life in fronta the mirror, and I never been that good. I never been there. If I could be like you, and not get hit —

GARNET: Oh I get hit. Every damn day of my life. Half the time they're talking through my set. Bust my gut, they don't give a good goddamn —

New 45 plays—Jackie Wilson classic side.

PEDRO: He's the King. (*sings along tentatively*) Help me out, wouldya?

GARNET: Naw, this ain't my key. (*gives in, sings a bit, then breaks off*) Nuh-uh. Can't touch that. Too good. (*beat*)

PEDRO: I better go.

GARNET: Lemme see you with the belt on.

PEDRO: No I can't. I don't wanna —

From the back, Garnet puts the belt around Pedro. Each backs away.

PEDRO: What? Does it look dumb? Is it that bad?

GARNET: It's beautiful.

PEDRO: It's what?

GARNET: You the man. No more doggin' around.

DRUMS. Spot on WILFRED VINAL as he hits the heavy bag—also curses, sweet-talks, even dry-fucks it. Jack and Alacrán watch.

JACK: Boy got more tricks than a hooker. And just as cheap.

ALACRAN: That's *El Chapo* Vinal. He's famous! He's from New York City! He's in the Top Ten.

JACK: Top ten?!! Top ten what? Public Ene-mies? You gotta be kidding —

ALACRAN: He's better than he looks. He come out here to fight Mantequilla and the wiener gets your boy—Quinn. For the title.

JACK: I'll be doggone. (*as VINAL exits flamboyantly*) He' a tomato can!

ALACRAN: So Mantequilla crush the tomato can, make a little *salsa*. Then he get the rematch *con* Quinn, and this time'll be different. This time we find out who's the better man. Who's the real champ around here. (*spits*) Quinn? *Chingao! Cabrón* think he's too good for us! We throw him a victory party, he hardly even show up! What? Something wrong with us? We ain't good enough? Little bastid got no respect!

JACK: You just sore 'cause he beat the flies offa your boy Mantequilla.

ALACRAN: *Wátchale, amigo.* Décima will be king again. (*DRUMS*) Vinal first. Then Quinn.

THE ARENA. TENTH and FINAL round. Mantequilla and Vinal at ring center. BELL rings. Mantequilla stalks Vinal, who thrusts, grabs, and clinches. To the beat of the drums, he makes a ballet out of fouling. Referee cautions him.

REFEREE: Watch the elbows!

VINAL: (*to MANTEQUILLA*) Watch the elbows!

REFEREE: (*pointing at VINAL*) You!

Mantequilla attacks. Vinal sidesteps, then punches him in the ass. They trade viciously. Vinal fouls him, then clinches.

VINAL: Don't clinch me, baby. I don't do no bendover.

REFEREE: You two wanna dance, do it in the dark!

VINAL: What are you, some kinda faggot?

Vinal blows him a kiss from a safe distance. Enraged, Mantequilla crushes him with the right hand, then punishes him in perfect rhythm with the drums. Vinal in trouble on the ropes as Mantequilla sets him up for the coup de grace—the Suzie Q. Vinal goes down. Takes the eight count. Rising, Mantequilla flurries and Vinal goes down hard. The Referee stops the contest.

VINAL: What're you doing?!! Don't walk away from me —

Referee raises Mantequilla's glove in victory. Vinal nearly hits the Referee, who exits fast.

VINAL: How could you stop it?!!! I wasn't hurt. I had him right where I wanted him! I was gonna knock him out! I had him! I had him right here in the palm of my hand!

Commotion in the ring. Vinal plays the crowd. Microphone drops from the rafters.

ANNOUNCER: The winnah, by knockout, Mantequilla Décima —!!

Mantequilla raises his glove. Vinal throws a tantrum, Into the microphone:

VINAL: Décima?!! That faggot? He din't knock me out!! You give it to that faggot?!! You can't give it to that faggot!! No, you can't give it to that faggot —!

MANTEQUILLA: Faggot?

VINAL: Faggot! *Tú*, baby! Let that little fag kick your ass. Fucking Pedro Queen! Ain't

no fag ever gonna beat me—(*rhythmic, as in a chant*) Come on, say it with me! ¡Ma-ri-cón! Ma-ri-cón!

As Vinal continues to chant in and out of the ring, TV REPORTER and CAMERAMAN approach.

TV REPORTER: (*on the move*) . . . The ex-champion definitely had the high-spirited New Yorker in trouble on the ropes . . . (*sidles up to MANTEQUILLA*) Here we are with the victor, Mantequilla Décima, in a bit of a wild scene. Were you bothered by Vinal's tactics?

MANTEQUILLA: Huh?

TV REPORTER: Tactics. He seemed to be talking to you during the contest. What was he saying? Was he trying to tell you something? I'm sure our viewers at home would be very interested to hear—Like the word he's saying now. *Marigold*? Perhaps you could translate. Go ahead, give us the gist if you can—

MANTEQUILLA: (*grabs the mike*) I win this fight no problem, *pero* I no rest till I get *la revancha con* Quinn.

TV REPORTER: You want to fight Pete Quinn again?

MANTEQUILLA: I want to fight Quinn. I prove I am a real mang. I dead him. I promise. (*Exits*)

TV REPORTER: Well there you have it! And just remember you heard it first on—

VINAL: (*grabs the mike*) He din't beat me! He's a fag! They're all fags! And Pete

Quinn, he's the biggest fag of all!

TV REPORTER: Cut it, for chrissakes!

VINAL: (*into camera*) Hi *Mami*.

DRUMS. MUSIC, mixed the ongoing chant of MA-RI-CÓN gives way to the sounds of the gym. Pedro skips rope. Radio plays James Brown. Alacrán and Jack watch from a distance.

ALACRAN: *¡Mira, cabrón!*

JACK: What am I looking at?

ALACRAN: See? There!

JACK: Where? Man I don't believe it.

ALACRAN: The way he moves. Look! That little sashay.

JACK: Man, if that's a sashay —

ALACRAN: It's right there in fronta your face —

BELL rings.

JACK: Say, Champ!

PEDRO: Say, Jack.

JACK: How ya feel?

PEDRO: I feel good.

JACK: You catch Mantequilla and Vinal? They stunk up the joint pretty bad. They didn't show me nothing. I think you got their number.

PEDRO: Don't jinx me. (*each knocks wood*)

JACK: I gotta admit, I wasn't sure we was gonna beat him, you being the unknown commodity and all that. But I like the way you do business. Real straight up. You done us proud.

PEDRO: Thanks, Jack. (*They shake hands boxer-style.*)

ALACRAN: Say, Champ.

PEDRO: Alacrán.

ALACRAN: *¿Comó está la novia?*

PEDRO: Huh?

ALACRAN: *La novia*. What? You no speaka Spanish? Your girlfriend. How's she doing?

PEDRO: Don't got one.

ALACRAN: *¡Qué no!* There's gotta be somebody. Come on! You can tell me. *¿Te gusta meter mano?*

PEDRO: Huh?

ALACRAN: *Meter mano?* Well. Ain't that a shame. Young fella like you and no *panocha* to be had. Don't you like a little tail between fights? After all, you the Man —

JACK: (*gets between them*) Don't mind him, Champ. He don't know nothing. Wetback always talking out his ass. (*BELL rings. Pedro resumes workout. To ALACRAN*) What the fuck you doing?

ALACRAN: I'm tryna show you something!

JACK: You mammyjamming old buzzard. You punch-drunk or what?

ALACRAN: You don't believe me? Are you blind?

JACK: I wish I was deaf!

Garnet enters. Alacrán and Jack instinctively form a human wall between him and Pedro.

JACK: Can I help you?

ALACRAN: You got business?

JACK: Um . . . I'll come back another time— (*about to exit*)

PEDRO: Hey! It's okay. Let him through.

He's with me.

Jack moves aside, but Alacrán doesn't budge. Garnet slides past him with a dance move.

PEDRO: Make yourself at home.

Garnet does another tight dance step.

PEDRO: Wow! What was that?

GARNET: You ain't the only one been working hard. I'm breaking in a new song tonight at the club.

PEDRO: Jackie? James?

GARNET: Just me. Been waiting a long time. Now it's my time. No more impersonating.

PEDRO: Cool.

Alacrán shadows him.

GARNET: (*looking around*) So this is it.

PEDRO: Not like the movies, huh?

GARNET: Place could use a good clean. (*ALACRAN slams a locker shut*) Where is everybody?

PEDRO: (*shrugs*) I prefer the quiet.

GARNET: (*as ALACRAN continues to shadow him*) I'ma go —

PEDRO: No! I mean it's okay. I never had a friend come up before.

GARNET: Hey, you the Champ. You got a million friends. (*ALACRAN scoffs.*) Well, there's a line of teenyboppers down the block waiting to get a look at the Champ.

PEDRO: I wish!

GARNET: You look good. (*ALACRAN whistles*) Here, I mean.

PEDRO: It's what I know.

BELL rings.

GARNET: (*awkward*) Pedro. Be at the club tonight?

PEDRO: I'll be there.

GARNET: All right.

Garnet exits quickly. Pedro works the heavy bag for a moment, then looks up.

PEDRO: That's my friend! (*resumes workout*)

ALACRAN: You see? You see?

JACK: What? It's a friend, ya damn fool! What's wrong with that?

ALACRAN: I knew it. It's what I told you, except it's worse! Fucking little chicano bastid! He's pissing on us. On the belt. On the game. On us. You shoulda listened to me.

JACK: You get outa his business.

ALACRAN: It's our business.

JACK: What the hell's it got to do with you?

ALACRAN: Everything, Jack. Every goddamn thing.

JACK: That boy deserves respect.

ALACRAN: Respect my ass!

JACK: Goddamn gossip! You're like some old woman! I'm sick of it —

ALACRAN: Now this is what we do. Cut him off. No talk. No warning. Just cut him off.

JACK: But he' my boy —

ALACRAN: Not if you know what's good for you. (*silence*) So. You with me?

JACK: Respect!

ALACRAN: Don't walk away from me!

JACK: (*to PEDRO*) I'll hold the bag for ya,

Champ.

ALACRAN: What you get angry with me for? He's the one! HE'S THE *MARICON*!!!

Pedro freezes. Feels all eyes on him. Then resumes hitting the bag one blow at a time.

JACK: That's it boy . . . Stay within yourself . . . Don't pay that fool no nevermind . . . That's it!

Pedro wears himself out on the bag.

ALACRAN: (*laughs at PEDRO*) He don't even deny it. He knows who he is! CUT HIM OFF!!!

DRUMS. MAMBO. Cuban flags. AIRPORT TARMAC. Mantequilla enters dancing with Sarita to the hottest sexiest mambo you have ever seen. Both of them dripping with style. They finish to applause. Mantequilla addresses a crowd.

MANTEQUILLA: I bery bery glad to be here in Miami. And to the Cubanos who are here, *¡le quiero decir que viva Cuba! ¡Que Viva Cuba Libre!*

SARITA: Give us room, please!

REPORTER: Say, Champ, the word was you were gonna retire before ya got beat. Care to comment? (*He doesn'.t*) Aren't you getting a little too old for the game?

MANTEQUILLA: (*smiling through anger*) I gonna be champ again real soon.

REPORTER: What about Quinn?

SARITA: What about him?

REPORTER: What about all this stuff coming from Wilfred Vinal?

MANTEQUILLA: Vinal? *Un imbécil. Pero* he

taught me something.

REPORTER: You mean it's true?

SARITA: *¡Payaso!* He just told you —

MANTEQUILLA: *Cálmate*, baby. (*They kiss, very sexy and public.*)

SARITA: He's all man! You see? You see? Get a picture.

Cameras FLASH.

MANTEQUILLA: We no' married yet, but we will be soon. (*motions for silence*) *Soy todo hombre. Todo hombre!* That's why I gonna win. You no can win *si es afeminado—como se dice*—un FAGGOT, *un maricón.* Vinal, he teach me you can no' trust the other guy. The other guy can be a bad mang. Or no mang at all. Now I have no mercy. Just like these beautiful Cuban people gonna have no mercy for *los malos Communistas! ¿Revolución? ¡Mierda¡* Buncha *maricón drogadictos, hijos de la gran puta se llama Communismo.* Castro? Guevara?!! Who are these guys? Get a shave. Put on some decent clothes! Then talk to me. Freedom fighters? *¡Aquí estamos!* The real freedom fighters! And me, I yam a freedom fighter! I fight for the goo' people—the normal people—of these beautiful *Estados Unidos!* How can I lose? T'ank you.

Applause, the million-dollar grin. Chants of MA-RI-CON mixed with DRUMS. Terrorizing nightmare sounds mixed with way-out jazz. As in a bad dream, images float past in darkness. TWO FIGHTERS, their faces obscured, are grabbing and clutching each other. The Referee appears.

REFEREE: I keep having this dream. I'm in there working, but it's like I'm in molasses. I can hardly move. And the fighters, well, they're just teeing off. Not just punches. I'm talking headbutts and elbows and laces and there's blood everywhere. I know I oughta stop it, I mean, hell, everybody knows. They're screaming at me. I feel like screaming, too, but I got the cotton mouth, can't get nothing out. And it's getting bad. The one fella, he's just getting ruint. Finally I get the feeling back, I can move. I can stop this thing. But the thing is, I don't. I let it go. I just let it go.

The fighters continue, more like they're fucking than fighting. DRUMS intensify. The fighters disappear as Mantequilla wakes from the dream. Sarita beside him. They are alone in bed.

MANTEQUILLA: *¡NO LO SOY!!!!*

SARITA: What?

MANTEQUILLA: *No lo soy.*

SARITA: What are you talking about?

MANTEQUILLA: *¿Por que maricón?*

SARITA: I don't know.

MANTEQUILLA: *¿Por qué?!!*

SARITA: Dammit!!

MANTEQUILLA: *¡Dime!!! Por qué?!!!*

SARITA: NOT YOU!!! *(silence)*

MANTEQUILLA: Quinn?

SARITA: Look, it's not true.

MANTEQUILLA: How you know?

SARITA: We went to school together. High school! They put all the Mexican kids in the same school —

MANTEQUILLA: D'YOU WENT WITH HIM?!!!

SARITA: You gotta be kidding! He's from El Monte, wrong side of the tracks. I'm from Montebello. We know these things. *(He stares at her.)* He wouldn't go out with me, okay? You satisfied?

MANTEQUILLA: He no go out with you?

SARITA: No he no go out with me. That bastard Vinal. He was just messing with your mind. He was just trying to hurt you, to make you mad, make you crazy —

MANTEQUILLA: Oh, no. *(slaps himself)*

SARITA: What?

MANTEQUILLA: I lose to a . . . ? No no no. *(slaps himself)*

SARITA: Don't do that!

MANTEQUILLA: *¡No me toques!* Everybody know. Now I know.

SARITA: Nobody knows anything! I mean, come on! This is the Fifties! What's the problem —

MANTEQUILLA: *(grabs her)* No lie. This Quinn—this Petey—*¿es macho o no es macho?* No lie. This cute guy. Did he . . . *?Contigo . . . ? (gestures lewdly) ¿Qué pasó,* baby? *¿Qué pasó —?*

SARITA: NOTHING! We did nothing!

He lets her go.

MANTEQUILLA: Then he is.

DRUMS.

Mantequilla grabs his pants and gym bag and

exits in a rush.

LIGHTS, LIVE MUSIC INTRODUCTION

GARNET: (*onstage at the club*) I'd like to do something different and dedicate this to a special friend.

Garnet launches into song. An Edith Piaf standard in a rhythm and blues version, sung in his own voice. Garnet hits the high notes as best he can—no imitation, just him—we can tell how much it means to him. He sounds great, but the CROWD boos him off the stage. Down and dirty stripjoint sax in the distance. Pedro finds Garnet in the Green Room.

PEDRO: You were great!

GARNET: Muthafuckas!

PEDRO: No, you were great.

GARNET: Two-bit bastids —

PEDRO: You'll get another gig —

GARNET: I was good!

PEDRO: A better gig!

GARNET: They wouldn't know talent if it kicked 'em in the ass.

PEDRO: You could even play the Apollo Theater —

GARNET: You gotta be kidding.

PEDRO: I was just tryna —

GARNET: Well, don't. Don't be so got-damn positive about me. When I sang that song, the Boss said, "What the fuck is that? Who the hell do you think you are? Josephine Baker? Some piece of French toast? You think we wanna hear you? See you? Singing in French? Singing in your own sorry-ass voice? What the fuck is that?" And he

fired me. And he was right. (*silence*) There won't be any more gigs.

PEDRO: But —

GARNET: Look. I'm an impersonator. Get that in your head, please. I fake Jackie Wilson. I fake James Brown. I shoulda known. Nobody wants to hear me. That's the way it is. That's who the hell I am. And that's it.

PEDRO: But—That's the thing. You don't have to be yourself. (*silence*) The rest of us, we gotta be ourselves all the time.

GARNET: You're not getting it —

PEDRO: I got it. I felt it when you sang. When you moved. That—thing. You got it, man. You hit me right between the eyes. You knock me out.

GARNET: But you're not getting —

PEDRO: You.

They are close together. Garnet looks at Pedro conflicted—confused, flattered—not sure what to say.

GARNET: So what do we do now?

PEDRO: We do the best we can.

DRUMS. Mantequilla at the gym on the heavy bag. With each blow he sends it swinging. Alacrán watches.

ALACRAN: You look beautiful! *¡Como chocolate! ¡Qué lindo eres!*

Mantequilla suffers his attentions with some embarrassment. BELL rings.

ALACRAN: *¡Precioso! ¡Chingonazo!* You look like a fucking god! That little half-breed *pendejo* —! (*spits*) He's dead! Listen *m'hijo— quiero hablar contigo*—I need to talk to you—

Sarita appears. Tension in the room. Long pause.

SARITA: Hey. I figured you oughta get the lay of the land. So here I am.

ALACRAN: *¡Pinches rucas!* It ain't like I don't like girls, I like 'em fine. *Pero en la cocina con una pata rota.* (*The men laugh.*)

SARITA: In the kitchen with a broken leg? Is that how you want me?

ALACRAN: Come on, *mamacita*, it was joke—

SARITA: Who the hell are you, Cantinflas? (*to* MANTEQUILLA) Is that how you want me? (*thrusts her leg out*) Then break it. I'll call you when dinner's ready.

MANTEQUILLA: *Siempre con las bromas.* (*bangs the bag hard*) No more jokes.

SARITA: Who's joking?

ALACRAN: I thought it was purty funny.

MANTEQUILLA: (*suddenly dangerous, commanding*) You shut up, okay? *¡Pa' fuera!* Get outa here! (ALACRAN *exits, hurt*) What the hell you doing here?

SARITA: What am I supposed to do?

MANTEQUILLA: No come to the gym no more. *Por favor.* Is hard . . . *es duro.*

SARITA: You no like me no more?

MANTEQUILLA: I got to stay clean! I got to beat this guy! This Quinn! Is my last chance!

SARITA: What? You see me you gotta lay me right here? In the ring? Not a bad idea.

MANTEQUILLA: I got to be strong!

SARITA: I love you.

MANTEQUILLA: I no wanna lose.

SARITA: Nobody's gonna lose. (*She takes off items of clothes. He tries to look away.*) Baby . . .

MANTEQUILLA: No, *chica* —

SARITA: No more losing —

MANTEQUILLA: *Por favor*, no —

SARITA: It'll be okay. You fight better when you're relaxed —

She touches him. He reacts as if from electric shock.

MANTEQUILLA: No, *¡coño!!!*

SARITA: I know you. If you hold it in too long, you'll explode —

She has both hands on him. By now he's caving in.

MANTEQUILLA: *Ay yi yi* —

SARITA: And you know me. I'll explode —

MANTEQUILLA: *Ay, no.*

SARITA: Yes.

MANTEQUILLA: Please.

SARITA: I'll handle everything.

They grab each other like hungry animals. She goes to her knees.

SARITA: You're beautiful —

He hears the chant of MA-RI-CON.

SARITA: You're the champ —

He looks away in pain.

MANTEQUILLA: *¡NO LO SOY!!!*

MANTEQUILLA Exits.

SARITA: You're not gonna cut me off!!!

DRUMS. Flashbulbs. Vinal jumps rope wildly, masterfully. A display of utter ballet and con-

tained violence. Reporter watches.

REPORTER: So who you gonna call a fag today?

VINAL: You. (*unsure laughter*) I tell it like it is. (*takes the speed bag*) See that? That's Pete Quinn's little head. And this is what I'm gonna do to it. (*bangs it*) I ain't no mixed blood. *¡Yo soy boriqua! Puro sangre.* I gots the blood of some kick-ass cannibals in these veins. (*displays forearm*) See that? That's *Indio*, baby. *El Carib*. Quinn fucks with me, I'ma stick him in a pot and make chicken soup.

REPORTER: You wanna fight Pete Quinn?

VINAL: You want me to fuck him instead? Sure! Mantequilla don't deserve no rematch! Gimme the fight. I'll show the world. I'll tell you this. I better not bump into him in no men's room, 'cause my *papi* told me don't stand for no *patitos*.

REPORTER: (*writing in his notepad*) Potatoes?

VINAL: You want the truth, you come to me. Straight up, no chaser.

REPORTER: You use me, I use you.

VINAL: Come back tomorrow for some more. Okay?

REPORTER: (*exiting*) Okay.

VINAL/REPORTER: Loser.

Jack enters.

VINAL: No autographs.

JACK: I don't want your chicken scratch!

VINAL: Then beat it, old man!

JACK: They call me Three Finger Jack —

VINAL: You got all five fingers, you old bastard —

JACK: Course I do! I'm tough but I ain't stupid!

VINAL: Listen, Tough Guy. I ain't got time—

JACK: Neither do I. So how do you know?

VINAL: Know what?

JACK: You don't, do ya? Don't know a gotdamn thing.

VINAL: You gone punchy?

JACK: You ain't good enough to shine Pete's shoes. I bet you' the freaky deaky one. (*walks away*)

VINAL: What'd you call me —

Vinal spins him around. Jack turns fists raised. Vinal cracks up laughing.

VINAL: You guys from El Lay are crazy!

JACK: You got any idea what you done to that boy?

VINAL: You mean that *mariconcito*?

JACK: How the hell would you know?

VINAL: It's obvious, man. You can see it a mile away.

JACK: I don't see nothing.

VINAL: You prob'ly ain't got a hard-on in ten years. What's it matter anyway?

JACK: You don't SAY that, not in this line of business. You KNOW that. You tryna destroy him? Somebody put you up to it? Why, you damn fool, why?

VINAL: Look, you in the ring with a dude, you get to know him all kinda ways. Like if he eats garlic, or goes heavy on the greasy kid stuff, or if he don't wash under the arms so good. You get to know these things. You was a fighter, you know this. Gimme a little credit here.

JACK: What, he had a hard-on, what?

VINAL: You come to a stinky gym like this for a reason. It's always something. Some assholes, they just like to fight. Other guys, they got to prove something. The little ones, they got a complex. Big ones, they got a complex, too. Some of these clowns like to beat on other guys to impress the chicks, like it'll make their dick bigger or something. Then there's the other kind. They here 'cause they like the smell of men. They like to share sweat. They like the form, man. The way a dude looks when he throws a blow, his muscles all strained and sweaty, his ass all tight bearing down on the blow, his mouth all stopped up with a piece of rubber, and only a pair of soaking wet trunks between his johnson and yours. They like it. And they like to catch a whupping for liking it. That's just the way it is. I'm surprised, man. I thought you knew the business, oldtimer.

JACK: You don't got a shred of evidence.

VINAL: What do you want? Pictures? Come on! I'd fuck him! I'd fuck you.

JACK: You 'sick.

VINAL: I tell it like it is. If some dude wants to go down on me, bring him on! I'll fuck anything! But ain't nobody fucking me. I draw the line, baby! (JACK pushes him) Hey,

what's that for? (JACK pushes him again) Look, old man—(again) I'm warning you —!

JACK: Of course I know what goes on. Been going on since the beginning of time. So what. You gotta go wreck a man's life?

VINAL: It worked, didn't it?

JACK: I oughta kick your ass.

VINAL: You go for the other guy's weakness, right? Am I right? He got a cut eye, you gonna hit him in the elbow? Come on! You jam your glove in there, you rip the fucker open. Tell me I'm wrong. (silence) When I fought Décima, that piece of trash called my mamita some dirty-ass names. I got mad. I din't fight so good. Okay, he found my weakness. I can live with that. I love my mami. But I vowed to God I'd get him back one way or the other. That's how I turned the fight around. All it takes is a single word. Hey, one look at him and I knew that macho crap would make him go crazy. Guy like that is stupid enough to think we really care where he sticks his two-incher. He ain't so great as everybody thinks. So, a little word, I got his mind messed up. And then I kicked his ass! I shoulda got that decision, too! I wuz robbed, baby! I wuz robbed! (beat) But the guy to worry about is Décima, not Quinn. Quinn is what he is. But I'll bet Décima is a little confused.

JACK: You got it all figured out.

VINAL: I'm a student of the game.

JACK: This ain't what the game's about.

VINAL: Nothing's about anything.

JACK: Take it back. Get the TV people. Tell them what you told me.

VINAL: Fuck that.

JACK: It ain't too late!

VINAL: Come off it, old man. Only need to say that kinda shit once. It sticks. Like glue. Like a cheap suit. Hey man. It's business. You talk to me when I'm champ, maybe I'll throw a few bucks your way . . . If you bend over. (*blows JACK a kiss*) So long, *maricón.* (*exits*)

JACK: I shoulda KICKED his ass!

DRUMS. Extreme light change. Alacrán joins Jack. Stripped to their undershirts, they assume fighting poses.

ALACRAN: *¡Le diera partido en la madre!*

The Referee moves in and out, as if working a fight. CROWD NOISE punctuates their stories. They speak to us in a place outside time.

JACK: Back in my prime, be like taking candy from a baby! Hell, I'da been champ if they'da let me!

ALACRAN: *¡Yo tambien! ¡Chingao!*

JACK: But they wouldn't fight us.

ALACRAN: *Pinches* white boys.

JACK: Dempsey wouldn't fight colored!

ALACRAN: Woulda kicked his ass!

JACK: Woulda knocked the flies offa that cheating lug! Only reason he hit so hard was he had a roll of nickels in his glove— see, white folk are like that.

ALACRAN: Colored too. And I got the scars to prove it. *¿Ésto?* (*his hand*) *Un* sparring session *con un negrito* de Detroit name of Ray Robinson. He come out here *para pelear con* Baby Arizmendi. He wanna spar *con Mejicanos.* So they get me, dollar a day. They call him The Dancing Man. Well that's all he did, dance! *Pero* I watching him, I watching him alla time. I cut off the ring, he dance right to me, I catch him on the ropes and—POW!—*la izquierda, y*—WOP!—*un derechazo como relámpago!* Now he dancing all right, *pero* like he drunk or something. End of the round, nigger in a suit come up to me gimme ten bucks and tell me to get out.

REFEREE: Punch and get out!

ALACRAN: Ray Robinson? I coulda taken that *pinche como-se-llama* any day of the week. Din't even know my hand was broke.

JACK: This?(*runs a finger across his nose*) This one I got first time I fought at the Hollywood Stadium. Richie Lemos. I was hot outa Cleveland. They sent me out here to whup me some Messicans. Only Messicans I ever seen was doing stoop labor out fronta the white folks' house. At the weigh-in the greaser he outweighs me eight pounds. Shoulda backed out right there, but I was a damn-fool youngblood. I said "Bring him on" —

BELL. Referee finishes 10-count on him.

REFEREE: Yer out!

JACK: He kicked my ass.

REFEREE: I'm doing a fight down in San Diego 'bout fifteen years back. Joe Louis on the Bum of the Month tour. All white fellas and he's knocking 'em out right and left. Lemme tell ya, that was one powerful colored man, made people nervous. So just before the fight, this old geezer comes up. One eye is off and he's a weird-looking sonofabitch. Baggy plaid pants and a red tie, and his hair greased on the sides and shaped like devil horns, and he's making like this—(*extends pinkies and forefingers*) And he's screaming Cockadoodle doo! Cockadoodle doo!

ALACRAN: *Lo estaba embrujando.*

JACK: Making some whammy.

REFEREE: He was putting the whammy on Ol' Cotton Eye Joe. And Joe didn't much like it neither. See, fighters is like kids. They believe in all that bunk. Especially them black and Latin types. Somebody figured the old bastard might get under Joe's skin, spook 'im, you know, give the Bum a chance to send Joe back to the cotton fields.

ALACRAN: Hey, you get any edge you can.

JACK: But it cuts both ways.

REFEREE: So King Joe comes out and puts the Bum to sleep in no time flat. Didn't want to be in that ring any longer than he had to. Walked right outa that arena, didn't even take a shower. Left town before you could say Jack Robinson. Whammies and cockadoodle doos. Maybe that's why they call 'em spooks. That's the fights for ya.

JACK: We was jinxed. But it'a be different for Pete—

ALACRAN: It'a be different for Mantequilla—

JACK: They gonna RESPECT us!

ALACRAN: They gonna give us what we deserve!

JACK: (*confronts the audience*) You hear me? RESPECT. You are gonna respect us.

ALACRAN: *¡O le diera dado en la madre! ¡A la chingada!*

REFEREE: Come on! Pick it up! What the hell you think this is?

JACK/ALACRAN: It's a fight.

Light change. DRUMS give way to mariachi music. Alacrán joins Mantequilla in a seedy Mexican bar. Renderings of boxers from yesteryear on the walls.

ALACRAN: *¿Te gusta?* Purty good, no? (*looks around*) *Boxeadores Mejicanos, Cubanos—Latinos—los mejores del mundo.* They got you over there. Looking good. I useta have my pitcher here too, *allá—Campeón nacional de México.* I was Number Two in the world for a whole year. Hombre, I useta get free drinks alla time. *Cabrones.* Can you believe it? I come in here, they painted it over. Put up some little *mayate*, little black guy *comemierda* —

MANTEQUILLA: Sugar Ray Robinson?

ALACRAN: Yeah, that's the guy. (*toasts*) *Arriba, abajo . . . cualquiera.* Here's to the real champ.

MANTEQUILLA: *Oye, viejo.* Tell me what

you got to tell me.

ALACRAN: *Pero* I got so much. *Información.* I got *tácticas.* I know how to beat Quinn.

MANTEQUILLA: I know how.

ALACRAN: *¡Pues si!* You're the better man. The moves are sweet, and that right hand of yours is just like a *machete.* Two years ago you'da cut him down like a buncha sugar cane.

MANTEQUILLA: (*bristling*) Two years ago?

ALACRAN: Hey, it happens to everybody.

MANTEQUILLA: I gonna be champ again —!

ALACRAN: Sure!

MANTEQUILLA: I gonna get him! Dyou hear me? I gonna dead him —

ALACRAN: Sure, you will. But different. You gonna get him with *tácticas.* (drinks) I been watching him. I know how to break him down. You got to find the angles. You got to make him think. Start by going downstairs.

MANTEQUILLA: It no work last time.

ALACRAN: (*indicating the groin area*) I'm talking low. *Le tienes que romper las bolas. Los putos huevos.*

MANTEQUILLA: I no fight dirty!

ALACRAN: Not dirty! *Tácticas. ¿Tú sabes? TEATRO.* (silence) 'Cause Pedro Quinn, he don't know nothing about *teatro.* That boy don't got no sense of humor. He can be taken. No sense of humor.

MANTEQUILLA: Then how come he smile at me?

ALACRAN: Huh?

MANTEQUILLA: He laughing at me! How come he laughing at me?!!!

ALACRAN: Laughing? He just looking at you like you' something good to eat. He prob'ly got the hots for you. Can't wait to clinch you! That's as close as he gets to you know what! That's what I'm telling you! Don't fight this guy straight on. Play with him. Make him think one thing—(*leaps in suddenly with a punch*) Then do the other. BOOM. *El Martillo. El Suzie Q. El Campeón.* (*drinks*) *Teatro.* (*Both are quiet, awkward.*) Hey, *es que,* I'm your *compadre.* I'm doing this as a friend. I'm doing this for *La Raza.* In my day, Quinn, he'd be dead. You get to be my age, you know what's right and what's wrong. Nobody got to tell you. You just know. I mean, the little shit can't even speak Spanish! Don't even speak his own language! Too many *cabrones* like that running around these days, breaking all the traditions. No respect! Don't know who the hell they are. That's what's wrong. He ain't pure.

MANTEQUILLA: Pure nothing is pure.

ALACRAN: The way we feel about you, that's pure. That's real. That's how come you got to win for us. We love you, son. We love you to death.

He embraces Mantequilla too hard and for too long. When there is no response of affection, he pulls away.

ALACRAN: Hey. *Cabrón* like me sticks around the gym as long as me, he must have some kinda reason, no? He must be good for something. Not like I'm some kinda stiff, some kinda *pinche* has-been . . . They forget . . . I was Number Two in the World for a whole year—(*breaks off, suddenly like little boy*) But it ain't like I'm asking for nothing . . .

Mantequilla rises, about to exit. Looks at Alacrán a while.

MANTEQUILLA: *Oye.* You come. You work my corner.

ALACRAN: You mean it? (*MANTEQUILLA nods, exits*) Teatro.

DRUMS. Garnet and Pedro together, alone.

GARNET: Useta be like that. Like you. Getting smacked around. Fighting all the time, fighting myself. I had to fight to find the music. I had to fight. That's why you gotta stay focused, man. That's why you gotta keep your head. That's why you gotta be who you are —

PEDRO: You ever had a dog?

GARNET: Say what?

PEDRO: Have you ever had a dog?

GARNET: Been bit too many times.

PEDRO: Had a bull terrier.

GARNET: Got bit by one of those. Muthafuckas don't let go.

PEDRO: That's what they're trained to do. Fighting dogs don't let go. But you don't have to fight 'em. Mine was a good boy. Useta sleep together. I ain't ashamed. He was my friend. So when he got old, I wanted to be there for him. I just wanted to be there. So this one time he sorta arched his back like he was stretching and real slow he just sorta fell over. I was shouting "Come back! Come back, boy!" but he wasn't breathing. His lips were blue. I never seen a dog turn blue. And all I could do was hold him and tell him to come back . . . And he did. (*silence*) After that, the both of us kinda lived closer. So that, when he finally did . . . die . . . I cried, sure. But it wasn't outa fear. It was just for missing . . . that closeness. That—(*can't find the word*) Whatever that thing is. (*silence*) Since then, I never really been that close to anybody. I never let myself. I never had the chance. Till now.

Pedro touches Garnet. After a moment, Garnet moves away.

GARNET: Why'd he come back?

PEDRO: He came 'cause I called him. I guess what I wanna know is—Can you get that close? Is it all right? I feel it—that stretching—I feel it coming on. Coming closer every day. And I don't have anybody. Nobody to call me back. (*beat*) What I wanna know is, if I should ever come to that—that thing, that place —who's gonna be there for me? Who's gonna call me?

A moment, then:

GARNET: Pey-dro. (*like calling a dog*) Here, Peydro. (*moves close*) Here, Pedro.

PEDRO: Will you?

GARNET: Will you?

Tenderly they come together, hold each other

close. Slowly they kiss. At first it's brotherly, sweet. But more and more each man's desire takes over. Both are scared. Both are hungry. Garnet takes off Pedro's shirt, then his own. They slowly go to their knees. Up to this point, it's very romantic. Then, Pedro steps up the activity. Almost like rough trade, both men start to grab and clutch. It's confusing, part turn-on, part actual fight. It starts with a bite by Pedro, which causes Garnet to cry out in pain and pull away, which leads to Pedro hitting Garnet, pure reflex. A trickle of blood comes from Garnet's split lip.

PEDRO: I'm sorry. I'm sorry.

GARNET: (*wiping the blood with his hand*) That's all you know. You poor dense muthafucka. You're just like your dog. But you're not a dog. Time to sleep in your own bed.

PEDRO: What?

GARNET: Get outa here.

A dog barks. DRUMS. The gym. Mantequilla trains slavishly, savagely. Alacrán urges him on with a new cocky attitude. Reporter interviews Vinal. DRUMS drown out the words, but we can see him speak with his hands—colorful, nasty. Then Pedro enters. Hitting the mitts with Jack.

JACK: Jab, jab, jab—Here I come—That's it!—Now add the hook!—To the body— Yeah!—Now finish him off —!!! (*BELL rings. Jack pulls off the mitts, but Pedro keeps punching the air hard as he can, sweat pouring off him.*) Hey. Enough already. (*no response*) Quit it now. What you tryna do, kill yourself? (*no response*) Jesus, Kid —! (*throws his arms around him*) What the hell you doing?!!! (*slaps him*) WAKE UP!!!

PEDRO: I'M AWAKE!!!

JACK: Good! Shit. (*winded*) What you working so hard? Ain't gonna have no fight left in ya! Now sit your ass and down and don't get up till I tell you, or you wanna see me mad? What the hell is wrong with you —?

PEDRO: I can't tell y—

JACK: Did I tell you to speak? Now you listen. You the Man. You don't got to prove nothing to nobody. Least of all me. 'Cause I think you're beautiful. Hell, I think you're the tail of the dog. So don't be showing off to me. Save yer strength.

PEDRO: Jack, I —

JACK: Nuh! You save it. And *use* it. You a fighter! All you need to do is eat, and sleep, and dream good dreams. That's all you need.

PEDRO: I need to sweat this outa me.

JACK: This is life and death we're talking! (*throws him a towel*) Grab a shower. And cool yer damn heels. (*stops him*) I am here for you.

PEDRO: Are you?

JACK: 'Course I am. Dammit, you won the title for fighting, not fucking! Long as you defend your title like a man—(*breaks off*) Sorry, son. I'm sorry.

PEDRO: Now I see. You are what you were before. Just everybody knows. (*nearly crying*) I thought the belt was supposed to protect me.

JACK: Naw. See, it's you got to protect the belt. (*beat*) What? You don't want it no more? Hell, I'm half-dead and I still want that fucking belt. Shit, Kid. You' the champ! We'd give our lives to be you. To be you. Don't that make you feel nothing? (*PEDRO exits*) What the fuck this world coming to?

Sarita enters. Jack jumps up startled.

JACK: What can I do for ya?

SARITA: I'm looking for Petey. (*no response*) Petey. Pete Quinn.

JACK: You mean the champ?

SARITA: Petey to me.

JACK: (*laughs*) He'll be right back. (*looks her over*) Don't get too many women 'round here, 'cept of course the lady boxers. I seen a lady knock a fella down, not once but twice, right there in that ring.

SARITA: What? Supposed to let the guy win? (*throws a blow*) Spare me.

JACK: Say, you all right.

SARITA: I'm washed in the blood. My dad boxed.

JACK: Would I know him? (*She shakes her head no.*) We boxers hang tight.

SARITA: Richie Lemos. (*JACK involuntarily rubs his nose*) You knew him?

JACK: Only by reputation. Only by reputation.

SARITA: Dad liked dogs. Petey raised 'em. Dad showed Petey how to box.

JACK: (*snaps fingers*) I knew I'd seen that style of his!

SARITA: Yep. He was a banger and a comer.

JACK: Like you. The thing your dad had is what the Spanish fighters call *mackismo*.

SARITA: *Machismo*.

JACK: Yeah, that too.

Pedro enters.

SARITA: Hey.

PEDRO: Hey.

JACK: Hey! Well, all right. I'll leave ya with the fine lady. (*to SARITA*) Come around again. I'll tell ya a coupla stories about your dad. (*exits, to himself*) Hot dog! I knew that boy flew straight! Thank you, Jesus.

PEDRO: How's your dad?

SARITA: Sick.

PEDRO: Sorry.

SARITA: Don't be. It's just tequila. The dog?

PEDRO: Buried him.

SARITA: Boy, that dog was a sex fiend. Remember, he used to —

PEDRO: You remember that?

SARITA: Prop up one leg and whack off with the other! Who could forget a thing like that? That was hot stuff! Who taught him that, I wonder?

PEDRO: He's the one taught me.

SARITA: Yeah, right. Remember that fight? That big black shepherd with the scars? Your boy was so dumb he tried to mount that killer dog! Jeez. All that blood spurting out of your boy's head, but his tail was wagging! I guess he didn't feel it. Crazy . . .

So is it true? You know . . . Queer? 'Cause I mean, I been scouring my brain for clues, and it's not like you wore high heels or carried a purse or —(PEDRO motions for her to stop.) So I'm nervous. But you wouldn't go out with me. And I wasn't that bad then, was I?

PEDRO: I don't go out with people.

SARITA: You oughta try it sometime.

PEDRO: I hurt people.

SARITA: Love hurts people. Sometimes I feel just like your dog, trying to make love, and just getting bit. Just getting cut off. And like some stupid dog in heat coming back for more. Trying to feel that close, that—

PEDRO: That feeling—that thing? It can't last.

SARITA: That's why you gotta grab it while you can.

Pedro leans in and kisses her. She kisses back. It gets passionate fast. Then each pulls away.

SARITA: No.

PEDRO: I can't.

SARITA: Whoa.

PEDRO: Sorry.

SARITA: Quit being sorry!

PEDRO: Well it's weird!

SARITA: Yeah, so?

PEDRO: So I want —(stops)

SARITA: What? (He struggles.) What do you want? Spit it out!

Amazingly, with a freedom he has not shown before, Pedro does a Jackie Wilsonesque dance move.

SARITA: What was that?!!!

PEDRO: I dunno!!!

SARITA: I'd like to see you do that in the ring!

PEDRO: I wish I could.

SARITA: Your dog. When he killed that dog, he jumped straight in the air. I'll never forget that. Straight in the air. I better go find my man.

PEDRO: Me, too.

Off her double-take, GUT BUCKET ROCK N ROLL. Green Room. Club door opens. Garnet smokes. Stained cummerbund, tie undone, hard-working man in show business. Pedro appears, out of breath, trying to smile.

PEDRO: Hey. Been looking all over. (icy pause) Got your gig back. I thought you weren't gonna impers —

GARNET: Hey, we all impersonate. (snaps fingers) And I'm pretty good at it, too.

PEDRO: I'm sorry. I'm really sorry for what I done. But I'm back. I'll make it up to ya. And I wanna —

GARNET: Don't do that. Don't get close.

PEDRO: I'm not gonna hurt you.

GARNET: I'm not afraid of you or any man. I just don't wanna get bit.

PEDRO: I'm sorry —

GARNET: I'm about sick of hearing you say you're sorry. Sorry for what? For your dreams? Please. You ain't the first or the last to dream about another man. For what you done to me? I've been through worse.

Be sorry for what you done to yourself. And what about you? You came to me, with your sorry-ass dog story. And I was there for you. I was there. But you wouldn't go there. No, you'd rather take a royal ass-kicking. Let the Cuban kill you for your sins. For your dreams. Being sorry. As if that'll wash you clean. Make you the man. Got no clue, Kid. Not a clue in the world. (*beat*) You know what I see when I watch a fight? I watch the men. Holding on as much as hitting. And I see them in their corners getting massaged and Vaselined and whispered in their ear. I see the closeness. And I see the fear. The fear of what you can and cannot touch. No wonder they go out and try to kill each other. And then I see you. And then I really see. No wonder they cut you off. No wonder they want you dead. If you're their champ, then what the hell does that make them? (*PEDRO about to touch him*) What are you gonna do, hit me?

PEDRO: Come to the fight.

GARNET: That's all you know. Grabbing and clutching and punching and kicking ass. That's love. Or the closest you've ever been.

PEDRO: It is love.

GARNET: It ain't l—

PEDRO: It's my love.

GARNET: Well it ain't mine. Look. Forget me. Forget all this. Get down to business. Don't be looking to nobody. And watch yerself in them clinches. That's what I forgot to do.

PEDRO: Come to the fight. Please.

GARNET: (*MUSIC vamps from within*) That's my set.

PEDRO: Come to the fight!

GARNET: Nope. You ain't gonna bite me twice. (*adopts his performance attitude*) Be who you are, man. Who you are. (*INTRO MUSIC*)

PEDRO: Come back.

GARNET: Gotta go.

Pedro reaches out, but Garnet brushes past him. A moment later he hits the stage singing a James Brown song to live accompaniment. Then he sees Pedro. Stops singing, drops the attitude, exits mid-song. DRUMS. The arena. An uneasy animal hum from the packed crowd. Ringside, hallways, dressing rooms.

TV REPORTER: It's Décima versus Quinn, and the Garden is packed to the rafters! Good evening fans, and welcome —

VINAL: *¡Oye nena!* Come on baby! *Dame candy!*

SARITA: Please.

VINAL: Wilfred Vinal, hundred fifty-eight pounds of love. *Venga a verme.*

SARITA: Listen, Wilfred, you're a walking catastrophe.

VINAL: I could go blind dreaming of you.

DRUMS. She rushes past him down the hall. Alacrán, dressed as Mantequilla's cornerman, stops her.

SARITA: Let me see him.

ALACRAN: See him after, *chula.*
SARITA: I wanna see him now.
ALACRAN: *¿Para qué?*
SARITA: None of your goddamn business.
ALACRAN: It is my business.
SARITA: *¡Hijo de la chingada!*
ALACRAN: Nice mouth you got there. If you were my girl —
SARITA: I'm not your girl. Please. I need to see him.
ALACRAN: He told me to tell you. He'll see you after the fight.
SARITA: That's a lie!
ALACRAN: Sometimes, *chula,* a man's gotta get down to business.
DRUMS.
TV REPORTER: There's a circus atmosphere due to the Vinal allegations, not to mention a certain amount of bad blood between the two —
ALACRAN: (*in the dressing room*) *¿Qué onda, chulo?*
MANTEQUILLA: Where my girl?
ALACRAN: How should I know? Prob'ly out with some other guy. (*MANTEQUILLA angers*) Who the hell knows?
MANTEQUILLA: She no come?
ALACRAN: She no come.
MANTEQUILLA: You sure?
ALACRAN: My business to be sure.
JACK: (*in the other dressing room*) Hey, Champ. You okay? (*PEDRO looks sick*) Butterflies. Be all right once you're in there.

PEDRO: Not butterflies.
VINAL: *Oye mami,* you come back for me.
SARITA: *¡Cabrón!* (*takes a swing at him*)
VINAL: That's what I call a dream match. You and me, baby!
SARITA: Goddamn this whole *chingadera!*
VINAL: *Munga munga,* baby!
DRUMS.
MANTEQUILLA: You sure she no come?
ALACRAN: How many times I gotta tell you —?
MANTEQUILLA: She always come. (*tears of rage*) She always come.
ALACRAN: Not always.
Mantequilla swats the air viciously. He's a lethal weapon.
JACK: Go throw some water on your face boy. Try to take a piss.
ALACRAN: *¡Ándale! ¡Vámanos!*
JACK: If you gotta throw up, do it now. When you come back, we gonna kick some ass!
DRUMS. The urinal. Pedro spits up. Then Vinal enters.
PEDRO: Exit's down the hall.
VINAL: Who's going? I got business.
PEDRO: Me, too.
VINAL: (*looks him over*) Not exactly god-like.
PEDRO: Get away from me.
VINAL: So you guys gonna fight or fuck? Betcha Mantequilla's getting some right now. That little bitch of his sucking on his

candy. Don't worry. She'll take the edge off. Better he gets fucked. If he don't he's liable to kill your ass. So he's taken care of. How about you?

PEDRO: What?

VINAL: 'Cause hey, I came to see a fight. I can watch guys fuck any time I want down by the docks—(*PEDRO tries to exit. VINAL blocks the way*) But hey. Here's everybody getting fucked but you. Poor little Piccolo Pete. So I said to myself, why not come down and see the Man himself? Find out what he needs. God knows he needs some, and he sure as hell don't know how to get any on his own. So here I am. (*VINAL kneels*)

PEDRO: Hey.

VINAL: Come on. Take me. (*kisses PEDRO's belly*) Go on. Take me.

PEDRO: What do you mean?

VINAL: What do you think? (*loosens PEDRO's trunks*)

PEDRO: What are you doing?

VINAL: (*kisses*) Letting you know. Who you are.

PEDRO: What?

VINAL: Who you are, man. Who you are.

PEDRO: What do you mean?!!!

They grab and wrestle.

VINAL: Oh, you like to clinch!! Almost like the real thing—(*yanks him close*) Except it ain't.

PEDRO: Goddamn Rican bastard *puto MARICON!!!!*

VINAL: I know who you are!!!

PEDRO: I'll fucking kill you!!!

VINAL: Everybody knows who you are!!!

PEDRO: I'll fucking kill you!!!

Jack enters.

VINAL: Now even you know who you are.

JACK: Get the fuck outa here. (*to PEDRO*) Time to go.

They exit. DRUMS loud and furious.

VINAL: (*checks himself in the mirror*) Put the blade to the heat.

DRUMS. The ring like a pit. The fighters enter to cheers and jeers. Microphone drops from the rafters.

ANNOUNCER: Ladies and Gentlemen— Fifteen Rounds for the Undisputed Championship of the World —

Sarita and Vinal separated by a single empty seat.

SARITA: *Amorcito!!!* (*MANTEQUILLA doesn't see her*)

VINAL: Hey, baby. You're sitting next to the next champion of the world, soon as these two fuck each other to death.

SARITA: It'll never happen.

VINAL: Don't jinx me, baby —

SARITA: (*stares right through him*) Never.

BUZZER indicates ten-second warning. DRUMS. Mantequilla goes to one knee, genuflects. BELL rings. Round One. They touch gloves. The fight begins. We see the action as a series of snapshots, an accelerated fight punctuated by DRUMS. Punches land both ways.

JACK: (*from his corner*) That's it!

ALACRAN: (*from his corner*) ¡Como martillo!

JACK: That's my boy —!

ALACRAN: Watch it now, watch it —!

VINAL: Wasn't nothing.

Pedro lands hard. Mantequilla clinches. Pedro doesn't take the fight to him. BELL rings.

VINAL: What the fuck was that?

JACK: (*as PEDRO returns to his corner*) Why you let him off the hook?

ALACRAN: (*as MANTEQUILLA returns to his corner*) Why you let him hit you like that?

VINAL: I could take both these guys on their best night.

ALACRAN: You need to do more!

JACK: Give me more!

BUZZER.

REFEREE: Round Four!

BELL rings. They fight. Pedro out of rhythm. Mantequilla scores well. Pedro gets hit flush on the chin.

ALACRAN: ¡En el hígado! ¡El hígado!

Mantequilla staggers Pedro.

ALACRAN: Qué chulo!

JACK: Aw, hell! (*BELL rings. Jack meets Pedro with a wet sponge, while Alacrán applies Vaseline to Mantequilla's face.*)

MANTEQUILLA: Dyou see that?

ALACRAN: What?

MANTEQUILLA: He smiling at me!

ALACRAN: Another round like that, he ain't gonna have any teeth left to smile. Looking beautiful. ¡Como chocolate —!

JACK: You okay? You okay?

SARITA: (*screaming towards MANTEQUILLA*) Baby, you look beautiful!!!!

BUZZER.

REFEREE: Round Seven!

BELL rings. Mantequilla flurries, then toys with Pedro, dancing and making him miss badly.

JACK: Hit him!

ALACRAN: ¡Muévete!

VINAL: What is this, a first date?

ALACRAN: ¡Muévete!

JACK: Hit him!

Mantequilla lands a five-punch combination. Pedro doesn't fight back. BELL rings.

JACK: What are you doing?

ALACRAN: Play with him!

JACK: What are you doing?

REFEREE: Watch the heads!

JACK: Tell the other guy!!

ALACRAN: One thing—then do the other!

JACK: You think this is a game?

ALACRAN: Play with him!

JACK: This is a fucking dogfight!

REFEREE: Watch the heads!

ALACRAN: ¡Vete a la chingada, idiota!

REFEREE: Just watch the heads!

JACK: You hear me? You hear me?

BUZZER.

REFEREE: Seconds out!

JACK: My God, Kid! You got it right there in the palm of your hand!

REFEREE: Round Eleven!

JACK: Chance of a lifetime —!

BELL rings.

JACK: All our lives! We been waiting all our lives!

The men fight viciously like dogs. Both are staggered. Again and again, they summon up their best. As the BELL rings, each man lands potentially his best shot. Neither goes down. Round over, Pedro grins, smiles all the way back to his corner.

MANTEQUILLA: He smiling at me!!!

ALACRAN: *¡Mátelo!!!*

JACK: Kill the muthafucka!!!

SARITA: Just hold on!

VINAL: FAGS!!!

REFEREE: (*hears VINAL*) May be a fag, but he got a helluva left hook!

BUZZER.

MANTEQUILLA: I go dead him.

REFEREE: Last Round. Touch gloves.

BELL rings. Pedro offers his glove. Mantequilla punches him instead, then slams home the Suzie Q. Pedro staggers, badly hurt against the ropes. Mantequilla hammers him mercilessly. Pedro won't go down. Mantequilla, exhausted now, stops. Both are weak, spent. Alacrán screams to get Mantequilla's attention.

ALACRAN: *TEATRO!!!!* (*Mantequilla leans in and kisses Pedro full on the lips.*)

FREEZE. Then Mantequilla lands the Suzie Q with everything he has. Pedro goes down. Slow motion as DRUMS beat out Pedro's heartbeat.

He's on his knees, unable to focus. Mantequilla in the neutral corner, exhausted. Crowd on its feet, cheers wildly, full of bloodlust. Pedro looks around. Then he sees Garnet in a perfect suit and pompadour, standing beside the empty seat. Pedro rises. Mantequilla's hand is hurt. Still he goes in for the kill. Hits Pedro once, twice. Then misses the third as Pedro slips the blow, and suddenly in regular speed, connects with a monster shot to the jaw. Now in vicious REAL TIME, Pedro punches Mantequilla over and over. Mantequilla is tangled on the ropes, unable to go down. Pedro hits him again and again. Finally the Referee steps in. Mantequilla hangs lifeless. Pedro in ring center, like a pit bull, bathed in sweat, rejoices and jumps in the air. Flashbulbs FREEZE this moment in time. Crowd noise explodes. Then all sounds stop. Pedro, now able to focus, sees Mantequilla falling slowly to the canvas, half-smiling, dying. Pedro goes to him like a lover, takes him in his arms.

PEDRO: Come back.

Garnet begins to sing, something hard and strong like James Brown's "THIS IS A MAN'S WORLD." Pedro kisses Mantequilla. The dog barks like crazy.

END OF PLAY

L to R: Dominic Hoffman and Ray Oriel. Photo by Craig Schwartz

You and a guest are cordially
invited to join us for the
opening performance of

BLADE
TO THE
HEAT

by Oliver Mayer
West Coast Premiere
Directed by Ron Link

Thursday, March 28, 1996, at 8 p.m.

Please RSVP to the Audience Development
(Mon - Fri, 10 - 6 p.m.) **no later than**
Wednesday, March 20. (213) 972-7625

Tickets not picked up by 7:30 p.m. will be released.
This invitation is not transferable. Reservations will be accepted
only for the person to whom this invitation was addressed.

 MARK**TAPER**FORUM

Gordon Davidson, Artistic Director

Blade to the Heat **Glossary**

Compiled by William and Rosalinda Nericcio

El gancho al hígado: The hook to the liver.

¡Tira, coño!: Hit him, damn it!

Corazón: heart; will.

¡Qué chulo!: How beautiful!

Todo hombre. ¡Cómo esto!: All man. Like my fist here!

Cabrón: asshole (literally, a huge goat).

Hijo de la gran Puta: Son of the "great bitch."

Con esa sonrisa comemierda: with that shiteating smile.

En la panza: in the stomach.

Oye: Listen.

Qué bien te ves, chica: Looking good, baby.

Tremendo golpe, como cañonazo: major blow, like a canon.

Me llamo Martillo. El ponchador martillo: They call me the hammer. The punching hammer.

Maricón: slur-term for a gay man.

¡Te gusta meter mano!: You like to get some?

Si es afeminado: if he is effeminate.

¡No me toques!: Don't touch me!

Pinche rucas: Damn wenches.

Yo soy boriqua. Pura sangre: I am Boriqua (indigenous to Puerto Rico). Pure blood.

Un derechazo como relámpago: A lightning-like right.

Latinos—los mejores del mundo: Latinos—the best in the world.

Desgraciado: Low-life.

Le debes romper las bolas. You should break his balls.

La raza: The [Mexican] people.

Dáme candy: Give me love.

Vénga a verme: Come see me.

¡¡¡Mátelo!!!: Kill him!!!

Raymond Cruz

The original glossary from the Mark Taper Forum program *for Blade to the Heat*, 1996; translations by Rosalinda Nericcio.

Blade to the Heat
entremeses | *intermezzo* | inter-acts

Cast, director, and playwright, *Blade to the Heat*,
Public Theater, New York, 1994.

Oliver Mayer and Ron Link, director,
Mark Taper Forum, *Blade to the Heat*, 1996.

Publicity card for the San Franscisco production of
Blade to the Heat, Thick Description, 1997.

Directed by...Madonna?

"Yeah, I got to meet Madonna," says playwright Oliver Mayer, author of the sizzling gay boxing drama *Blade to the Heat*, which scored a knockout this year at New York's Public Theater. "It was a trip," Mayer told The Buzz, recalling his meeting with La Ciccone. "I walk into her office, and she's sitting there at the desk. I sit down, and she's just looking at me. And then she says, 'I want to direct your play as a movie. Is that all right?' I think it over carefully, for about two seconds, and then I say, 'Sure.'"

Madonna hopes to shoot the film after she finishes work on *Evita*, says Mayer, who's already completed the script revisions she requested. *Blade to the Heat* may be the first American drama in which a gay character beats the hell out of a straight one. As one character puts it: "He may be a faggot, but he's got one hell of a left hook!"

And when can we see *Blade to the Heat* in our local multiplex? Madonna isn't saying. Her producer at Maverick Pictures "doesn't talk to the press about upcoming projects," a spokesman told The Buzz. For those who can't bear the mystery, Mayer's original play will be staged in spring 1996 at L.A.'s Mark Taper Forum.

DECEMBER 26, 1995
THE ADVOCATE 61

1995 *Advocate* story on Oliver
Mayer's collaboration with Madonna.

With Tupac Forever
BLADE TO THE HEAT
Hassan El-Amin, Ray Oriel

On *Blade to the Heat*

Tommy Tompkins

Anyone who saw the 1997 San Francisco production of Oliver Mayer's exhilarating *Blade To The Heat* left the theater knowing that boxing and soul music meant a lot to the young playwright. The opening scene has a hook rivaling anything Smokey Robinson wrote for his Motown sidekicks, the Miracles.

As the play begins, a tight spotlight reveals a supple, athletic young black man lip-syncing to an up-tempo Jackie Wilson number; then lights come up on a gym where fighters bang away at speed bags and at each other. Their rhythmic volleys echo Wilson's driving groove to create a powerful soundtrack that elevates the seedy world of fighters, hustlers, and hangers-on, in all its violence, grime, and desperation, and infuses it with the yearning and passion of their broken dreams so that it's about to burst. I saw the play eight years ago, yet the scene has stayed with me like it was yesterday. Mayer himself has something to do with that; we became friends after Blade's 1997 run in San Francisco.

I met him through my wife, who was then a principal in Thick Description, the San Francisco theater company that staged *Blade To The Heat*. Their friendship tended to be sandwiched between rehearsals and performances and was burdened by the tensions and demands of life in the theater. By contrast, ours was built on a foundation of rhythm and blues. Over the years, Mayer would come to our house when he was in town, we'd go into my office where the main prop was a CD player and some seven or eight thousand albums. We'd grab handfuls of CDs, stretch out on the floor and stay up all night listening to music. Sometimes, a song would prompt an anecdote, but more often than not, we'd lapse into a rich silence. The truth is you can learn a lot about someone from the music they love.

For both of us, soul and rhythm & blues allow us to cross into the rich treasure of experience of Black America, its daily struggles, its triumphs, its heartbreak. We're both fond of Jackie Wilson, from his early songs like "Reet Petite," written by Motown founder Barry Gordy, back when the company was still struggling. Wilson's incredible falsetto sometimes seemed almost to carry him away from the often mediocre material he recorded. We laughed about the singer who could make so much out of so little. In his finest moment, on "Higher and Higher," Wilson's voice reached a kind of majesty. Once or twice we talked about Wilson's fate, to collapse on stage and live in a comatose half-life for years, eventually dying without gaining consciousness.

I can't speak for Mayer on this—our backgrounds share some things, but in many ways we're quite different—but for me, the music was its own kind of theater, permitting me to share experiences that weren't my own.

Mayer was still a young man when he wrote *Blade*, which had its premiere at New York's Public Theater in 1994. Boxers are paid to settle matters with their fists; their fights aren't personal. Except for when they are. In *Blade*, this leads to the deadly encounter between Mantequilla—imbalanced by slurs about his manhood—and Quinn, struggling unsuccessfully to hide his sexual orientation from his public and from himself. It's thick, ugly stuff, made all the more so because it deliberately echoes Emile Giffith's deadly fight with Bennie "Kid" Paret. Paret, who had called Griffith "*maricón*" (faggot) at the weigh-in, died from the savage beating he received in the ring.

Mayer inherited his love of boxing from his father. He fought when he was young and is still passionate about it. He's drawn to the sport's elemental, masculine clarity—one man wins, another loses—and at the same time by the ambiguous sexuality that infuses an activity that celebrates the male body and demands its participants engage in physical contact verging on the intimate. Now approaching middle age, Mayer's work is as diverse and unpredictable as life itself. But we're never far from the forces that shaped us growing up, and if *Blade To The Heat* feels personal, that's because it is. He's telling us about the things he's struggled with: the mixed-race dilemma passed his way by a Chicano mother and Anglo father, the limiting—and sometimes frightening—straightjacket of gender and sexual orientation, perhaps even the splitting apart of the two people he loved.

If Mayer the artist used boxing in *Blade* to explore personal questions, Mayer the boxer still shadows the artist—at least I like to think he does. In fact, the artist has another boxing story that only a few people know—until now. Mayer has twice workshopped his plays at the prestigious Sundance Institute. One invitation to the Sundance Theatre Lab is the dream of many playwrights; a second invitation signals admittance into the elite class of the literati. For three-week residencies, Sundance provides an idyllic, eminently civilized setting for artists to explore their work collaboratively, away from the usual pressures and stresses of making art in a commerce-centered world. The atmosphere is intense, but rarely fractious. During his second stay at Sundance, Mayer got into an argument with another artist. They'd been getting on each other's nerves. Things got testy. Then they got hot. Then they got hotter. The two men had raised fists and were about to dive into a full-on fist-a-rama before cooler, if disbelieving, heads intervened. Had they brawled the Sundance community would have been scandalized (and excited) for

years. The idea of a real fight amidst the high minds in the Utah mountains is so incongruous that it would have become instant legend.

Maybe it's not much of a surprise that the passion Mayer displays so nakedly in *Blade*, and which is the lifeblood of his best work, could so readily bubble over and erupt into violence in life, as well. But if it happens again, save me a seat.

Oliver Mayer's dog, Balder.

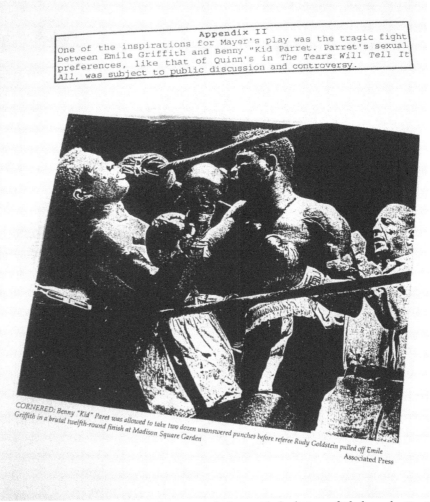

Appendix II

One of the inspirations for Mayer's play was the tragic fight between Emile Griffith and Benny "Kid Parret. Parret's sexual preferences, like that of Quinn's in *The Tears Will Tell It All*, was subject to public discussion and controversy.

CORNERED: Benny "Kid" Paret was allowed to take two dozen unanswered punches before referee Rudy Goldstein pulled off Emile Griffith in a brutal twelfth-round finish at Madison Square Garden

Associated Press

A xeroxed resource page from the *Prensa de la Vanidad* edition of *Blade to the Heat*.

Covers from *Prensa de la Vanidad* editions of Mayer's *The Tears Will Tell it All* and *Blade to the Heat*.

Blades, Tears, Music, and Laughter: A Fall 1996 Conversation

William A. Nericcio and Oliver Mayer

William A. Nericcio: Blade to the Heat *has been knocking around in your head for quite some time now. It began as a play called* The Tears Will Tell It All *and I wondered if you couldn't say a little something about where the play has come, how old the play is, and about its evolution from* The Tears Will Tell It All *to* Blade to the Heat.

Oliver Mayer: Well, it has been a while. It's been about five years altogether, although it's probably been my whole life. (laughs) I'll tell you, probably the truest answer is that the play really started when we were cleaning out one of my mother's closets and this Jackie Wilson '45 record fell on the floor and I said, "What's that?" And she said, "Oh, that's the music your father courted me to." I said, "Oh, wow." So I put it on and fell in love with Jackie Wilson and that sort of started everything going. That and watching my father watch the fights . . . and my grandfather as well. Between those things I started to get a sense of rhythm and blues and boxing. That became my big obsession. And I think about 1991 I was here in Los Angeles and was raking the leaves and I had a sort of thought come to me about boxing and sexuality and if there would happen to have ever been a gay boxer. I figured there must have been. I had even heard a little bit about a fighter . . . and so I began to think about it and I called a friend. Actually, I called the man who is now directing the play, Ron Link, and I said, "What would you think about a play about a gay boxer?" He said, "I don't know. Why don't you write it." And he sort of hung up. I think I interrupted a poker game or something. And so I said, "Oh, o.k." And I went back to raking the leaves and then I put the rake away and I started writing. And five days later, I had the play. And to be brutally honest, one thing that also helped with the play was the death of my great dog, Balder. He died about three days into the writing of it. And after people see the play, they'll know that my dog is in the play because I honored him throughout. He was very much on my mind and was very much in the play. In those days and weeks before and during the writing of the work, Balder was between death and life, and that was something I knew very well at that moment, something I wrote about. Anyway, so that was *The Tears Will Tell It All*, the name of a Jackie Wilson song. And I had some good luck with that—we had a couple of readings at the Mark Taper in the New Work Festival, and Gordon Davidson even did announce it once as a possible main-stage play back in 1992. It didn't happen

then. And that was really the life of *The Tears Will Tell It All*. I had a reading also at the Manhattan Theater Club, and then George Wolfe picked it up at the Public Theater and he told me to change the name so then it became *Blade to the Heat*. In a lot of ways there is something about the titles that has something to do with the feel of the plays. Something about *The Tears Will Tell It All* . . . I don't know. *Blade to the Heat* I think is a bit of a harder-edged play. I've actually been spending most of my re-writes now trying to bring some of the poetry and the emotion and the intimacy back into *Blade to the Heat*, to put *The Tears Will Tell It All* back into *Blade to the Heat*.

WN: *Can you tell me where the title* Blade to the Heat *comes from or what it refers to, specifically?*

OM: Yeah . . . "blade to the heat," Bob Dylan aficionados will recognize it as a line from Dylan's song "Joker Man." "Put the priest in the pocket, put the blade to the heat, take the motherless children off the street and bless them at the feet of a harlot." I just like that. I mean, I don't think Bob invented that phrase. I think he picked it up. I think it's a Blackism, a common street phrase. And I started to use it because when I had a paper to do or some deadline to meet, I would say, 'Oh man, I've got to put the blade to the heat.' 'I've got to get busy,' is what I meant. I just kind of liked it. And when George Wolfe told me to change the title or he wouldn't do my play, which is what he said, it came up and you know, it sort of sounds like a movie title, more melodramatic. But the good thing about the title is that I think it is thematic . . . because in metallurgy when you put a blade or some kind of knife or hard edge to the heat or the fire, you test the m-e-t-t-l-e of the m-e-t-a-l and judging from its amalgam, judging from how many parts iron to whatever, it will either break or it will get stronger. And for some obvious reasons, I thought in the world of cultural fusion that I'm writing about, in a world where Latin people live, where there's a man named, Pedro Quinn who is a mixed-blooded person, and where Latino and black people are trying to make it in this country in the 50s, I thought that they're living a trial by fire where they're constantly being put under the fire themselves. And either they'll break or they'll get stronger. And, uh, it's probably easier to break.

WN: This play of yours . . . it has characters who are Puertoriqueño, Cubano . . . you have a Mexican-American with an Irish surname, a Mexican-American woman who hates the word Chicano, you have an African-American character, etc. For an entertainment audience raised on stereotypes like Speedy Gonzales and Juan

Valdez, you've given them quite a lot to figure out in this play—people for whom Latinos are one stock type. Tell me about this. In other words, tell me about Latinos and the American theater, how it is the playwright works with all the types, or I would imagine, against type?

OM: Good question. How to approach this? Well, the unfunny answer is just that I want to write about those people in this country who haven't had plays written about them. And I'm sorry to say, there have not been enough plays about black and Latino people in previous generations. Thank goodness for the wonderful plays of Luis Valdez, Miguel Piñero, José Rivera, and Eduardo Machado. But I think there are whole groups of people who have yet to see themselves on stage. I think there's something exciting about celebrating the lives of people who are now dead, or some that have survived—like my grandfather and my mother, celebrating lives that would otherwise be forgotten. That's the unfunny side. The funny thing is I think that watching TV and reading comics and everything, the Latino character one expects to run into is going to be part-cootchee-cootchee girl and part-this and part-that, you know, part-Charo and part

. . .

WN: . . . oily, swarthy bandit rake . . .

OM: Yeah . . . Carmen Miranda and Emiliano Zapata rolled into one, I don't know. I don't know what the parts are. You know better than I with that archeology project on Speedy Gonzales and Rita Hayworth. So I was interested in actually breaking it down a little bit more. Also as a Latino man, I happen to know that there is a great deal of . . . well, definition, to be nice, but a great deal of bias from Latins on Latins. I don't know how to say that . . .

WN: *No, you say it well. In the play it's quite clear there's this sort of nation-specific animosity . . .*

OM: Oh, really?

WN: *Yeah*

OM: Yeah, patriotic kind of bullshit . . .

WN: *. . . between the Puertoriqueños and the Mexicanos, and the Mexicanos and the Cubanos. From the point of view of someone who studies the appearance of Latino characters, in all kinds of American entertainment vehicles, literature, television and theater, one thing that strikes me about* Blade to the Heat *is that your spectator is forced to come to terms with the fact that you can't just generalize about "Latins" or Latinos. These people are all different: Vinal is specific. He is not Cubano. He is not Mexicano. He is where he is from. And the same*

for the rest of the characters: Pedro Quinn, with that wonderful last name . . .

OM: (laughs)

WN: *. . . you know, just makes it that much more difficult for us to place these types, to place these characters.*

OM: That's the way I like it. I like the element of surprise. Particularly when it has to do with people of color. I like our audiences to have to listen to every word—and to be surprised at their actions. I learned about the schisms among Latin people through boxing, and I actually took part in it actively. Because you watch the fights long enough and you see the greatest fights are often between the Mexican champion and the Puerto Rican champion . . . the promoters have known this forever. You match the best white guy against the best black guy, the best Mexican against the best Black-American. In the old days, which is in the play, it was the best Irishman against the best Italian, whatever would improve the gate. And that's something essential in boxing, that is, the national side of it, the patriotic side. They are your champions, and that's why you love them.

WN: *Funny thing about the sport of boxing, it seems the perfect allegorical playground within which to explore the minds of men. From a playwright's point of view, tell me what the ring allows you to do on the stage.*

OM: What the ring allows on the stage?

WN: Well, it seems to lend itself to all kinds of epic or quasi-allegorical readings . . .

OM: It's a strong metaphor. And, you know, Brecht said that boxing is the best theater. Or he said something like that. (laughs) I probably missed something . . . but he was right. Thank goodness Ron Link, my excellent director, and I, we both can't help but think in boxing metaphors. I mean, before this play was even in existence, we were like that. So as men, for some reason we see our lives as a contest. We are not only fighting our opponents or many opponents, but we're fighting ourselves—trying to hit and not get hit.

WN: Right.

OM: . . . and to be beautiful and to be in sync. That's easier said than done. Usually only half of the time in your career you really are as good as you can be. So, yeah, it's a great metaphor for love and life and I hope I do justice to it.

WN: WN: Are you a Los Angeles writer, a Chicano writer, a Latino writer? How do you think

of yourself? Or are you just a plain old hack at the typewriter?

OM: I'm more often hack than not. (laughs). But I dabble. I dabble in all of the above. I have ten plays, and I'm glad to say that I think all of the readable plays I've ever written are different. Even if they have the same themes, they're very, very different in style, and they're about different kinds of characters and often in different time periods. I just don't want to write the same plays over and over again. I know it'll happen. But I'm going to do my best to be eclectic and broad-thinking. That's attractive to me. Without lying. I'm trying to be truthful and write from what I know, but I'm going to try to stretch those parameters as far as I can.

WN: Buzz Magazine named you as one of the . . . How did they put it?

OM: One of the hundred coolest . . .

WN: (laughs) Yes, one of the hundred coolest. And part of this recent rise in your celebrity quotient has to do with your rights to Blade To The Heat *being bought by a kind of important or, at least, well known person . . .*

OM: Yeah, I would say it's a seminal person of our generation . . .

WN: *I think she would like that. Seminal. A seminal woman. Yes.*

OM: A seminal woman. Definitely.

WN: *Tell us about it.*

OM: Well, Madonna came to see the play in New York and apparently saw it several times and liked it enough to buy it for a movie, to buy the option and to hire me to write the screenplay for a movie that, hopefully, she will direct. And we'll see what happens, for there's been many "a slip 'twixt the cup and the lip." It could really never happen. There's a million stories in this city about that. But I can say that in my dealings with Madonna, she's been fantastic. She's a wonderful, wonderful collaborator, very knowledgeable, and she really knows the subjects, really knows boxing, really knows the Latin culture, and obviously knows something about sexuality too. So if we ever do make this film, I think she's the man for the job, the right man for the job. I really do.[14]

---

[14] As of March 2008, as this book goes to press, Madonna still has not directed *Blade to the Heat* for the silver screen—this despite news reports from December 2006 that such a move was immanent: http://www.nme.com/news/madonna/25535

WN: *So Madonna's interest in the play led to some good "Buzz" . . .*

Mayer: . . . yeah, I do think that had a little something to do with my getting on the list, and I appear their alongside some really cool people, like Nick Van Exel of the Lakers, that gorgeous bus-poet Marisela Norte, and Tim Roth, the actor. I'm happy to be there. I hope they're coming on opening night. We've invited the so-called 100 coolest. You're 101. (laughs)

WN: *More like number 793. My digs are in San Diego, and I just don't rate on that list—I don't know what would happen if a professor of English got placed on a Coolest list—I might have to change professions. But let's leave L.A., as you did in your formative writing years: though your heart is in Los Angeles and you're a writer of the Southland, you did most, if not all, of your higher education on the East Coast and in England. Can you tell us a little about where you learned to write?*

OM: I was born in Hollywood, and I feel myself more and more like I'm glad to be back, because yes, I've been away for a long time. I lived in New York. I was in England, but I've been back now seven years, and I really feel this to be my home. I went to Cornell in upstate New York, and I went to Worcester College, Oxford, and then I did my Master's at Columbia University, so I'm totally over-educated. (laughing) But can you believe it? I tend to write about people who don't have a college education. But thank goodness I got to work in these places. I think that one thing that has held me in good stead is my great love for English and American literature. And that would include anything from Shakespeare to Nabokov and I guess even beyond that to . . . who do I like now?

WN: Tennessee Williams?

OM: That's it. Tennessee Williams is good. I'm a Eugene O'Neill man myself. But I have an incredible love for the classic American theater. That's in part due to my mentor at Columbia, Howard Stein, who really taught me to study the continuum of writers so that I don't have to invent the wheel every time. And I derive great strength from the plays of William Saroyan and Luis Valdez and basically am drawn to those tallest trees in our American theatrical forest. Also, I have to give credit to my mentor at Cornell, John Stallworthy, who I think will be a Poet Laureate, who really deserves to be Poet Laureate in England . . . Stallworthy, the great poet of love. So, yes, and that's of course where I met Carlos Fuentes, who's a friend, and his teaching assistant Bill Nericcio . . .

WN: (laughs)Yes, I was your teacher there, your

T.A. I guess I should take credit for all the good things that have happened to you—of course, truth be told, we drank more than we waxed eloquent in those days of fire and ice . . .

OM: . . . True, true . . .

WN: Moving on, I want to hear you say something about the soul of Blade To The Heat; *the play can be read as an exposé on homo-erotic desire set in that pre-eminent essential site of male essence, the boxing ring. I wonder if you might talk a little about homo-erotic, hetero-erotic desire in the boxing ring.*

OM: Desire in the ring is how I would say it, because it's not simply homo-erotic. The thing about it is that the ring is of course the place where men of power reside, but sexuality is somewhat taboo when you talk about the ring, and that's men or women. You know, old-timers will talk about how you're supposed to stay "clean," how you're not supposed to have sex before you fight. It's supposed to make you meaner. (laughs) And I think there's something to that. But beyond that, sex is said to dissipate your energy and your focus, which I think is probably true. And it's simply that: a taboo—something you wouldn't do in a gym. Of course, everything's been done everywhere— man/woman, man/man. When you begin to talk about men, and men in a place like a boxing gym amongst other fighters, then it really is beyond taboo. It's a really strong taboo, something really frightening. If you were to turn the sound down on the next boxing broadcast and just look at it as a sort of a piece of ballet, you would see the two men, half-clothed, leaning and clutching and grabbing as much as punching. And you would see, in their corners, older men with their bodies draped over the younger fighters, massaging or whispering into their ears. And if you were a Martian, looking at this picture, you would not see it as perhaps we've been conditioned to see it. I mean, it really is very much about love. I'm not talking about prurient stuff—it's about intimate connections, an intimate connection that is physical as well as emotional . . .

WN: Intimate connection, but focused upon destruction . . .

OM: Well, that, too. Yeah, that, too. Because, of course, it is one man against another and *the* perfect victory is a knockout. Not death, but maybe a little death. I saw a fight recently and got sad afterwards and told Ron Link, you watch a great fight, you watch any fight, but particularly a great fight, you see that both men die a little bit in there. I'm not talking about years of their life or anything, but I'm talking about the kind of sacrifice they have to

make in order to go the distance and entertain us as they do. They have to take terrible blows. They have to go beyond endurance. And this takes its toll. And that's one reason that I really do honor it and as much as I love boxing, it kind of hurts sometimes to watch.

WN: Two last questions: the epigraph to your play is from Robert Hayden: "Only the music. And he swings oh swings; beyond complete immortal now." This reminded me of something I just ran across in my reading. Recently I've been studying Julio Cortázar's Hopscotch, *(Rayuela) published in 1963 in Latin America and Spain, and in the United States in 1966. One of the things that's remarkable about the novel is the way that Cortázar orders the novel, or, better put, disorders the novel, using the music of Thelonious Monk as a kind of map or model—this allows all kinds of literary improvisation. Cortázar wants to use the tactics of jazz geniuses like Monk and John Coltrane and apply them to his fiction. I wonder if you could say something a little more about music in your work: I know you opened our conversation with a confession about your mother's Jackie Wilson '45. Tell us a little more about music and* Blade To The Heat—*I know it was the heart of the New York production.*

OM: Yeah, it will be again. We're lucky. We have one of the best men in L.A. music, Maceo Hernandez with East L.A. Taiko, is helping us with the play with live accompaniment. The play is full of not just rhythm and blues but sounds of the mambo, New York Palladium kind of Mambo Kings playing songs of love rhythms. And there's something about boxing that lends itself to music, the way the bodies move on stage, and the rhythms and the punches, the squeak of the feet on the mat and their exhalations. It is a kind of music, especially when there are two men, again, in sync. It's a really beautiful thing. It's not by accident that I set the play in 1959, which I think was, again, to use the word from earlier, a kind of *seminal* American year. I think a lot happened in '59. Not just in this country—that was the year that Castro took command in Cuba. Music in this country was at a particularly high level, just before the censors came in and Pat Boonized and Fabian-ized the music scene. So people like Jackie Wilson and James Brown were really kind of free and really gave some great performances. The Hayden epigraph is actually from a poem about Billie Holiday, who if I'm correct, died in 1959 and there's something of the time in that, there's sort of the quality of somewhere between blues and the beatnik period.[15] The experimentation of the beat generation with their fascination with

death is central to all this—the fact that death is a very attractive thing amongst the beats: that's why they wore a lot of black and why they would experiment with *peyote* and why people like Ginsberg would write gigantic poems like *Kaddish . . . and Kerouac*. It's a period in which music, literature, poetry, and sports . . . where there was a kind of darkness, a kind of very attractive darkness to the world. You know people think about the fifties and say they were boring, that it was the heyday of the Beaver Cleaver generation, and that may be true, for some unlucky few, but there were areas like San Francisco and Los Angeles and New York in the Village where there was incredible experimentation in artistry and self-expression that I'm interested in.

WN: Anything else about the music? Outside of local DJs and musician friends, you probably have the most eclectic collection of tunes of anyone I know.

OM: I have a new line in the play that sort of speaks to that; it's very new. It says, "I had to be a fighter in order to find the music." I had to be a fighter in order to find the music: that's the line. In the end, I think for me, I had to listen to music in order to find the writing.

---

[15] Born Eleanora Fagan in 1915, Billie Holliday died July 17, 1959.

Raymond Cruz as "Vinal" from the Taper's production of *Blade to the Heat*.

Raymond Saucedo and Oliver Mayer

Playwright Oliver Mayer has a lot on his mind. A native of Los Angeles, the Cornell and Oxford graduate was visiting San Diego for the sold-out, one-week-only showing of his play, *The Road To Los Angeles*. He sat down with me to discuss theater, identity, sex, and his new project, *Blade to the Heat*, which is currently in the works in preparation for the big screen. Madonna (yes, the Madonna), bought the rights to the story about a 1950s nobody-turned-championship boxer forced to confront his own sexuality after a dethroned champion accuses him of being gay.

Raymond Saucedo: You once said that some playwrights are afraid of or just don't write about the beauty and danger that is life today. What do you mean by that?

Oliver Mayer: Some playwrights, in particular some of the famous and successful ones, are writing in a very reductive style that they are famous for, and then they have to see the world through that prism, that style. That is unfair to the world, which is more interesting than those styles. I do have a style, but that style based on trying to get as much of a breadth of difference of population of characters as possible—to have a wide-angle, panoramic view of as many people as I could find, and then take it through history. I always write in the now. I have written plays that are set in the (19)40s and 1890s. The only reason to see a play that is set in say the 1890s is if it is about now; if we can see something about us that we can recognize: how history repeats itself, how we are replanting the seeds of whatever problem we want to talk about—slavery, racism, etc.

RM: Do you think that categorizing art is similar to applying a canon to literature? Do you see any right or wrong in that?

OM: I don't mind people who do categorize and evaluate art; it probably has to be done. But I think the artist is better off not knowing those evaluations—it's better it takes place in academia. Artists need to be free of checking over their backs to see if they're leading the race, or if they're behind. Contemporary artists, and I am guilty of this myself, tend to be rivals in contention with one another. As an artist, I should be in contention with myself—that's the real contest. I think that is the problem with such artists as Mamet and Wilson, who are canonized, and they believe it, so that now, they figure that "I'm so great, I'm going to continue to do the same

things I've been doing." It gets old; they stop; and in a certain way, they're dead. I don't want to die so soon; I've got a lot of work to do. I'm sure it'll probably happen to me one day, but I want to have gotten at least another 5 or 10 plays out.

RM: What do you try to accomplish with your plays?

OM: The theater belongs to us and is not a museum. It should be alive and represent live people. I think Shakespeare is so good because he is so contemporary. Shakespeare's London was not unlike this very campus: lots of violence, lots of sex, lots of death. I believe that is the world we live in today. We are all worthy subjects, and if I write lovingly and deeply about life today, then perhaps people in the future will see my work as a window to what it is like to live life today.

RM: Let's talk about that identity thing. Your mother is Mexican, and your father was, as you call him, an "American mutt." Did you struggle with your own identity growing up?

OM: I didn't even realize there was a struggle until I was 11 years old. In junior high, I had to fill out one of those forms where you had to check Black/White/ Latino/Whatever, and I didn't know what to do. I hadn't checked my box, and we were in Physical Education, so we were standing in line out on the field. Standing in front of me was this black guy whom everyone was afraid of because he was so much bigger and stronger. Well, he checked the white box because one of his parents was white. Everyone started laughing, and he wasn't scary anymore. I don't even know why, but I picked Latino—I made the choice. I could have picked "White"—my name is Mayer. But something about the experience, him shamed and confused, made me embrace the "darker" side. People don't ask me so much about my ethnicity anymore. When I was younger, in my twenties, some of the Chicano activists in L.A. were not as warm as others. But I've done my time. It doesn't even matter if someone calls me a Latino writer or just a writer—but they do have to deal with my body of work.

RM: So how does being bicultural affect you today? Does it inform your work?

OM: It influences me all the time. I have some political soap-boxes that I get on. Here I am making fun of Wilson and Mamet for having a singular style, and yet I've got my own. Like one thing you can always count on with a play of mine and that is there's going to be a lot of people of color in it. That's something that I can give to the world. The people who do this play thank me because many of them would never be in a play on this stage because they can't get roles. There aren't roles for them. That's seems to be something I hear over and over again, and it seems wrong to me. I happen to think they should all play in the Shaw and Ibsen plays, but apparently, they can't get the roles. But they can get the roles in a play by me that calls for mixed-blooded people, black people, Latin people. So, I've got to give them some work because they deserve the opportunity. I'm not saying they're better than anybody else, but they are at least as good. So that's one of my political themes that I do think of all the time. It may not even be my strongest thing; maybe I should just write and forget about it. But I think that it's something that I can do that will change the world in a good way, even incrementally. I think about this bicultural phenomenon every day. That's one reason I live in L.A. It's very, very exciting to live in California, because more and more it means you have to be bilingual. You have to eat in more than one language.

RM: Yesterday, you wore a shirt with one of the words from your play, "Califaztlán." Aztlán is the legendary origin of the ancient Aztecs. By merging the word with "California," are you saying that maybe Aztlán is somewhere in California?

OM: Yes, I think it is—symbolically and possibly literally. Perhaps so many of us who have Latin blood in our veins come here, being the second largest place for Mexicans, Guatemalans, and Salvadorans, outside of the capital cities in these places. So many people toil and put their blood and their spirit into this world of southern California. Why shouldn't our resting place, our paradise, our heaven, our dream world rest here? I think it ought to. Aztec peoples passed through here a long time ago also. Maybe there are some very deep ties. Maybe there is a reason we all come here besides the weather and the jobs. Maybe this is where we should be.

Is that your word? Did you coin "Califaztlan."

I've heard it once before, but never again. It's a good idea to stick California and Aztlán together. I've found another one for all the people from Oaxaca who come to work in California—they call it "Oaxa-California."

RM: What prompted you to write a play about a young Latino struggling with his own sexual identity?

OM: The thought came to me and scared me. I was at an age, in my twenties, when it was scarier than it is now. I thought about the identity of a male boxer. I wondered if in my experience and my knowledge if I've ever seen a gay boxer before. I thought "No, there couldn't be." Then I thought, "Of course, there must be." I didn't know who. I wasn't out to out anybody. But I was thinking about what kind of life such a man must have—not very unlike that of a marine. I was scared for the person, whomever that might be. Talk about danger. Then I thought if that guy's a really good fighter, then that's one thing they can't take away from him. I love boxing. There's a famous line—I don't even know who said it. Somebody said that a fighter was a "fag." Then somebody else responds, "Well, he may be a fag, but he's got a helluva left hook." I sort of thought about that, and if he's good, then he is a champion. Gay or straight, that's something they can't take away from him. In the end, what do we know about anybody? Unless we go to bed with them, how do we know? We don't know. Then again, we happen to know people who identify as straight who are, in fact, gay. I personally believe that it's our choice to do what we feel like doing. It's about warmth and flesh and blood. Today, we have the freedom to be with whom we want. In this play, I realized it would be hot and scary if this person didn't have those kinds of freedoms. So I thought it had to be pre-Stonewall. That was really important. If it was post-Stonewall, he might have had the sense that he was freer because he'd know that there were other people like him. I wanted him to be alone. I wanted to jack it up to make it as scary as I felt when I first thought of it. Then I had to write at that pitch—it's a very intense play. There's lot of sex and violence, but not just gay sex. I think with most straight men, they're constantly thinking about gay people. It's a contest thing—comparing and contrasting. This guy who loses to the gay guy, his macho identity is shaken to its very roots. He can't even get it up with his girlfriend. Everyone laughs at him. So now he has to kill this guy—beat him to a pulp. I think that's real. You have to watch a Latin guy if he feels like his machismo has been interfered with. It's extremely dangerous. You're talking about life and death at this point. After the blood has been cleaned, he realizes how stupid he was. Playwrights just have to watch what people do, and the stupid, crazy things they do are really worth putting on stage sometimes.

RM: What is the main characters' name?

OM: Pedro Quinn. Again, there's that mixed blood thing going on.

RM: If you had the choice, which actor would you chose to play Pedro?

OM: Oh, good question. In Hollywood, you have to be very brave to play anything other than your typical hunk. Whoever it will be, he should be in his early twenties. The point about him is that he hasn't had experience in life. His experience is in the ring. He's put his entire life into winning that title. He hasn't had a girlfriend, hasn't had a boyfriend. He hasn't lived—he's a virgin to all this. He's innocent. Then, he's disavowed of innocence in the course of the play, being beaten up for it. Really, the ring is the safest place he could be . . .

LA Prod 1996
Blade
Ray Oriel as Pedro
Dominic Hoffman as
Mantequilla

Glossary (In order of appearance in the play)

¡Tira!	Hit him
El gancho al hígado	The hook to the liver
¡Tira, coño!	Hit him, damn it!
Corazón	heart; will
Como-se-llama	what's his name
Quién sabe	who knows
¡Qué chulo!	How beautiful!
¿Y tú, qué sabes?	You, what do you know?
Tú	you
Todo hombre.	All man.
¡Cómo ésto!	Like *this* fist!
Cabrón	asshole (huge goat)
Hijo de la gran puta	Son of the "great bitch"
Come mierda	Eat shit
Por favor, chica	Please, girl
Las gané todas...	I beat them all with
con ésto, con el Suzie Q	with *this*, the Suzie Q
¡No, tonta!	No, stupid,
Mi inteligencia	my brain/intelligence
sonrisa comemierda	shit-eating smile
¡Seguro! ¡Sin duda!	For sure! Without doubt!
En la panza	in the stomach
Oye	Listen
Qué bien te ves, chica	How good you look, baby.
Pero	but
Algo	something
Como se dice	how do you say . . .
Tremendo golpe,	a major blow,
como cañonazo	like a cannon
—y nada	—and nothing

¡Espérate!	Wait
¡¡¡Carajo!!!	Damn!!!
Chicanas/os	Politicized, left of center Americans of Mexican decent, (antonym: Hispanic)
Me llamo Martillo.	They call me the hammer.
El ponchador martillo	The punching hammer.
¡Chingao!	Fuck!
Maricón	slur-term for a gay man
¿Cómo está la novia?	How's the girlfriend?
¿Te gusta meter mano?	You like to put in the hand/get some?
Panocha	pussy/vagina
Pendejo	idiot/asshole
¡Payaso!	Clown!
Cálmate	Calm down
Soy todo hombre	I'm all man
Si es afeminado	if he is effeminate
Aquí estamos	We're here
No lo soy	I am not
¡¡¡Dímelll !!!¿ por qué?!!	Tell me!!! why?!!
¡No me toques!	Don't touch me!
¿Es macho o no es macho?	Is he a man or is he not a man?
¿Contigo?	With you?
¡Qué lindo eres!	How beautiful you are!
Pinche rucas	Damn women
¡No coño!	No damn it!
Yo soy boriqua. Pura sangre	I am Boriqua (Puerto Rico) Pure blood.
Un derechazo como relámpago	A lightning-like right
Latinos—los mejores del mundo	Latinos—the best in the world
Campeón nacional	National champion
Desgraciado	Low-life
Le debes romper las bolas	You should break his balls.
Los putos huevos	His fucking balls.

La raza	The [Mexican] people
Dáme candy	Give me love.
Venga a verme	Come see me.
Hijo de la chingada	Son of the fucked woman
¿Qué onda, chula?	What's up, gorgeous?
Chingadera	Fuckin' thing
Andale, vámanos.	Hurry up, let's go.
¡Muévete!	Move!
Vete a la chingada, ¡idiota!	Go to fucking hell, idiot!
¡¡¡Mátelo!!!	Kill him!!!

From the private collection of Oliver Mayer,
an original '45 by Jackie Wilson.

Period Reviews, *Blade to the Heat* (1996)

"It begins with the growling of wild beasts and ends with a boxing match as brutal as you are likely to see on a stage. In between, the lights throb, the bloodthirsty crowds roar, and two drummers, as if possessed, beat a mad tattoo on the congas. Flashbulbs rip holes in the darkness, already fouled by clouds of smoke. Even the scene changes are explosive."

The New York Times

"Oliver Mayer uses the bare aggression of boxing, the clarity and inevitability of the battle, to examine broader issues about the time in which we live, issues about what defines a man and the price men pay for the rigid delineations of a macho culture ... Oliver Mayer is out to reclaim the ring as heroic dramatic territory."

The Los Angeles Times

"BLADE TO THE HEAT ... packs a helluva wallop ... With Mayer, the metaphor of boxing is used to explore the ethnic and cultural worlds of the boxers.... And Mayer doesn't stop his probing until he's into the very minds of the combatants ... It's searing and soaring theater."

The Hollywood Reporter

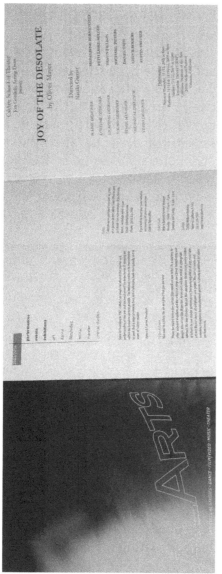

A reproduction of the program spread from the CalArts production of *Joy of the Desolate*.

JOY OF THE DESOLATE

World Premiere performed at the Apple Tree Theatre, Chicago, 2000

Directed by Geraint Wyn Davies

DC	Michael Gotch
JAHA	Kwaku Driskell
HRMF	Si Osbourne
DAN	David Laurence
HOLLY	Aasne Vigesaa
BRIGID	Kate Goehring
CYNTHIA	Ora Jones
MOM	Mierka Girten
DONNY	Sean Blake

West Coast premiere performed at CalArts School of Theatre, Valencia, CA, 2003

Directed by Nataki Garrett

DC	William Figueroa
JAHA	Nicholas Grimes
HRMF/DONNY	Jin Suh
DAN	Michael Hanggi
HOLLY	Ariane Owens
BRIGID	Shai Schneider
CYNTHIA	Carla Nassy

Why did they shut me out of heaven?

Did I sing too loud?

Emily Dickinson

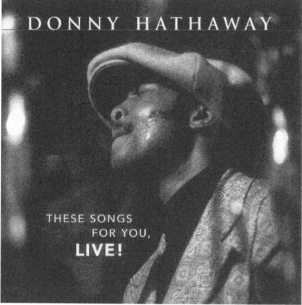

Classic Donny Hathaway.

Darkness.

The piano lead-in to Donny Hathaway's "A Song For You."
Lights rise.
D.C. sits atop a single bed. Seventeen, a freshman student in all his poverty, wearing a tee-shirt with the insignia of a prestigious Ivy League school. Textbooks strewn on the bed.
The phone RINGS in the hall.
D.C. freezes. Waits. Someone OFF answers it. Breathes deep, but can't get enough air in his lungs.
D.C.: Dad . . . ?
The phone RINGS.
Then JAHA enters. Black, studious, grave.
JAHA: It's for you.
D.C. rises like a man on his way to die.
As he goes to the phone, —
BLACKNESS. Not blackout, but the blackness of death itself.
Then, a massive door creaks open. Cold night air like a windshaft. D.C. enters.
In the lack of light we see a chapel, empty at this late hour. Smell of incense. Old wood pews, stained glass windows. An introspective place, pregnant with silence.
D.C. breaks it. He has been crying. More retching than crying. Now, he falls into a pew awkwardly, unused to prayer.
No more tears. He laughs bitterly. A more permanent shade of mourning taking over fast.

Then a sound. Magnified by stillness.

D.C. freezes. Nothing, no one.

D.C.: Aw, Dad. Couldn't you have held on a little longer? (*beat*) I guess I should go home. But I want to stay. What am I gonna do? (*genuflects clumsily*) Aw hell. Amen.

The sound of various pockets releasing air.

Then, amazingly, Bach played on the church organ.

D.C. rises to leave, but the music stops him, washes over him, and makes him listen.

The single light reveals HRMF, the organmeister. Small and handsome and dour, dapper and outdated, prissy and macho. Playing with great physicality, doubling over arms and legs to play the music.

The music ends.

Sound of air pockets releasing.

HRMF rises. Then sees D.C. — D.C. sees him, too.

D.C.: My dad died.

A long stare. A nod. Then HRMF exits.

D.C. breathes deep.

A TENOR sings hard and strong:

DAN: THE LOWLINESS OF HIS HANDMAIDEN —

HOLLY scoffs.

HOLLY: Lowliness of his what?

Dan is Italianate, beefy, in his mid-twenties. Holly is Black Irish, impressive as hell.

DAN: Hey, I just sing it.

Dan shuts her up with a kiss. They grind together a moment, two lovers in mid-relationship.

D.C. enters by mistake. Clears his throat.

D.C.: Auditions here?

DAN: Around the corner.

D.C.: Thanks. (*beat*) You sound great.

HOLLY: Don't tell him that!

DAN: She thinks I'll get a swell head. But I can't help it if I sound good.

D.C.: I could never get that high.

DAN: You mean . . .

He demonstrates, showing off his tenor range.

DAN: Pavarotti says . . . (*doing Pavarotti*) "The voice is an 'orse!" (*in his own voice*) An elegant, delicate, dangerous horse.

HOLLY: The voice is an animal. Sometimes you gotta let it out of its cage. (*slight pause*) You sing?

DAN: Great place to sing. Strongest choir upstate. Live radio broadcast every Sunday—

D.C.: (*losing heart*) I don't even know what I'm doing . . .

D.C. starts to exit.

Holly catches him by the arm.

HOLLY: Wait.

D.C.: I'm just — I'm looking —(*runs out of air*) My dad sang. (*pause*)

HOLLY: Good reason.

DAN: Stick with us. We'll keep you outa trouble.

HOLLY: Or get ya into some.

A look passes between D.C. and Holly. Then she smiles.

HOLLY: This big lug is Dan. I'm Holly. And you are?

D.C.: D.C. (*pause*)

DAN: Which stands for?

D.C.: Don Carlos. (*clears throat*) I know. Stupid.

HOLLY: No, it isn't.

DAN: Don Carlo. Kinda like the opera.

D.C.: The what?

Dan and Holly share a look.

DAN: Let's take the chicken under our wing.

D.C.: How do I audition?

DAN: You meet the man.

As they speak, we see HRMF at his desk.

HOLLY: He doesn't bite.

DAN: Not too hard, anyway.

HOLLY: That's just the way HRMF is.

D.C.: Harrumph?

HOLLY: Harold R.M. Fitzpatrick — HRMF.

DAN: Himself.

HOLLY: His Nibs.

DAN: The Very One.

D.C.: So what do I do?

HOLLY: You sing. (*slight pause*) You do have something to sing?

D.C. doesn't answer. Holly responds by searching through sheet music. He puts his hand out to stop her. Their fingers meet by accident.

D.C.: It'll be all right. I'll just let it out.

HOLLY: Let what out?

D.C.: The animal, I guess.

As Dan and Holly exit, —

MUSIC — Brahms introspective choral stuff. HRMF fiddles with his record collection. Leans into the speaker, listening, studying the polyphonies, trying to find some hidden key in the chords.

Then D.C. enters.

(*When HRMF speaks it is with an exacting enunciation, pompous if weren't also a bit funny.*)

HRMF: A lean and hungry look.

D.C.: Pardon me?

D.C. hands him an application form.

HRMF: Mister . . .

D.C.: Nodora. Call me D.C. (*beat*) Initials — like HRMF!

HRMF: Indeed.

D.C.: We met the other night. (*beat*) Funny, I never really been to church.

HRMF: Funny.

D.C.: Never really sang either.

(*beat*)

But my dad? He sang. He sang his ass off.

HRMF: (*tries to picture that*) I'm sure he did.

D.C.: Yep, Dad could sure hit the high notes.

HRMF: And you?

D.C.: Me? I'm in the middle range somewhere.

HRMF: The heart of the music. (*clears throat*) Now you realize this is a place of sacred music.

D.C.: Do I have to believe in God?

HRMF: You must sing for those who do. (*gesticulates*) The choir is searching for a certain bigness of sound. We do not cater to any one musical tradition. Rather, we search for great music and strive to sing it greatly. And by singing greatly, I mean with the requisite faith—

D.C.: You mean you like it hard and strong?

HRMF: (*clears throat*) In a manner of speaking.

D.C.: I can't promise faith. But I'll give everything I got.

HRMF stares at D.C. like a piece of music from a foreign land, recently discovered and hard to decipher.

HRMF: We may not be the most beautiful singers. But we sing from the very bottom of our hearts. (*beat*) At least we try.

HRMF motions. Time to audition.

For a moment D.C. looks like a Little Leaguer on his first at-bat. But he finds strength from within.

D.C.: This is something Dad used to sing. In the bathtub. I don't know how sacred. Dad was a communist. (*HRMF clears throat*) And proud of it. Don't get too many communists on the Rez. (*slight pause*) Reservation. He was Native. Pima Indian. A red man, I guess you could say.

HRMF: Indeed.

D.C.: He used to forget the words. But Mom—

D.C. stops dead.

Stops breathing.

It soon becomes alarming.

HRMF: Mister Nodora?

D.C.: Nothing. (*breathes*) This is for Dad.

D.C. sings a capella with a strong young voice, untrained but expressive.

D.C.: DERE'S AN OLD MAN
CALLED DE MISSISSIPPI
DAT'S DE OLD MAN I DON'T LIKE TO BE
WHAT DOES HE CARE
IF DE WORLD'S GOT TROUBLES
WHAT DOES HE CARE IF DE LAND AIN'T FREE—

HRMF: If I'm correct, those are not the words Mister Hammerstein had in mind.

D.C.: Paul Robeson. He changed the words. After what this country done to him, I figure he earned the right.

HRMF: Yes. Well. Continue.

D.C.: I'll skip the famous stuff. This is what I really want to sing . . . (*belts it out*)
BUT I KEEPS LAUGHIN'
INSTEAD OF CRYIN'
I MUST KEEP FIGHTIN'
UNTIL I'M DYIN' —

As D.C. shouts out the climax, —

HRMF: That will do. (*pause*) You have an untrained but perfectly serviceable baritone. You will fill out the baritone section, and, I believe, enhance it mightily. You have much to learn. But then so do we all. I will instruct you as best I can. If you care to join us, perhaps we can help you find your voice.

D.C.: Indeed.

HRMF turns away. The meeting has ended. D.C. backs off, running down the hall. By accident runs headlong into BRIGID. Blonde, page-boy haircut, full of fire. Knocks the Bible out of her hand.

D.C.: Sorry!!!

BRIGID: Don't be.

D.C.: I gotta—

BRIGID: Go.

He goes in. Brigid reacting from the force of the blow; not necessarily the physical force, but something else.

D.C. backs his way back to his dorm room.

Jaha is studying on the bed. In his underwear. Incense is burning.

JAHA: Hey. Look what the cat drugged in.

D.C.: (*cold*) Hey.

JAHA: So. You in? (*mock-sings*)

D.C.: I'm in.

D.C. ignores Jaha despite their proximity. The phone RINGS. Even though D.C. is closer and only just got in, he makes no effort to answer it.

Jaha sighs. Goes to the hall to pick it up. Then returns.

JAHA: It's for you.

D.C.: What now? (*cold*)

Did you ask who?

JAHA: Well, it can't be your dad. (*laughs*) It's a woman. Ivy, Holly, one of those.

D.C. heats up fast, jumps out of bed and out the door.

MUSIC — Opera records, played loud.

Dan and Holly are preparing pasta.

D.C. joins them on the run.

HOLLY: Now the fun starts.

DAN: Listen to the best singers. Fischer Dieskau, Hermann Prey —

HOLLY: Jussi Bjoerling.

DAN: Oh, yeah, play the Bjoerling!

D.C.: The who?

DAN: (*to HOLLY*) We got a lotta work ahead.

HOLLY: (*finds record*) Surround yourself with beautiful things. The richest voices. The most exquisite songs —

D.C.: I brought my Donny Hathaway tape.

He pulls out a cassette from his pocket.

Dan laughs. Continues cooking.

D.C.: But I don't know how sacred it is.

He starts to pocket the tape. She stops him.

HOLLY: It's all sacred. If it's beautiful, then it's sacred.

D.C.: I like it. My dad —(*struggles*) Makes me think about him.

HOLLY: Let's hear it.

She plays the tape. Over the piano intro:

D.C.: There's a lotta great singers. But Donny, he has my heart. Sometimes this song really takes me away . . .

HOLLY: Where?

D.C.: I don't know. Home.

As they listen—

We see DONNY HATHAWAY, or his spirit, in shadow. Apple Jack rakishly atop his head. He sings LIVE:

DONNY: I'VE BEEN SO MANY PLACES
IN MY LIFE AND TIME
I'VE SUNG A LOT OF SONGS
I'VE MADE SOME BAD RHYMES
I'VE ACTED OUT MY LIFE IN STAGES
WITH TEN THOUSAND PEOPLE WATCHING
BUT WE'RE ALONE NOW
AND I'M SINGING THIS SONG TO YOU —

There is an air of death about him.

It is attractive.

HOLLY: I think I see what you mean.

D.C.: You can almost see the kind of man he was, you know?

HOLLY: What happened to him?

D.C. struggles to answer.

DAN: Come on! Let's have some real music!

D.C. ejects the tape.

The spirit Donny Hathaway lingers on, slipping slowly into the growing darkness.

HOLLY: (*to DAN*) Charming.

Dan comes over. Finds the Jussi Bjoerling album with the duet from Bizet's PEARLFISHERS.

DAN: There's men. Then there's Jussi. Sometimes you get to hear the voice of God. Maybe once a century. If you're lucky.

He pours wine.

Holly fixes the pasta.

DAN: (*listens*) If you wanna sing, listen to Jussi. Sometimes I just sit here and pretend he's me. You know—like Michael Jordan or something. And when he hits that note?

Points at the stereo as Jussi sings:

DAN: That note only dogs can hear? That Joe Cocker note that just crinkles you up like cellophane? That one?

Dan contorts Joe Cocker style:

DAN: That's God.

Holly sets out the food.

HOLLY: Time to eat.

D.C. joins her at the table.

Dan continues to sing along with Jussi. Dan has a lovely tenor voice, but he's thin up-top. He breaks off, tries, breaks off again.

HOLLY: Come on. Break it up.

Dan keeps trying to hit the high note. The harder he tries, the worse he sounds.

Holly joins him.

DAN: Dammit. I can.

HOLLY: Sure you can.

DAN: Just gotta warm up —

HOLLY: Later.

DAN: Just gotta —

HOLLY: LATER.

Hot pause.

Then Dan turns the volume down. Sits at table. Begins to eat as if nothing happened.

D.C. watches them like they're from Mars.

Dan downs his wine. Pours another.

HOLLY: Duet from PEARLFISHERS. Bizet.

D.C.: There's two guys singing.

DAN: Very perceptive.

D.C.: Who's the other guy?

DAN: Robert Merrill. Baritone. Like you.

HOLLY: That's your part. You two oughta sing this.

D.C.: You think?

DAN: (*pouring more wine*) Why not.

HOLLY: Merrill was great.

DAN: Not as great as Jussi. (*off HOLLY's frown*) Hey, it ain't easy being great. Before a performance, Merrill useta havta walk Jussi around and around the block at the Met.

D.C.: Why?

DAN: (*downs his glass*) Because Jussi was a drunk. Hey, it all goes hand in hand.

HOLLY: Singers are under a lot of pressure. To sing like that, to really sing, it can kill you . . .

D.C.: Merrill, too?

HOLLY: No.

DAN: There's gods and then there's men.

HOLLY: You need them both.

DAN: We can't all be gods. You gotta know your place. In the scheme of things. You gotta know how far you can go. Steady, like ol' Robert Merrill. Or on fire like Jussi. Blaze of glory. Then pffft!

D.C.: You mean he's dead?

DAN: This ain't heaven. Gods just don't cut it on earth. But hey, you gotta go sometime. So why not go in style? (*to HOLLY*) Ain't that right? (*then toasts*) Blaze of glory.

D.C.: Blaze of glory.

Dan and D.C. drink. Holly does not. They listen to the end together.

We hear a cacophony of LECTURERS declaiming on all subjects undergraduate. In particular whatever sounds pretentious and esoteric.

He walks away alone.

Now he is on the suspension bridge between school and town. He is about to cross when CYNTHIA appears from underneath the bridge. Black, attractive, but not young anymore.

CYNTHIA: You driving?

D.C.: Just tryna get home.

CYNTHIA: Student? (*following*) I'm just tryna survive. Watch people's cars, you know how it is, nothing safe no more no way. I'm just tryna get out of the rain. In the old days I had one date after another all night long, but tonight the shit is dead. This a dead city, boy. (*stops him*) For a coupla bucks I'll suck your dick.

D.C.: What?!!

CYNTHIA: Just a blowjob. Nothing personal.

D.C.: I-I-I don't think so.

CYNTHIA: Maybe next time.

D.C. fishes for a dollar bill. She takes it.

CYNTHIA: Just tryna make an honest living. (*as he tries to get away*) I'm not here to beg. I'm willing to do my part.

D.C.: Next time! (*exits*)

CYNTHIA: (*calling after him*) We'll call it a raincheck!!!

She returns to her home beneath the bridge. Darkness. Then the massive door swings open again. D.C. slumps into a pew. Genuflects half-heartedly.

D.C.: I don't know about this place. I kinda had a different picture of the Ivy League. (*beat*) But I'm learning how to sing.

Then HRMF takes the choir lectern. Baton in hand.

D.C.: Everything's about God. But the music. Music's pretty cool.

Dan and Holly enter, take their places on the choir stand. D.C. watches Holly's every move. HRMF raps the baton.

D.C.: Oops. Gotta go.

Genuflects. Then runs up to the choir stand. D.C. takes his place.

HRMF: Welcome, Choir. Let us begin on Bar One.

Taps baton. CHOIR comes to attention.

HRMF: (*sets baton down*) Perhaps a moment. Let us welcome our new voices. I expect you to help these newcomers find their way. You were once in their position. As was I. Yea, back unto pre-history. We were all young once. Not yet ourselves. Who we would become. (*beat*) Even the divine Johann Sebastian.

D.C.: (*whispering*) Who?

DAN: (*whispering*) Bach!

HRMF: Bach! Yes. Papa Bach. Yes Virginia, there was a time when even Bach was but a rank beginner. Even Bach. Someone was there to help him on his way. Someone had to be. You see, a person is a person through other persons.

Throats clearing from the CHOIR, the sound of awkward embarrassed young people.

HRMF: So we sing together. No one voice above the others. Rather, we sing in one voice. And, to borrow a phrase, we sing it HARD AND STRONG. (*taps baton*) And—

The CHOIR sings a Magnificat.

CHOIR:
MY SOUL DOTH MAGNIFY THE LORD
AND MY SPIRIT REJOICETH
IN GOD MY SAVIOR —!!

HRMF cajoles, intimidates, nearly jumps out of his clothes as he conducts.

HRMF: Tenors? Together!! (*keeping time*) Baritones! Look at me!!

CHOIR:
FOR HE HATH REGARDED
THE LOWLINESS OF HIS HANDMAIDEN
FOR BEHOLD —

HRMF: Come on, now, Sopranos!!! (*stops them*) People! You must listen. I know what you're thinking. You're wondering, who is this madman? Why is he waving his arms so? Well, listen. (*intones, imbues*) MY SOUL DOTH MAGNIFY THE LORD, AND MY SPIRIT REJOICETH IN GOD MY SAVIOUR.

(*beat*) MAGNIFY. REJOICETH. SAVIOUR. Not—(*repeats in monotone*) My soul doth magnify the lord and my spirit rejoiceth in god my saviour are you hungry let's get a burger. NO!! Not that.

A titter from the choir.

HRMF pounds the lectern.

HRMF: Search for the meaning! Only then can your spirit soar!!

HOLLY: Kinda hard when I'm singing about the lowliness of some guy's handmaiden.

DAN: Some guy?!!

HRMF: Holly, dear. What exactly is your objection?

HOLLY: Handmaidens? Lowly?

HRMF: In relation to God, my dear. In relation to God.

HOLLY: Look. I'm here to sing, not to bow before any man.

DAN: What about God?

HOLLY: Him neither.

HRMF: What disgrace is there in that? I do not ask you to believe. But I ask you to feel. Sing the feeling.

HOLLY: My feelings are my own.

HRMF: Not if you're a singer. To really sing, you must make the private public.

(*beat*) That's what "Magnify" means.

(*beat*) After all, this is a Magnificat.

D.C.: (*clueless*) Magnifi-Cat? Isn't that a Disney movie?

BRIGID: God, no.

Brigid appears, now in the robes of Chapel Pastor.

HRMF: (*clears throat*) Newcomers — Pastor Brigid Peters Johannsen —

BRIGID: Call me Brigid.

HOLLY: (*to BRIGID*) You know what I'm trying to say.

BRIGID: Of course I do.

Despite her raiments, she makes herself comfortable.

BRIGID: People read the Bible and wonder where the heck the women are. Of course they're there. To beget — and be got. And of course there's Mother Mary. A paragon of women if there ever was. And Ruth. Rebecca. Rachel. And then there are those who think of God as decidedly female. Well, I feel a little different . . .

(*beat*) The truth, Holly, is that women were handmaidens. And often still are. And it is upsetting. Repeating the old moldy lies. Keeping ourselves from being free. (*beat*)

But the music. That's something different altogether. No, it is not a Disney movie, thank God. It is a sacred text. And it was meant to be sung. A Magnificat is a kind of expression of joy. Not simply of faith, but of the feeling that one is blessed, and can bless.

She joins HRMF at the lectern. He seems shy.

BRIGID: As my learned friend can attest, I wrestle with my faith almost every night. After much thought and many sleepless nights and a few too many scotches on the rocks, I've come to this rather incomplete conclusion. (*to HOLLY*) We're all of us handmaidens. Men, too. But there are Gods amongst us. And we should wash one another's feet every once in a while. (*beat*) Just in case. Just for the hell of it.

Silence.

Then HRMF raps the baton.

HRMF: Choir?

Brigid smiles, touches HRMF as she withdraws. He recoils, ever so slightly.

HRMF: Bar Ten. And—

CHOIR

FOR HE HATH REGARDED

THE LOWLINESS OF HIS HANDMAIDEN

FOR BEHOLD FROM HENCEFORTH

ALL GENERATIONS SHALL CALL ME

BLESSED

HRMF stops the choir.

But D.C., eyes closed, sings on in his raw enthusiastic voice:

D.C.: (*solo*) FOR HE THAT IS MIGHTY

HATH MAGNIFIED ME —

HRMF raps the baton.

HRMF: MISTER NODORA!

D.C. stops, embarrassed.

HRMF: This is not a solo. (beat) Not yet.

CHURCH BELLS. Choir disperses.

Holly approaches Brigid.

Dan and D.C. hover uneasily.

HOLLY: This is for you.

She gives Brigid a bookmark.

BRIGID: Guess now I gotta go and read a book.

HOLLY: Well, you got a Bible.

BRIGID: That old thing?

HOLLY: I want to believe. I got a voice. I want to use it. I want to be an instrument. A living breathing human trumpet! But it's like there's a rag stuck in a valve somewhere inside. Sure, I can sing. But it keeps me from really going there. And if I can't go there, they're just a bunch of words. (*beat*) What is joy?

BRIGID: Being free.

HOLLY: What if you're not? If you're caught? Can you still find joy? Or do you gotta chew your own foot off, whatever it takes to be free?

BRIGID: Maybe you don't have to go quite that far. But if you do, then go with God.

Dan clears his throat, attitudinal. Holly exits with Dan. D.C. stands there. Brigid reads the bookmark.

BRIGID: Hmmn.

HRMF: What is it?

BRIGID: The Saint Francis Prayer.

HRMF: How does it go?

BRIGID: I'll read it to you sometime. When you need it.

They exit together.

D.C. sits alone in the back pew.

D.C.: I dunno, Dad. Singing is scary. I dunno what's gonna come out. Sometimes it's like my voice isn't even mine. Like a

burp, or a yawn. I can't control it. And when I try — well, it just sounds like shit.
He sits back. Trying to figure it out.
D.C.: Guess it's like sex! Not that I'd know. It's all such a mystery. And I know it's gonna happen. It's gotta happen. But it hasn't happened. When's it gonna happen?
D.C. finds himself at the bridge.
Then Cynthia emerges from under the bridge.
CYNTHIA: Raincheck?
D.C.: What do I do?
CYNTHIA: You don't gotta do nothing.
D.C.: Where do we go?
CYNTHIA: Under the bridge. (*off his balk*) No one's gonna see us.
She takes his hand. Leads him down with her.
Mid-way he stops. LIGHT CHANGE, Native American drum.
D.C.: I had this dream. Even as it happened. I was in a dark room. Couldn't see. So I stood up and opened the window. And I just stepped out. Stood on the roof. Just stood there in the light and looked into the sun. And the world was so big. I'd been inside so long I'd never seen the view. Never been free. The sun was shining. The room had been so small and dark. (*beat*) But now I was a man. And the world spread itself before me. Its mysteries revealed. And all I had to do was just let go.
D.C. holds out his hand, like letting go of a tether, or a balloon.
Then he goes down after Cynthia.

She stops. Drum.
CYNTHIA: Sometimes you're glad for a good day. This had not been one. But something about this boy . . . Made me wanna keep on keeping on. Mostly you don't wanna touch another person. They weigh you down. Somehow he lightened my load. How I do not know. Kinda like a muscle I'd forgotten I ever had. Hadn't had to use it. And now it hurt. But I liked the ache. 'Cause I knew it was mine. Belonged to me. Funny how much a couple minutes can mean. How much feeling can pass from one body to another. Then just clear away, like a cloud over the moon. If only you could feel like that a moment longer, that much knowledge, that much pain, like a god on earth. If we only had the guts to just let go. (*beat*) Aw, hell.
The spirit of Donny Hathaway wafts through, along the suspension bridge, humming "A Song For You."
Then D.C. returns to the dorm room.
Jaha sits in boxer shorts, bare feet on the windowsill. Listening to Donny Hathaway on tape.
D.C.: (*RE: the tape*) Who said you could listen to that?
JAHA: I did.
D.C. turns the music off.
JAHA: Look, man. We don't gotta like each other. We don't even gotta talk. But if you don't start growing a little respect for me, then I'm havta put my foot up your ass. And I will, too.

D.C.: Do us both a favor. Stay on your side of the room.

JAHA: Man, what's your problem?

D.C.: No problem, I just don't like you.

JAHA: 'Cause I'm gay?

D.C.: Partly.

JAHA: Which part?

D.C.: I dunno. Up to the bellybutton.

He lies down. Tries to ignore Jaha.

JAHA: What's wrong with being gay? Think I'm gonna turn you on? Make you my woman?

D.C.: Get off my back!

JAHA: Cooties on the toilet seat?

D.C.: Shut up!

JAHA: What's the other part?

D.C.: The other part is—(*explodes*) Maybe you haven't noticed, but there's about ninety-nine-point-nine percent white people in this dorm, right? And yet here we are. A black dude and an Indian.

JAHA: Indian?

D.C.: Yeah, Indian.

JAHA: East Indian?

D.C.: No!

JAHA: West Indian?

D.C.: You're starting to get on my nerves.

JAHA: Indian Indian. Hmn. You don't look it.

D.C.: Shut up! I'm trying to tell you something! They stuck us together. And it wasn't by accident.

JAHA: So?

D.C.: So that's fucked up! I didn't come to the Ivy Leagues to be ghettoized.

JAHA: Why did you come?

D.C.: Well— (*stammers*) I didn't come for this.

JAHA: So you're gonna take it out on me.

D.C.: No, but—Look, hell, it's just that I mean you're black and you're gay—

JAHA: Well, you're red and she gave you head.

D.C.: What?!!

JAHA: Bridge is a pretty public place. Kinda famous, too. Among certain crowds.

D.C. blushes. Busted.

JAHA: Don't worry. Your secret's safe with me. So you don't like gay people?

D.C.: I never met a gay person.

JAHA: Hi. (*waves*) And you don't like black people.

D.C.: I like black people. I always wanted to— (*trails off*)

JAHA: What?

D.C.: (*embarassed*) Be black.

JAHA: Well, maybe, I can teach you how someday. (*beat*) What about the other part.

D.C.: What other part?

JAHA: The part about your dad dying. (*beat*) My dad died.

D.C.: Sorry.

JAHA: Why? You didn't do it, did ya? Look man. We don't gotta bond or get touchy-feely or pink tutus or none of that.

But this is a small room. And hey, I dig Donny Hathaway, you know? Feeds my gay black soul.

Off the cuff, he sings the refrain from Donny Hathaway's "The Ghetto."

D.C.: I didn't know you sang.

JAHA: What you don't know could choke a snake.

Pause.

D.C.: Wanna beer?

JAHA: Don't you got choir practice or something?

D.C.: I got something. But it can wait. (*slight pause*) I thought the Ivy League was gonna be like the movies. And you weren't in the movie I saw. But then neither was I. (*slight pause*) Did you really see me?

JAHA: Next time scoot down a little more.

D.C.: There won't be a next time.

Jaha flashes him a look — "I don't believe you."

JAHA: Somebody oughta have some fun around here. Come on. Let's get shitfaced.

D.C.: In the movie, they said inebriated.

They do an Alfonse and Gaston routine at the door.

D.C.: After you.

JAHA: No, after you.

D.C.: Oh no, after —

JAHA: Get the fuck out!

D.C. does.

Then Holly in spotlight, singing:

HOLLY: FOR HE HATH REGARDED THE LOWLINESS OF HIS HANDMAIDEN

D.C. enters, listens. Holly sees him.

HRMF sits on his organ bench.

HRMF: Very nice indeed. (*slight pause*) Do you feel better . . . about the song?

HOLLY: I like the song better than the words. But — yes. I feel better.

HRMF: (*stands*) The Christmas Concert is shaping up quite nicely. Remember to dress warmly. The weather's changing. Button your coat to the top. (*approaches her*) Wear a muffler.

He almost touches her.

She moves past him.

Approaches D.C. as HRMF recovers and putters at the organ, pretending not to eavesdrop.

D.C.: (*sputters*) I-I hope you don't mind — I-I just wondered — maybe you'd —

HOLLY: How about a beer?

D.C.: What about Dan?

HOLLY: Let him work on his high notes. Come on. I'm buying . . .

They are about to leave together, when —

HRMF: (*clears throat*) Mister Nodora.

D.C. freezes. Holly squeezes his hand.

HOLLY: I'll wait.

D.C. joins HRMF at the organ.

D.C.: Yes sir?

HRMF: Now then, —

D.C.: I know, I'm sorry. I've haven't been singing so good. I haven't been doing anything so good. I'm having some trouble in Biology. Actually, I'm really bad at it, sorta threw me into a tailspin, and I caught a cold. My roomie leaves the window open. Guess I need a muffler, but I promise, sir, I'll do better. I'll work harder. I —

HRMF: Mister Nodora. (*silence*) I want you to sing a solo. For the Christmas Concert.

D.C.: Pardon me?

HRMF: I have something in mind for you. Particularly after hearing you sing the Robeson. To free your voice —

D.C.: You mean I got singing talent?

HRMF: I wouldn't go that far. You need to sing. For whatever reason, it's as if your very life depends on it. You need this. So I will help you the best I can. If that's all right. (*D.C. nods*) This is new for me as well. (*clears throat*) That's all.

D.C.: Thanks. I'll work hard. I mean to magnify. I mean myself — magnify myself. I mean —

HRMF: Thank you, Mister Nodora.

D.C.: I feel blessed!

HRMF: (*RE: HOLLY*) Don't keep her waiting.

D.C. nods. Returns to Holly. They exit.

HRMF sits on the organ bench. Then, for himself, he begins to play Bach with an air of self-searching and meditation. As he plays—

Holly and D.C. sit together with a sixpack under the stars.

HOLLY: (*pointing*)
You see? Orion.

D.C.: Where?

HOLLY: (*showing him*) There's the belt . . . and there . . .

Their faces are close—they feel each other's breath.

D.C.: (*pulling away*) That opera? DON CARLOS? What's it about?

HOLLY: (*chuckles*) Lovers' triangle.

D.C.: Whoa.

HOLLY: Pretty sexy stuff.

D.C.: How come you're in the choir if you love opera so much?

HOLLY: I love to sing.

D.C.: Sing opera.

HOLLY: Not so easy. I'd have to move to New York City. And the competition is beyond cut-throat.

D.C.: So? You're great.

HOLLY: You just don't know.

D.C.: You're free. You can do whatever your heart desires.

HOLLY: Free? (*she drinks*) My dad had this friend. Used to say the same thing. I could do whatever my heart desired. But he didn't mean what I thought. He wanted me to touch him. That's what he desired. It's all right. I'm okay about it. It's a wonder anyone can sing at all for all the crap in the way . . . It's a wonder I don't sound like a frog! I do sometimes. I'm not that good

. . .

D.C.: (*drinks*) I still say your voice kicks ass.

HOLLY: Takes more than a voice to sing. I love the music. But the words keep getting in the way.

D.C.: But you gotta have the words. They make the spirit move. (*beat*) My people? They live in a flatland. Just a buncha dirt and gravel. And so dry. We had a river, we were fishermen, but it got dammed up. Town fathers of Scottsdale, Arizona, dammed it up for themselves. My people never really got over that. We needed that river to make things flow. Now things just stay put. The Rez doesn't move. Got no flow. That's why I came here. I gotta move. I wanna flow.

HOLLY: What's that have to do with words?

D.C.: I figure if I can just find the right ones, I can get that river flowing. Inside. I just gotta find the right ones . . .

HOLLY: The words will come.

Meanwhile, Brigid joins HRMF at the organ bench. He stops playing. They hold hands in silence like two teenagers.

BRIGID: I was trying to pray. I got bored.

HRMF: Just like my choir. They lose interest mid-song.

BRIGID: Such is life in the new millennium. Fate of a fatherless generation. Searching but not finding. Boredom masking death beneath —

HRMF: You're in a mood.

BRIGID: Just feeling tired of being a handmaiden.

HRMF: Do I make you feel that?

BRIGID: Not you. God. I find it harder and harder to believe. And if I can't, then how am I to shepherd others? I just can't seem to break through. (*beat*) It's different for you. You have the music. You don't have to think. The music takes care of your desire. Takes you away from yourself. The sadness. The booze. All the bullshit. Music is a drug.

HRMF: I prefer to think of music as the true expression of man's faith.

BRIGID: That's nice, dear. (*rises*) Shall we? Scotch on the rocks?

HRMF: I have to work. I'm looking for something. A spiritual.

BRIGID: Rather unlike you.

HRMF: For a particular voice. A voice that doesn't quite know what it is.

BRIGID: D.C.?

HRMF: He knows so little!

BRIGID: He's learning to be a man. Remember? You did it once yourself. (*beat*) You're not his father. So he makes a few mistakes, —

HRMF: Some mistakes you don't survive.

As he says this—

D.C. takes Holly's hand. They breathe together. Holly and D.C. kiss. Then start to make out. Brigid starts to leave.

HRMF: What's your favorite spiritual?

BRIGID: (*thinks, then*) DEEP RIVER.

HRMF plunks down the melody. Immediately starts working.

HRMF: Yes.

BRIGID: If you want me, I'll be praying. I'm gonna give it another shot.

As she leaves, —

D.C. pulls away, laughing.

HOLLY: What?

D.C.: The Rez seems about a million miles away. Useta sit on the bleachers listening to them old traditional Indian songs. They'd sit in a circle with a drum in the middle and they'd sing. With an edge. A don't-fuck-with-me edge and they meant it, too. So I didn't. I listened to them songs, but I never joined in.

HOLLY: Why not?

D.C.: Didn't know the words.

HOLLY: But — (*stops mid-thought*) Maybe one of them could teach you.

D.C.: Nah! I wasn't in the circle.

HOLLY: But maybe —

D.C.: I'm in this circle. (*pause*)

HOLLY: What did they sing about?

D.C.: Tryna raise the spirits.

HOLLY: That's what songs can do. Maybe when you sing your solo, you can do that.

D.C.: What?

HOLLY: Raise your dad. Or your mom.

D.C.: My mom?

HOLLY: Or your dad.

D.C.: Why my mom?

HOLLY: I don't know, I —

Silence.

Then D.C. reacts. D.C. rises, cold.

D.C.: It's getting late.

HOLLY: Look, I didn't mean —

D.C.: I don't talk about my mom.

HOLLY: Fine.

D.C.: That's just the way it is!

HOLLY: I said fine! (*pause*)

D.C.: Sorry.

HOLLY: You have your reasons.

D.C.: I just wish . . . I wish we could just start today. Our lives begin today. We'd be free. We'd get everything right. And we wouldn't have to feel sorry. There wouldn't be any reason. We wouldn't make the same mistakes.

HOLLY: No. We'd make new ones.

She breathes the air next to him. Then exits.

D.C. watches her go.

Then Jaha sings along with the recording:

JAHA: THE GHETTO
TALKING 'BOUT THE GHETTO
THE GHETTO —

In between breaths, he gets high on an evil-looking joint. LAUGHTER tells us he is not alone.

D.C. enters the dormroom. Smells the reefer.

D.C.: Shit!

He feels the other person in the room. Turns to go.

JAHA: Where you going?

D.C.: You got company.

JAHA: We ain't doing the nasty or nothing!

CYNTHIA: Not yet anyway.

D.C.: Wait a minute!!!

D.C. turns on the light.

Cynthia is sitting on his bed.
D.C.: What in the hell are you doing here?
JAHA: Cool out. She come bearing gifts. (*tokes*) Excellent gifts. I let her in. I was brought up that way.
D.C. looks disgustedly at the weed.
D.C.: Come on, man. We could get kicked out.
JAHA: This? This is baby stuff! This is grade school! I oughta write a book — The Ivy League Cartel — 'cause if you're looking you can get some shit in back of the library. If I'm lyin' I'm flyin' —!
D.C.: Quit the Harlem bullshit.
JAHA: Harlem, my ass. I'm from Binghamton, baby!
CYNTHIA: Cool out, y'all.
D.C. grabs her arm and ushers her out.
D.C.: Look, Cynthia. Nothing personal, but I don't want you here.
CYNTHIA: You want me under the bridge. (*beat*) But I'm gone.
She walks by D.C., placing his wallet in his hand.
D.C.: What the hell —?
CYNTHIA: Left it on the bridge.
JAHA: Musta fallen out your jeans or something.
D.C.: (*as it hits him*) Oh, shit.
JAHA: Yep. She brung it to you.
D.C. looks to see if any cash remains.
CYNTHIA: I cannot tell a lie. I took me a fiver. For my troubles.

JAHA: And with it she scored some very gentle shit.
CYNTHIA: No hard feelings. Your ID's still there. You oughta get yourself a new drivers license — I swear you look just like Charles Manson.
JAHA: (*sneaking a peak*) Oh, shit — he does!
CYNTHIA: It's been fun.
She starts to leave. He stops her.
D.C.: Stay.
JAHA: Oooh. Now he wants her to stay.
D.C.: Please stay.
CYNTHIA: This a work night. Turning cold fast. Gotta get some dates lined up, get some bucks —
JAHA: Maybe if we gave you a coupla bucks, you'd stay.
D.C.: Two dates in a row.
JAHA: Maybe?
CYNTHIA: What kinda thing you two bad boys got in mind?
Donny Hathaway's recording of "Be Real Black For Me" with Roberta Flack.
Jaha grooves and sings along:
JAHA: OUR TIME SHORT AND PRECIOUS YOUR LIPS WARM AND LUSCIOUS
CYNTHIA: Well, when you put it like that.
D.C.: YOU DON'T HAVE TO WEAR FALSE CHARMS
JAHA: CAUSE WHEN I WRAP YOU IN MY HUNGRY ARMS
D.C.: BE REAL BLACK FOR ME
JAHA: All right!!

Jaha slaps D.C. five. Jaha and Cynthia dance. D.C. watches, even smiles, but his mind is elsewhere.

D.C.: Be right back.

CYNTHIA: Don't be gone too long now.

JAHA: You safe with me, black woman.

CYNTHIA: But you ain't safe at all with me, black man.

They dance.

D.C. goes to the phone.

Then we see Dan and Holly mid-argument.

DAN: I don't think it's too much to ask!

HOLLY: So I was late, so get over it!

DAN: If you're gonna have a beer with someone, have it with me.

HOLLY: What beer?

DAN: I can smell it on your breath. Next time invest in a pack of gum.

HOLLY: Look. This is boring. I'm bored!

DAN: Of me?

She does not answer.

The phone rings.

DAN: Saved by the bell. *(answers)* Hello? Hello? *(to HOLLY)* Musta been for you.

HOLLY: Why me?

DAN: He didn't talk. But I could smell beer on his breath.

D.C. hangs up the payphone. Gnaws on a thumbnail.

Returns to the dorm room.

Cynthia is singing, gyrating over Jaha:

CYNTHIA: YOUR HAIR SOFT AND CRINKLY YOUR BODY STRONG AND STATELY

JAHA: Keep talking, mama.

CYNTHIA: YOU DON'T HAVE TO SEARCH AND ROAM 'CAUSE I GOT YOUR LOVE AT HOME —

D.C. turns off the stereo.

JAHA: Hey!!!

D.C.: That's enough for tonight.

JAHA: *(in his face)* Who do you think you are?!! Mu'fucka! Someone oughta kick your ass —!

CYNTHIA: Easy now.

D.C.: It's late and I'm just real tired.

JAHA: I'm watching you!

CYNTHIA: That's right. You watch his back. He watch yours. Nobody else gonna.

JAHA: Kimo sabe bastard . . .

CYNTHIA: *(to JAHA)* Quit that shit!

The two boys sit on their beds, in a truce.

CYNTHIA: Now both of you get some sleep. You're good boys. And you're far from home. That ain't easy. Don't make it harder.

She kisses each of them like a mom.

CYNTHIA: Stay warm now. Just remember to stay warm.

She starts to exit.

JAHA: Hold up, girl.

Jaha gives her cash. D.C. does the same.

D.C.: See ya later.

Cynthia stares him down hard.

CYNTHIA: Maybe it's time you started getting serious. Get yourself a real girlfriend.

She exits. Soon as she's gone, they miss her.

JAHA: One cool lady.

D.C.: Why? 'Cause she stokes your habit?

JAHA: No, you fucking dolt! She's the first real person I've met since I came to this overrated godforsaken shithole. (*grabs his head*) Oh, man. I got me a marijuana headache.

Jaha hides his head under his pillow.

Meanwhile, Dan puts on his coat.

Bad-ass Indian DRUMS accompany him.

DAN: I'm going out. For some air. (*no response from HOLLY*) I love you too, babe.

Dan exits.

Jaha sleeps like a stone. Dan wakes up D.C.

DAN: Hey.

D.C.: Hey.

DAN: Drink?

D.C.: Gotta sleep.

DAN: Drink first.

Dan nudges D.C. in the ribs. He is not fooling around.

They walk across the suspension bridge.

Cynthia appears from underneath.

CYNTHIA: Watch yer car —!

She sees D.C. — smiles. He blushes.

DAN: Did you hear the one about the horticulturalist? You can lead a whore to culture, but you can't make her think.

D.C. bows his head. They walk on.

Sounds of a crowd as they sidle up to the bar.

Dan swigs wine.

DAN: I come here the other night with Holly. Bartender tries to pick her up. Right in fronta me! I mean, it was funny. "Come back later, I'll take ya dancing"—We could be married for all he knows. So I ask her, does this happen to you all the time? She nods. Aw, hell. Every man deserves a shot, I guess. If he don't get caught. (*grins*) My pop says if you ever have too much wine, women, and song — then cut down on the singing.

D.C. notices Brigid of all people sitting across the bar sipping a scotch and reading a book.

DAN: (*seeing her, too*) Oh look. Mrs. Johnnie Walker.

D.C.: (*uncomfortable*) Say, do you think maybe we could sit somewhere else —

DAN: My pop is a cop. His beat? Lovers Lane. Sixty dollar ticket for parking in a restricted zone. All steamy windows and unbuckled bra straps. Talk about a cushy job. Just goes down the road, one ticket after another. Doesn't even need a gun. (*drinks*) You ever do a thing like that? Take a piece of ass into the back seat, or under the stars . . .

D.C.: Not really.

DAN: You oughta. I would. I truly miss the time when a man could be with two three women at the same time with no shame. Cause hey, I'm Italian. A man ain't nothing unless he's got at least one woman. I mean, back me up here. You're Latin—

Native— whatever! Hey, come on, we're men! We're highly sexed! It's historical. You're reading English Lit, right? The Romantic poets? Forget about it! Byron? The Original Bad Boy. Coleridge? Shelley? Sex Incorporated! Have Pen Will Travel. (*getting loud*) And what about our very own choir? If music be the food of love, play on, say I. And what about that precious organ? There's a play on words. And why's old HRMF play so much Bach anyway? 'Cause it's a goddamn aphrodisiac! Why do you think they called him Papa Bach? The dude had twenty-one kids! He was a famous fucker, man. Feel sorry for Mama Bach. (*drinks*)

D.C.: Why dontcha go easy on the sauce.

DAN: I'm an exuberant drinker. I'm having this great Hollywood affair with red wine—

D.C.: Like Jussi?

DAN: Yeah, like Jussi. Helps me hit the high stuff. (*beat*) Free advice? Sing from here. (*his crotch*) You know where that is? Holly showed me. Oh, yeah. Put her hand right down there and out I came. You play your cards right, maybe Holly will show you, too—

D.C.: (*rising*) I'm outa here.

Dan pushes him back down.

DAN: Don't leave now. It's just getting good. See, she showed me how to sing. Guess that's why I stayed. I still dream about other women, but you can't bed 'em all. Or maybe you can. Maybe you got the touch, kid. Is that it? You catch my drift?

D.C.: You think I'm stupid?

D.C. drains his glass of wine.

DAN: You know, we really oughta sing that duet sometime.

He hums a bit of PEARLFISHERS.

DAN: It's all about two guys who dig the same chick.

D.C.: Who gets her?

DAN: Who do you think?

Dan exits singing.

D.C. sits alone.

Then Brigid sidles up next to him.

BRIGID: Demon wine.

D.C.: Pardon me?

BRIGID: One of those apt phrases. Minnesota wisdom. For times when something untoward occurs.

D.C.: Untoward?

BRIGID: Don't worry. I wasn't listening. I've got a very good book. So they say.

D.C.: (*eyeing the tome*) The Bible?

BRIGID: *Confederacy of Dunces.* I keep waiting to laugh. It's supposed to make you laugh till your belly aches. I keep waiting. Guess that makes it a page-turner of sorts. The writer died. Suicide, I think. The mother saved the manuscript from the ravages of time. The way of all flesh.

She is staring at D.C. — making him blush.

BRIGID: So you're going to sing a solo?

D.C.: I guess.

BRIGID: You've entered our collective imagination.

D.C.: What?

BRIGID: Fantasies. Dreams. Don't worry. It's not your fault.

D.C.: You're saying I'm in your dreams?

She shrugs, not saying.

Then HRMF enters, very much out of place.

BRIGID: Look fast.

D.C.: Huh?

BRIGID: His Nibs. Don't want him thinking you're making time with me.

D.C.: Making time?

BRIGID: Another one of those apt phrases.

HRMF approaches, ill at ease.

HRMF: Mister Nodora. Brigid.

BRIGID: Hey, Cutie.

D.C.: I-I was just — I gotta go —

D.C. backs off and exits.

BRIGID: Bye. (*to HRMF*) God what I'd give to be D.C.'s age and know what I know now. Oh, man . . . The fun I'd have. (*drinks*)

HRMF: Let's go.

BRIGID: Relax. Have a drink.

HRMF: I don't like it here.

BRIGID: I do. I can pray here. (*finishes her drink*) That's not a joke. I really can.

HRMF: You just like the drink.

In response she orders another.

BRIGID: How about this? You go.

HRMF: You waste yourself.

BRIGID: Is that wasteful? I embrace it. I've seen legions of sad and lonely people drink their lives away — and guess what? Now it's my turn. Christ teaches that people should share. Well, I'm sharing a scotch with the people.

HRMF: You're a pastor, for godsakes!

BRIGID: Don't I know it. (*drinks*)

HRMF: (*embarrassed at raising his voice*) If you must drink, then do so in private.

BRIGID: Like you? No thanks. It's more fun airing out my dirty laundry.

HRMF: I don't like you like this.

BRIGID: What don't you like? The tippling? (*mockingly*) The bite of the hair that dogged me? (*beat*) Or the looking for mindless sex —

HRMF: (*embarrassed*) Quiet . . .

BRIGID: Putting the Devil in Hell —?

HRMF: QUIET. (*beat*) Your flesh is weak.

BRIGID: Go home.

HRMF: What about you?

BRIGID: I have a good book to read.

She tries to read.

HRMF stands alone. Then walks into the darkness with the weight of the world on his shoulders.

As soon as he is gone, Brigid looks up. Drinks. Very alone.

D.C. stops where he kissed Holly. Lingers. Then moves on, humming the Magnificat to himself.

HRMF walks alone, then stops at the suspension bridge.

Cynthia stands waiting.

CYNTHIA: You driving?

HRMF stops, shakes his head.

Brigid hums to herself. Then sings.

BRIGID: DEEP RIVER
I WANT TO CROSS OVER . . .

(trails off)

D.C. enters his dorm room.

Jaha still sleeping dead to the world.

Then D.C. feels a presence in the room. He experiences a sudden lack of air.

D.C.: *(gasping)* Dad?

A FIGURE moves in shadow on his bed.

Cynthia walks up to HRMF.

CYNTHIA: I'm just tryna make a few dimes. *(She knows him.)* Whatdya say, Professor?

She touches his hand.

HRMF nods. Together, like two children, they go hand in hand beneath the bridge.

Brigid talk-sings, running out of air.

BRIGID: I WANT TO CROSS OVER
INTO CAMPGROUND . . .

She drinks alone.

D.C. chokes as the FIGURE stands on the bed and assumes the shape of a person. Then begins to dance.

Then Donny Hathaway returns:

DONNY: I KNOW YOUR IMAGE OF ME
IS WHAT I HOPE TO BE
I TREATED YOU UNKINDLY
BUT DARLING CAN'T YOU SEE . . .

The Figure disrobes.

A sexy, catlike, frowsy, dark-skinned, long-haired woman emerges from the shadows. Staring back at D.C. in an arrestingly sexy manner.

DONNY: THERE'S NO ONE MORE
IMPORTANT TO ME
BABY, CAN'T YOU SEE THROUGH ME
WE'RE ALL ALONE NOW
AND I'M SINGING THIS SONG TO YOU . . .

Mom stands on the bed, a vision of sex and motherhood.

Dancing.

D.C.: Mom . . . ?

END OF ACT ONE

ACT TWO

Darkness.

HRMF plays Bach with great introspection. The sound is otherworldly.

Standing on the bed, MOM dances to the music. A creature from another time. Another planet.

D.C. sits, head in hands.

MOM: Bach is a trip. *(listens)* Listen to that. You can feel the planets in space. See the notes coming off the page. Curling up and around like DNA. Like the double helix. Feel it. Feel it in your blood. Don't it make you wanna feel? *(beat)* Got any grass?

D.C.: Fuck.

MOM: That's okay. I don't need it just yet. (*looks him over*) Don Carlos.

She moves to touch him. He recoils.

D.C.: Don't call me that!

MOM: It's the name I gave you. Don Carlos. Like the opera.

D.C.: What the hell do you know about opera?

MOM: I know how it makes me feel.

D.C.: Get off my bed.

She lies back on it. Listens to the music.

MOM: Puccini. Hendrix. When you were a baby I played PETER AND THE WOLF just for you. (*beat*) And lots of Los Lobos too.

D.C.: You weren't even there.

MOM: I'm always there. (*beat*) You done good. Long way from Pima College, eh? I sure couldn'ta done it. Your dad couldn'ta done it, either—

D.C.: Don't talk about Dad.

MOM: Your dad could hardly get outa bed. (*picks up a textbook*) You read this? I can hardly pick it up. We didn't read back in my day in Indian School. We weren't gonna get jobs. I couldn't even waitress. They might wanna fuck me but they sure as hell weren't gonna hire me . . . (*beat*) I know it hurts. But it's true.

D.C.: Please. Go.

MOM: I'm your mom. What I did I did for you.

Mom finds Jaha's marijuana stash.

MOM: What do we have here?

D.C.: Get away from his bed! You'll wake him!!

MOM: No chance. Got a light? Guess not. Good thing I brought my purse. What's that the Scouts say? Be Prepared.

She lights up.

He watches her disgustedly.

MOM: What?

D.C.: You left.

MOM: So? I was a bad Indian. (*tokes*) So shoot me. It was so dry, you know? So dry. I picked lettuce for a while. Didn't like it much. I wanted to watch TV, smoke in bed, drink beers, and dance. I wanted a life.

Offers him the pipe.

D.C.: You kidding?

MOM: Then I met your dad. (*silence*) He was Fuckin' A, eh? Long hair and sexy belt buckle. His hair was soft. Hair on his chest, and a beard — he was mixed. Anyway he looked real good.

D.C.: He was fat. Look, I loved the guy, but he was pretty damn ugly.

MOM: He looked like you. (*silence*) I was drinking a lot. Way too much time in cerveza-land. I just wanted to be free. He freed me. For a while. (*beat*) We sat in bed and played music. Lots of music. "Bridge Over Troubled Water" by Aretha Franklin—

D.C.: Simon and Garfunkel.

MOM: Aretha done it better. More sex, you know?

D.C.: No, I don't wanna know. I don't wanna hear about your sex life —

MOM: Then we made you. (*silence*) We had hope then. It was a hopeful time. Cripes, you coulda been the Second Coming. Not like I was the Virgin Mary or nothing, but hell, I mean, you never know. And here you are. Lo and behold. (*with pride*) The next Chief Joseph. Neil Young with a doctorate. (*beat*) I mean, hell, I didn't plan on leaving.

D.C.: But you did.

MOM: I wanted to be free.

D.C.: Free, my ass.

MOM: Like to chew your own foot off just to be free. Even for a minute.

D.C.: When you left, I useta break bottles out in front of the house. By the riverbed. The rocks and old syringes. All the empty bottles of beer and Chivas and wine cooler laying out there with the busted condoms and twisted nylons. And the ghosts of all the drunks and rapes and overdoses. All the death. (*beat*) I'd toss rocks till the bottles broke. That's when I felt free. Hearing the glass break. That sound? Reminded me of your voice. When you left us.

MOM: Had the urge for going. Your dad had to let me go. It's my *Opus Moderandi*.

D.C.: *Modus Operandi*!! Criminy. Sometimes you sound so dumb —

MOM: I am not a ditz. (*beat*) Look, it was another time.

D.C.: Don't blame your weakness on the times. You left us. You.

MOM: That was the hardest part. Looking into your eyes was like looking in the mirror. And I looked so ugly, so beaten down, so not the way I dreamed I'd be. For you. So I hit it. Yeah.

D.C.: And now my dad's dead.

MOM: Baby. He died a long time ago. (*beat*) Maybe it's an Indian thing. We drink 'cause it's too hard looking in the mirror. We commit suicide 'cause if we didn't we'd fucking kill ourselves. (*beat*) Didn't know your mom was a stand-up comic, did ya?

D.C.: I didn't know my mom.

MOM: You know I love you. You're the only thing I do love. You. And artichokes. And Miller Draft under the stars. And Hendrix. But you the most.

D.C. jumps to his feet.

D.C.: I gotta get outa here!

MOM: Where you gonna go?

D.C.: I'm gonna rub the slate clean! I came all this way to rub it clean. What a concept, a clean slate! No drunken dads, no whoring moms. No racist bullshit —

MOM: Baby, they got all that here, too.

D.C.: Don't you know why I worked so hard? All the extracurriculars? Acing those fucking tests? Cramming before class? Academic Decathlon and Mock Trial and fucking Student Council and all the other hoops they made me jump through? I knew. Hey, I knew, mom. If I filled my life with stuff to do, if I got good enough grades and lathered up all those career advisors I despised, if I could just hold my breath and ENDURE, then I could go away.

MOM: I been all over. (*smiles*) But the best place? Pima Country.

D.C.: It's shit. It's death.

MOM: It's home.

D.C.: (*wildly*) It killed Dad!

MOM: Have to die somewhere.

D.C.: Where did you die?

She looks at him. No answer.

On the bridge, Donny Hathaway stares down into the abyss.

DONNY: I LOVE YOU IN A PLACE
WHERE THERE'S NO SPACE OR TIME

Mom tries to smile.

MOM: I dunno.

D.C.: Raped in a ditch? O-D'd in a toilet? Wasting away in some hospital ICU . . . ?

MOM: I don't like to think about it.

D.C.: You bring me down. I'm on a tightrope, Mom. If you break my concentration, I'll fall. And it's a long way down. I'll be back on Pima, trying to make it in Scottsdale. And I'll be dead soon. I'll be dead, too.

MOM: I won't let you fall. (*beat*) You know how people are afraid to die? How they

dream they'll come back as another person? Or a bird? Or something pretty?

DONNY: I LOVE YOU FOR MY LIFE
YOU'RE A FRIEND OF MINE
AND WHEN MY LIFE IS OVER
REMEMBER WHEN WE WERE TOGETHER

MOM: I was one of those people. I dreamed of coming back. And I think I got my wish. I think I came back in the music. When it gets good, you know? The part that makes you think back. Your heart like you're on a rollercoaster . . .

DONNY: WE WERE ALONE
AND I WAS SINGING THIS SONG TO YOU

MOM: I always wanted to be a song. I couldn't do it in my life. I had a lousy voice. Work didn't cut it. Sex didn't get me there. Even having you, good as you are, didn't take me where I dreamed I'd be. But when you sing —? When you really sing? I'm there. I'm there, son. I'm there for you.

Then she begins to sing along with Donny.

MOM/DONNY: WE WERE ALONE
AND I WAS SINGING THIS SONG —

D.C.: No!

D.C. grabs his coat and leaves the room.

MOM: For you!

Mom slips back into shadow.

D.C. walks alone in the growingly intense cold. Then he hears drumming. Men's voices. A traditional Indian song carried on the wind. Just out of view.

D.C.: Goddammit. Goddamn fucking Indians.

He finds himself at Dan and Holly's house. Stands frozen outside. He can hear voices within. Watches from the window.

HOLLY: You did WHAT?!!

DAN: Come on. It was just a threat, —

HOLLY: You threatened him?!!

DAN: It was a guy thing. Look you had to be there—

HOLLY: Who do you think you are?

DAN: Your man.

She walks away.

DAN: Come on. Wasn't that the right answer? (*silence*) Hey, I give a damn who you sleep with.

HOLLY: I didn't sleep with him!!!

DAN: I didn't know!!!

She rummages through a closet.

DAN: Look, it's cultural. (*silence*) I was drunk. That's all. (*silence*) I did it for you, babe.

Holly removes a suitcase.

DAN: What's that for?

HOLLY: It all comes down to a question of faith.

She starts packing.

DAN: Hey, I got faith. Look, just 'cause I got faith doesn't mean I'm smart! I'm stoopid! Jealous! Scared, all right? I'm a singer, a tenor, for chrissakes! We tenors got short-changed when God passed out brains. But, hey, we got more room to resonate.

He tries to stop her packing.

DAN: I told him to stay away. I told him in the old style. I'm old school. Kiss me. I'm Italian! I was— (*beat*) I was so damn scared.

HOLLY: Of him? Or me.

DAN: (*thinks, then*) I guess you.

Pause. She starts to leave.

DAN: Don't.

HOLLY: It's time to go.

DAN: It'll be all right. Just make love to me. Yeah.

HOLLY: Make love?

DAN: If we make love, it'll be all right.

HOLLY: It won't be all r—

DAN: Please.

Intense Native American drum.

Holly grimly gets astride Dan. Intense, severe, her mood deep and black and scary.

Dan, on his back and out of his depth, closes his eyes.

More than sex. Or maybe not even sex at all.

Then Holly sees D.C. at the window looking in.

Not stopping, still atop Dan, she stares D.C. straight in the eye.

D.C. cannot turn away.

Dan comes, crying out.

DAN: OH, GOD!!!

D.C. runs off.

Now he is on the suspension bridge.

Depth of night. No one anywhere near.

D.C.: Cynthia? (*beat*) Cynthia!

(looks beneath bridge) Damn, you really can see everything.

He looks down at her perch.

Then at the gorge below, one hundred feet down.

He relaxes. Leans over. Seduced by a feeling.

D.C.: Oh, man.

He starts to go over.

D.C.: Man, I could just let go.

Then a voice nearby:

BRIGID: You could.

D.C.: Oh hell.

It is indeed Brigid, but a Brigid of the mind. Freed of vestments, looking sleepy and frowsy and ready for sex. Oblivious to cold, a figment of libido. Like Mom, a spirit who just won't go away.

BRIGID: Shuffle off this mortal coil.

D.C.: I'm thinking about it.

BRIGID: Fantasize. Good for you. But fantasies can only take you so far.

She reaches out to touch him, but touch is not possible. More like a breeze, felt but lacking substance.

BRIGID: You can't touch them.

D.C.: (gulps) I'm your fantasy?

BRIGID: Well, you're not my only one.

D.C.: How come I see you?

BRIGID: Maybe it's your fantasy, too.

D.C. checks himself for fever, looking embarrassed and more confused than ever.

BRIGID: Don't beat yourself up. It's not so bad. It's a little like eating out. Get a little tired of the same old same old. Sometimes you wanna go . . . Southwestern. Sometimes you eat a jalapeño by mistake. Your mouth on fire. Tears in your eyes. But the taste . . . Oh, it's good.

D.C.: I don't eat out much.

BRIGID: That's not what I heard.

D.C.: (flaring up) Look, Holly and I, we didn't, I mean, I didn't, I mean —

BRIGID: But you thought about it. And that's okay. You're stressed. Sleepless. And horny as all hell. Poor baby. No one to mother you, and here it is nearly Christmas. You wanna be wrapped in swaddling clothes. Lowliness of your handmaiden? I can do that.

D.C.: All right, yes! I thought about you.

BRIGID: Like that?

D.C.: Like that. I guess I just like older women.

BRIGID: Well, duh! What are ya, eighteen?

D.C.: But what's with wrong me? Am I sick? I mean, you're a pastor.

BRIGID: I'm a woman. (beat) I wish to God I could kiss you.

D.C.: But what about HRMF?

BRIGID: The name says it all. Sure he's cute. But with him it's all so Euro-centred, so lily-white, so proper, so damn Ivy League. That's why you shook us up so. I guess that's why I came . . .

D.C.: I'm trying not to.

BRIGID: People do that, try to take the sex out of the Gospel. Christ loved humankind, I assure you. And Mother Mary? She was all woman. And it's all right.

She smiles. One last ephemeral kiss.

BRIGID: Don Carlos. It's all right.

The wind blows.

Brigid is gone.

D.C. shivers.

D.C.: It's not.

He moves into chapel.

D.C.: This has got to stop. (*grim*) Maybe if I don't sing. If I stop singing. Yeah. (*beat*) I thought we could talk through the music, Dad. But it's something I can't control. I can't live like this. What am I, some kind of animal? I can't let myself be an animal. (*beat*) So I'm gonna stop. I'm gonna put it to bed. You're dead. And Mom is dead. And God is dead.

HRMF appears from the shadows. Still in muffler and coat. Definitely not a figment of anyone's imagination.

HRMF: We are animals.

D.C.: Pardon me?

HRMF: I apologize. I didn't mean to—I thought I'd be alone. Trying to make my bit of peace with my own demons . . . But that's another story. One makes one's peace as best one can. But there is no real peace. The demons come back twice as hard.

D.C.: It's like that for you, too?

HRMF: It's much worse. But then I'm much older. It's very hard to sing. One must learn everything all over again. How to breathe. Stand. Talk. One's very thoughts. A lifetime of habits, peculiarities, the things that make a person feel special. All must change. All must work together, if one is to truly let go. Because underneath the habit lies the soul. (*beat*) I sang once. But I was afraid to let go. The true voice is a manifestation of one's own soul. I was afraid of mine.

D.C.: But what about the organ —?

HRMF: Easy to hide behind. It makes a grand and joyous noise. So big you never have to see me. I like that. In the end I prefer not to be seen. I'm not important. But Bach is. And Sweelinck. Praetorius, and Purcell. Cesar Franck and Walford Davies, Stanford and Howells and Donald Patterson. But Bach the most. (*beat*) Bach never achieved what one might term popularity. He spent his life in chapels like this, working on the music. Like I do. His children called their dad "Old Wig" — an apellation not unlike "Stuffed Shirt" or perhaps "His Nibs" . . . And perhaps he was. In his best broadcloth suit and neatly powdered wig. Seated at the house organ, the music would flow. Perhaps like a brook, its origin in the melting snows of some Rhineland mountaintop. Then broadening into a stream and that stream turning into a river, and that river into an ocean. Into the goodness of God and all his works, in lovers, and boys becoming men, and growing old, and dying in one's own good time. In essence — Joy. This is how he played. Even at his most desolate. (*clears throat*) As Brahms pointed out, quite rightly, this strange man was not a *Bach*— not a brook—but a *Fluss*—a full-fledged river. This strange man with the old wig had a lust for music. He put his life into it. And so should we. (*beat*) When in my life I stupidly and grossly lose my way — then through Bach I find my way back. At least I try. (*silence*)

D.C.: Did he really have twenty-one kids?

HRMF: Bach? Indubitably.

D.C.: Wow. (*slight pause*) Weird, us here.

HRMF: We had things to work out.

D.C.: Did you?

HRMF: No, but that's not the point. Some people, in their woundedness, play the blues. That's what they feel. I feel the Baroque organ masterworks. And I feel them best, or worst, at night. When I'm alone, and the spirits come out to play.

D.C.: Spirits?

HRMF turns and walks away.
D.C. reaches the dormroom. Jaha still snoring.
D.C. climbs into bed. Sings:

D.C.: DEEP RIVER
I WANT TO CROSS OVER . . .

He lies back and sleeps.
Morning light.

Jaha rises, pissed, goes to the bridge.
Shares a smoke and a caffe latte with Cynthia.

JAHA: Dude's insane! I can't sleep there no more. He talks in his sleep! To his mom or something! All hours of the fucking night! This morning, not even dawn yet, he's singing in bed! I swear it's freaking me out!

CYNTHIA: Cut him some slack.

JAHA: And just try eating with him! We go chow down at the cafeteria, the fool won't eat nothing with butter, or canned meat, or cheese. And we got us some damn good cheese up here!

CYNTHIA: Native people. Obesity's a problem. Diabetes too. Not to mention alcohol — fetal alcohol syndrome. Gets passed down in the blood. Literally. Born alkies. Give 'em a coupla drinks, they'll break a chair over your head.

JAHA: Boy don't get drunk though.

CYNTHIA: (*surprised*) Really? Hmn.

JAHA: Dude is scary!

CYNTHIA: His peoples was warriors. But that was a long time ago.

JAHA: How come you know so much?

CYNTHIA: No secret. I'm older than water.

JAHA: Warrior? He's a butthead.

CYNTHIA: You like him. (*JAHA blushes*) You do.

JAHA: Don't grin at me. All right, what if I do? I've always liked difficult men.

CYNTHIA: (*laughs*) You're a good boy, Jaha. (*beat*) You know what your name means?

JAHA: No. Duh! What kinda black man you think I am? Means warrior.

CYNTHIA: Damn right.

JAHA: D.C. and me—warriors—be afraid; be very very afraid.

The tower BELLS ring in the day. Jaha rises.

CYNTHIA: Have a good one.

JAHA: You too, Mom. (*beat*) You don't mind me calling you mom?

CYNTHIA: Up here you need a mom sometimes.

A moment's awkward affection.

JAHA: Stay warm.

Jaha splits.

Holly appears. Alone. Lugging a suitcase.

CYNTHIA: Need a hand?

HOLLY: No thanks. Bus stop?

CYNTHIA: Greyhound?

HOLLY: New York.

CYNTHIA: Over there.

Holly goes. They stand across from each other.

CYNTHIA: Tough town. Got a place to stay?

HOLLY: I'll be fine.

CYNTHIA: Money?

HOLLY: I'll be fine.

CYNTHIA: I'll leave ya in peace. Go with God, girl.

HOLLY: I'll go it alone. But thanks.

Cynthia returns to her place on the bridge.

D.C. runs on, grabs Cynthia's hand. Kisses it.

Holly watches.

D.C.: Cynthia!

CYNTHIA: Hey baby. You looking for Jaha, you just missed him —

D.C.: I'm looking for you. I came last night.

CYNTHIA: Got kinda busy.

D.C.: I got worried. I thought the worst. I dunno. I was afraid you'd—(*tries to laugh*) I was afraid.

CYNTHIA: Well, I'm here. Like always.

D.C.: Maybe we can get a cup of coffee—(*sees the coffee cup*) Or whatever. I just wanna . . .

Then he sees Holly.

CYNTHIA: What?

D.C. lets go of her hand. Too fast.

Holly turns away.

Cynthia also turns away. Feelings hurt for all concerned.

CYNTHIA: Oh. Well, go to her.

D.C. hesitates. Start to go, turns back.

D.C.: Cynthia, I —

CYNTHIA: (*to someone else*) Watch yer car for ya! (*exits*)

D.C. turns to Holly. Tense pause.

D.C.: Where you going?

HOLLY: I'm getting outa here.

D.C.: Does Dan know?

HOLLY: He ought to.

D.C.: You weren't gonna tell me?

HOLLY: Why should I? (*beat*) Don't take it to heart. No harm done.

D.C.: Is it 'cause of me?

HOLLY: Everything doesn't happen 'cause of you. I'm just leaving. Shoulda done this a long time ago.

D.C. sits on the curb.

D.C.: Just like Mom.

HOLLY: I'm not your mom.

D.C.: As if it's any better out there. As if you can ever get away.

HOLLY: What the hell are you talking about?

D.C.: Mom left. You're leaving. Chasing dreams. You gotta wake up sometime.

HOLLY: When are you gonna wake up? *(beat)* You left, too. You came here. You ran so far from home you can't even talk about it. You're so full of dreams you think this place is heaven. If that's not a dream I don't know what is.

D.C.: This is not a dream.

HOLLY: Okay, call it a vision quest, whatever term your people use, —

D.C.: My people? No vision quests for us. We just don't dream.

HOLLY: Everybody dreams.

D.C.: Not everybody. Some places have no air. And you just gotta have air.

HOLLY: I need to breathe too.

D.C.: I know you do.

We hear a BUS braking as it rounds the corner.

HOLLY: Listen. Don Carlo. To really sing, let go. I'm not talking red wine, or sex. I mean inside. Let it out. The reason why you sing. The animal in all its beauty. All its shame.

The BUS comes. Holly gets on. D.C. is alone. Brigid sits reading. A moment, then she laughs. A moment, then another laugh. After the third laugh, HRMF enters.

HRMF: People tell me the Bible can be a very funny book.

Brigid shows him her book.

HRMF: *Confederacy of Dunces?* Indeed.

HRMF exits, unsure.

BRIGID: *(to herself)* It is funny. It just takes a while.

The CHOIR assembles. Dan and D.C. among them.

HRMF takes the lectern. Taps the baton.

HRMF: The Magnificat, please. And—

CHOIR: ALL GENERATIONS
SHALL CALL ME BLESSED
FOR HE THAT IS MIGHTY HATH
MAGNIFIED ME, AND HOLY —

Then Dan breaks down. Weeping.

D.C.: I got him!

D.C. walks Dan outside. Dan hunches over like an old man.

DAN: I gotta get drunk.

D.C.: You gotta sing. We need your high stuff.

DAN: I don't got any high stuff left. Not no more. Not without Holly. *(beat)* I got nothing. What do I know about singing? I got no taste. She got the taste. I'm just a lump of flesh. I'm putty. I'm cookie dough. Holly told me how to stand, to breathe. She touched me here — *(his diaphragm)* I shoulda waited on her hand and foot. That woman is a God. I feel low, man. I'm nothing. Just a voice. Not a clue what to sing.

Pause. Then D.C. begins to hum. Then to sing:

DAN: No way, man.

D.C.: AU FOND DU TEMPLE SAINT   PARE DE FLEURS ET D'OR

UN FEMME APPARAIT —

DAN: She is a goddess.

D.C.: She is.

Together they sing the duet from PEARLFISHERS. Not Bjoerling and Merrill, but they sound pretty good.

BOTH: OUI C'EST ELLE

C'EST LA DEESSE

PLUS CHARMANTE ET PLUS BELLE

Dan cannot sing the high note. Stops.

D.C.: Will she come back?

DAN: Not to me. (*breathes deep*) Come on. Let's go.

They reenter the chapel, return to the choir. HRMF clears his throat.

HRMF: Gentlemen! We cannot tolerate interruptions.

He frowns down on them. Then relents.

HRMF: Perhaps a moment. There has been a change, due to the unexpected departure of Miss — of Holly. It would be easier if we lived in a world where life did not interfere with art. But music is no place to hide from life. (*sets down his baton*) And this chapel, this place of music, should be able to withstand the slings and arrows. Even if I haven't been able to.

He leaves the lectern. Stands among them.

BRIGID: Amen.

A moment passes between them. The HRMF returns to the lectern. Raises the baton.

HRMF: Shall we return to the Magnificat? And—

DAN: (*interrupting*) I just wanted to say, thanks.

HRMF: Then perhaps we might begin? (*raps baton*) And—

DAN: And I'll miss her. (*starts to lose it*) And, I mean, I —

HRMF: We will all miss her. Now. Everyone. Breathe.

They do.

HRMF: And, —

CHOIR: HE HATH PUT DOWN THE MIGHTY FROM THEIR SEAT, AND HATH EXALTED THE HUMBLE AND MEEK. HE HATH FILLED THE HUNGRY WITH GOOD THINGS, AND THE RICH HE HATH SENT EMPTY AWAY. . .

D.C. and Dan sing hard and strong.

But HRMF leaves the lectern.

He is perspiring. Sits heavily in a pew. Reciting the John Donne poem as a prayer:

HRMF: Wilt thou forgive that sinne, where I begunne,

Which is my sinne though it were done before?

Wilt thou forgive those sinnes through which I runne

And doe them still, though still I doe deplore?

When thou hast done, thou hast not done, For I have more.

He struggles to breathe.

Brigid enters in pastor's robe.

HRMF: I'm sorry.

BRIGID: For what.

HRMF: For everything I've done.

BRIGID: For all that?

HRMF: Let's start with last night.

BRIGID: What exactly did you do?

HRMF cannot speak. He blushes.

BRIGID: Forgive us our trespasses.

HRMF: As we forgive those who trespass against us.

BRIGID: You mean me?

HRMF: Perhaps in your mind? Thoughts? (*now BRIGID blushes*) You mean my fantasies? Geez, does that count?

HRMF: In God's eyes or mine?

BRIGID: Oh, let's have a bit of privacy from God. Let's just be you and me. No trespasses. Just love . . . Or whatever it is you feel for me. (*beat*) We're free. I wash your feet. You wash mine.

HRMF: But I'm not free.

BRIGID: I'm not, either. But let's pretend. (*beat*) Anyway, I like you a little bad. Just as long as we're bad together.

They touch.

CHOIR: WORLD WITHOUT END, AMEN!

HRMF returns to the lectern.

HRMF: Quite nice. (*beat*) Now get some rest. The Christmas Concert approacheth. (*beat*) It's a good time to make your peace.

The Choir disperses.

D.C. starts to cough. The coughing fit escalates. He leaves the choirstand.

Walks out into the cold. Towards the suspension bridge.

D.C.: Cynthia?

He looks over the edge.

Then he feels someone near.

D.C.: Cynthia?

The spirit of Donny Hathaway joins him at the rail, looking down.

D.C.: Donny? Holy shit! Wow. Donny. I know you . . . fell. They say maybe you were pushed, or maybe it was an accident. But I think you did it to yourself. And I can't help wondering why. I listen to your songs over and over. I know death is in them. I'm not afraid of it anymore. You helped me not be. But it seems like everyone I know ends up on this precipice. And the ones I love the most, well . . . They tend to be the ones who just let go.

Soft and low, Donny hums from "For All We Know."

D.C.: Is that what letting go means?

Donny responds with the song.

DONNY: WE WON'T SAY GOODNIGHT UNTIL THE LAST MINUTE

I'LL HOLD OUT MY HAND
AND MY HEART WILL BE IN IT
FOR ALL WE KNOW,
THIS MAY ONLY BE A DREAM . . .

D.C.: We can't all let go. Can we?

Then Mom appears.

MOM/DONNY: WE COME AND WE GO
LIKE THE RIPPLES OF A STREAM . . .

She touches Donny, one spirit to another.

MOM: Tomorrow may never come. For all we know. So who's this Cynthia? Why you looking so hard? You need sex?

D.C.: It's going down below zero. She needs a place to stay.

MOM: What's come over you?

D.C.: (*screams*) CYNTHIA!!!

MOM: It is sex.

D.C.: I just don't wanna get left anymore.

MOM: Cynthia?

D.C.: No! Holly. I had this fantasy. I guess it was a dream. I just wonder where the dream ends.

MOM: There are infinite dreams. Chances to make peace. This is one.

Mom breathes on him. They slow dance.

DONNY: FOR ALL WE KNOW
THIS MAY ONLY BE A DREAM
WE COME AND WE GO
LIKE THE RIPPLES OF A STREAM
SO LOVE ME, LOVE ME TONIGHT

D.C.: Oh, God, I wanna have sex with you.

MOM: Me too baby.

D.C.: Tell me it's not right.

MOM: You're pretty hard to let go of.

D.C.: Good.

He stops dancing.

Donny stops singing, stares down at the abyss.

D.C.: You're my home.

MOM: I thought you didn't like home.

D.C.: I love home. That's what's so sad.

MOM: Your dad had the voice. But he couldn't remember the words. Me, I couldn't sing. But I loved the words. (*talk-sings*)

WHAT DOES HE CARE
IF THE WORLD'S GOT TROUBLES
WHAT DOES HE CARE
IF THE LAND AIN'T FREE

D.C.: Oh, man. The song? It was you.

MOM: It wasn't any one of us. It was all of us together. That's what a song is. (*beat*) And we passed it on to you.

Cynthia enters. Bundled up from the cold.

CYNTHIA: Whatchu doing?

D.C. does not hear. He leans over the rail, looking down. Mom on one side of him, Cynthia on the other.

CYNTHIA: Hey! Kid! You crazy? It's cold out here!

D.C. talks into the abyss. Neither to Mom, nor to Cynthia. Or else, perhaps, to both of them.

D.C.: I'm just . . . I'm just—

CYNTHIA: What baby?

D.C.: I'm just so sorry—

CYNTHIA: Oh, shit.

Cynthia runs to him.

CYNTHIA: Don't jump! Don't do it. It'll get better, boy. I promise. Please. Kids come up here all the time. But you don't wanna do that.

D.C. suddenly sees how close he is to falling. He jumps back into Cynthia's arms.

D.C.: Oh, man!

CYNTHIA: You got so much to live for. So many people love ya. So much love.

MOM: Older woman.

D.C.: I wasn't gonna— (*beat*) It's too damn cold. Come home with me.

CYNTHIA: What? You mean, for sex?

D.C.: No!—Well, maybe. But mostly I think we both oughta just get warm.

CYNTHIA: You think this is cold? I been through worse. River froze over a long time back. Earth cold as iron. Water like a stone. But I'm fine. 'Cause the real warm? Comes from inside, boy. (*beat*) So go inside.

She lets go of him.

D.C.: Cynthia, come home —

CYNTHIA: This is home.

Cynthia goes under the bridge.

MOM: Go on. Go home.

MOM/CYNTHIA: Get warm.

Then she too turns away and leaves him.

D.C. is alone.

Then he sees Donny still looking into the abyss.

D.C.: Why did you kill yourself?

DONNY: Sometimes it just be's that way.

D.C. leaves him staring off the bridge.

HRMF on the organ. Bach's "Jesu Joy of Man's Desiring."

D.C. dresses in a choir robe. As he does, Brigid takes the lectern, dressed in her best vestments.

Candles glow, holly and ivy.

BRIGID: Welcome to Sage Chapel. And Merry Christmas.

Brigid pulls out Confederacy of Dunces, but instead reads from the bookmark.

BRIGID: A beloved member of the choir gave me a bookmark with the Saint Francis Prayer, and, uh, to thank her I would like to read it to you. Let us pray.

(*reads*)

Lord, make us instruments of thy peace.

Where there is hatred, let us so love.

Where there is injury, pardon.

Where there is doubt, faith.

Where there is despair, hope.

Where there is darkness, light.

And where there is sadness . . .

Joy. Amen.

D.C. takes his place on the choirstand. Dan by his side.

Jaha and Cynthia sit in the congregation. They look not unlike a mother and child.

HRMF takes the lectern.

HRMF: The First Reading is taken from the Gospel According to Saint Luke . . . And it came to pass in those days that there went out a decree from Caesar Augustus that all the world should be taxed. And Joseph also went to be taxed. With Mary, his espoused wife, and she brought forth her first-born son, and wrapped him in swaddling clothes and laid him in a manger, because there was no room for them at the inn . . .

JAHA: This is long.

CYNTHIA: Hush up and learn something.

JAHA: Now if this was a Baptist minister we'd have some big fun.

HRMF frowns down at them.

HRMF: And there were country shepherds abiding in the field keeping watch over their flock by night.

JAHA: I'm listening!

HRMF: And lo! The angel of the Lord came upon them, and the glory of the Lord shone round about them and they were sore afraid!

JAHA: What's he looking at me for?

CYNTHIA: 'Cause you talk too much!

HRMF: And the angel said unto them "Fear not, for behold I bring you tidings of great joy, which shall be to all people."

CYNTHIA: All people.

JAHA: Shush!

HRMF: And it came to pass as the angel was gone away from them into heaven, the shepherds came in haste, and found Mary, and Joseph, and the babe, lying in a manger. And when they had seen it they made it known abroad. (*beat*) But Mary kept all these things and pondered them in her heart.

He looks to Brigid. Brigid looks to D.C.

D.C. looks down. He looks scared and very very young.

HRMF perspires. He clears his throat.

HRMF: Here ends the First Reading.

HRMF goes to the choirstand.

D.C. stands forward.

JAHA: It's his turn!

CYNTHIA: Hush now.

JAHA: Stand and deliver, baby.

CYNTHIA: Baby?

HRMF raises the baton. D.C. looks to him. Their eyes meet full of fear. Then he downbeats.

The Choir sings a singular arrangement of "Deep River."

D.C. breathes irregularly as he awaits his cue.

The sound of his breathing MAGNIFIED — more like a wheeze, not near enough air in his lungs to make a sound.

The sound of the Choir fades out.

All we hear is the labored breathing.

Then HRMF points the baton at D.C. — eyes wide.

Silence.

Time stops.

D.C. opens his mouth. Nothing comes out.

Then Mom appears.

MOM: Let go.

D.C. shakes his head vigorously "no."

MOM: Breathe.

D.C. unable to breathe. His face turning color.

MOM: You have to breathe. Dad's dead. I'm dead. One day even you will be dead. But not now.

D.C.'s body beginning to suffer, beginning to writhe.

MOM: You can do it. Breathing is believing.

HRMF points the baton once again, also holding his breath, eyes bugging out of his head.

MOM: Because eventually you gotta believe in something. Look, you don't gotta reinvent the wheel. You just gotta breathe. Let go!

Mom touches his diaphragm.

D.C. reacts as if from an electric shock.

Her hand firmly on his groin.

D.C. chokes, coughs — then breathes, gulping.

MOM: Now sing.

D.C. opens his mouth. His voice crackles like dead twigs.

D.C.: I'm dry.

Mom leans in. Kisses him. Life flows.

D.C.: God help me.

MOM: Let it flow.

JAHA: Shouldn't he be singing by now?

CYNTHIA: Hush!!!

D.C. breathes down to his toes, then sings:

D.C.: DEEP RIVER
MY HOME IS OVER JORDAN
DEEP RIVER
I WANT TO CROSS OVER INTO
CAMPGROUND —

Now HRMF can breathe.

The sound of the Choir returns.

Now finding his true form, singing out like a champion, a modern-day Robeson, proud and strong, beautiful and free.

D.C.:
OH DEEP RIVER,
MY HOME IS OVER JORDAN
DEEP RIVER LORD
I WANT TO CROSS OVER INTO
CAMPGROUND!

D.C. vibrates as the song ends.

D.C. and HRMF lock eyes. Both clear their throats.

DAN: Yeah!

D.C.: Thanks, Mom.

CYNTHIA: Paul Robeson would be proud.

The room still vibrating, the Choir stands and departs through the congregation.

D.C. first, then Dan. D.C. walks by Jaha and Cynthia. They give each other love. D.C. looks up, feeling Mom near. She does not appear. Instead, she joins Donny Hathaway on the bridge.

Together, they look down.

Then, quietly, they hold hands.

JAHA: (*to CYNTHIA*) Merry Christmas, Mom.

CYNTHIA: Back at ya, Son. (*then to D.C.*) Just remember now. Your penis? It's not your only organ.

D.C. sees Holly.

Dan sees Holly.

Holly walks past D.C. to Dan.

HOLLY: I just thought I ought to come.

DAN: Thank you.
HOLLY: I'm not staying. I just — I just wanted to —
Dan kneels at her feet.
HOLLY: I guess I just wanted to.
DAN: Thank you. (*losing it*) Thank you forever.
D.C. watches them. Then he leaves them alone. HRMF plays the organ. Bach floods the room. Brigid joins HRMF on the organ bench. HRMF plays on, without words. Eventually, Brigid leans her head on HRMF's shoulder. He plays on. The music flows.
D.C.: (*looks up*) Amen.
D.C. opens the chapel door and walks out. On the wind, he hears Native American traditional songs. As he walks towards them—

END OF PLAY

Joy of the Desolate
entremeses | *intermezzo* | inter-acts

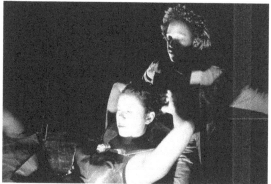

Carla Nassy and Nicholas Grimes in a scene from
the CalArts production of *Joy of the Desolate*.
photography, Nataki Garrett

Jin Suh in another scene from the
CalArts production of *Joy of the Desolate*.
photography, Nataki Garrett

Some Notes on *Joy of the Desolate*

Geraint Wyn Davies

Joy of the Desolate is an evocative, provocative piece of theatre. This is one of my favorite works by Oliver Mayer in a collection of many challenging and insightful studies of our human condition.

JOY is a young man's play, full of the bravado, no-fear, no-compromise, unconditional love of topic that a mind "in heat" can produce.

Working together on both the workshop and full production of the world premiere at the Apple Tree Theatre in Chicago, I was embraced constantly by an excitement and commitment to the production by Oliver. Through many a too-hot jar of sake and many televised games of hoops, we laughed and worked our way into allowing this play to take its own shape—or life, if you will.

The willingness of our cast to embrace the ideas and celebrate them made the journey even more of a joy.

A play where a young man finds his voice, complete with sex, drugs, R&B, family, tradition, loss, ghosts, religion . . . Wow!

We have a rollicking visual delight as well as an aural treat. Donny Hathaway with music—Oliver Mayer Hathaway with words.

The frontispiece of the *Prensa de la vanidad* edition of *Joy of the Desolate*.

Natsuko Ohama

Dear Reader, the preceding plays have blood pumping through them. Vital blood. The extended fist, the open hand, the dark thoughts, the exposed heart, the shadowy words, make actors hunt down and find the space between language. These are not easy plays, but plays in the sense of the meaning of the word itself—like sport, like play. The mystery of creating character is just that, and in an Oliver Mayer play this is not stamped out and laid before you like a robe to put on. You have to dig in, up close to the characters, get to know them, smell them, sense the whys and wherefores. What is not said is almost as important as what is said. One looks for the answer in situation and in the what-ifs when you are wrestling with words. This means it is a workout for the reader; no skimming, but leave time to let things breathe and imagine. This work is theatrical—get up on your feet and duck and weave with it. There is pleasure in discovering what you are really saying. The world you bring to play is the answer to his invitation to collaborate. His world is the world of boxers, misfits, mixed race, the child, lovers, loneliness and longing. The heart is worn on the sleeve, and the sleeve is rolled up to work. It demands exposing and revealing for the performer, and one can only say, what a joy to be so desolate.

Promotional poster for the Chicago, Apple Tree Theatre production of *Joy of the Desolate.*

Ad for the East Los Angeles Repertory Theatre Company's production of Bananas and Peachfuzz and other works.

Bananas and Peachfuzz

by Oliver Mayer

directed by Sara Guerrero
produced by Jesus Reyes
world premiere at East Los Angeles
Repertory Theatre Company
at El Gallo Plaza Theater, Los Angeles
from Sept. 28-Oct. 21, 2007
LATINO Jose Esqueda
LATINA Karen Anzoategui

SCENE

A LATINA ADULT WOMAN looks in the mirror. She examines herself with poker-faced interest. She feels her face. Checks her eyes. Rearranges her hair.

Her interest goes deeper. Beyond the surface of the skin. She searches for something difficult to locate inside. Something she cannot easily find.

Then a MOMENT as she finds what she's looking for. A memory of MUSIC—sexy, steamy rocknroll Orisha.

The sense memory makes her put her hand to her heart. It takes the breath out of her lungs. It parts her lips. The MUSIC grows.

It conjures a MAN IN SILHOUETTE. He dances supercoolly, underdoing rather than overdoing, but unmistakeably rolling his hips in the universal language of attraction.

She doesn't look at him—yet she sees him.

Despite herself, she rises.

He beckons her, supercool, quiet, not to be denied. As she is about to go to him—

SOUND OF A SCREEN DOOR CREAKING AND SLAMMING.

The MAN IN SILHOUETTE disappears.

The WOMAN catches her breath. Sighs. Pats her heart.

Sits and looks again into the mirror as—

A LATINO TEENAGE BOY enters. Nearly a man, but not there yet. Nothing supercool about him. Still, he's a cute kid.

As soon as he sees her, he grows awkward. He fights between looking away and staring at her.

His voice keeps breaking, particularly when he says anything revealing.

LATINA: Hey, Handsome.

LATINO: Shut up.

LATINA: Charming. Nice technique. You say shut up to all the girls? You must have to beat 'em off with a stick.

LATINO: Don't call me handsome. That's all.

LATINA: Why not?

LATINO: 'Cause I'm not.

LATINA: Oh, yeah? Who says?

LATINO: Use your eyes! I got pimples.

LATINA: Yeah, you got a couple. I didn't really notice under the peachfuzz.

LATINO: That's a moustache!

LATINA: Oh. Excuse me.

LATINO: It's still coming in.

LATINA: You got a lifetime to grow a moustache. Get a shave. Let us girls have a look at your pretty face.

LATINO: Shut up!

LATINA: We really gotta work on your lovetalk. Get you listening to some Al Green, Marvin Gaye, may some Luis Miguel. I don't think any of 'em say Shut Up when they get to slow grooving.

LATINO: Arggh!!

LATINA: Don't take it all so personal! Jeez. *(she looks at him)* Why do you want to be grown up so bad?

LATINO: I'm not a kid.

LATINA: No, you're not.

LATINO: I want a moustache. And a low voice. I want respect!

LATINA: You want a girlfriend?

LATINO: Shut u—

LATINA: You shut up. If you wanna be a man so bad, then learn how to talk to a lady.

LATINO: Sorry.

LATINA: What do you got there?

She motions to the bag in his hands. Lots of fresh fruit and vegetables, canned goods, tupperware.

LATINO: Mom went shopping.

LATINA: Tell her she doesn't have to buy extra for me. She doesn't have to do that.

LATINO: She doesn't listen to me.

LATINA: Set it down.

He sets the bag down. Suddenly self-conscious about a growing bulge in his jeans.

LATINA: Is that a banana in your pocket? Or are you just glad to see me?

LATINO: I'm going.

LATINA: No! I'm just kidding.

He lingers.

LATINO: It's not what you think it is.

LATINA: What do you know what I'm thinking?

LATINO: It's my body! I can't control it any more! It keeps surprising me! Embarrassing me! I just want to quit being a kid so I can be a man and get control of my life!

LATINA: Oh, baby. You're never in complete control. It's like a burp (*he reacts*) or a fart. (*he reacts*) No matter how hard you try to hold it back, it's gonna come out. Louder than ever and probably at the very worst time. Don't worry about control. Just learn to relax. It's all right.

LATINO: Is it?

They lock eyes through the mirror. She looks away.

LATINA: So! Are you driving yet?

LATINO: Just got my learner's permit.

LATINA: You wear a seatbelt?

LATINO: Seatbelts are stupid.

LATINA: Seatbelts are sexy.

LATINO: What?!!

LATINA: Seatbelts are sexy.

LATINO: You're weird!

LATINA: Surviving is sexy. Dying isn't. Just remember that when you're behind the wheel. Do you drive the speed limit?

LATINO: Now you're gonna tell me that 55 miles per hour is sexy, right?

LATINA: How'd you know?

LATINO: I guess I'm smart.

LATINA: I guess you are. Smart is definitely sexy. And that's no joke.

LATINO: You really think I'm smart?

LATINA: I hope you're smart. (*beat*) Do you use a condom?

LATINO: SHUT UP!

LATINA: Do you?

LATINO: No!

LATINA: Then you're not very smart.

She gets up. Picks up the bag of food and starts

to go.

LATINO: Wait! I didn't mean no like that. I meant—(*struggles*) I didn't mean I don't use condoms. I meant that I wouldn't know how. I've never had the chance. (*embarrassed*) Talk about stupid.

He starts to leave. She reaches out to stop him.

LATINA: Don't go.

LATINO: Feels like I'll never get the chance. You know? Like it'll never happen.

LATINA: It'll happen.

LATINO: And I keep thinking that when I finally get the chance I'll mess up somehow. I'll lose out. I'll do it wrong. It'll break or something. I'll mess up. But I'll be so stupid I'll do it anyway. And I'll get sick!

She reacts. As soon as he's said it, he stops.

LATINO: Hey. I didn't mean to—

LATINA: You're a very smart kid.

LATINO: Look, uh. Are you feeling all right?

LATINA: I'm fine. (*beat*) It's a little like a seatbelt. You don't have to wear it. You can lie about it, tell your mom or me that you wear it when you don't. But when you're in the middle of an accident, it'll be too late to put it on. Your life will be in the balance, in the air, and there won't be any safety belt to protect you from the crash.

LATINO: Um. Did you? Did you get sick—? How?

LATINA: (*smiles ruefully*) I didn't wear my seatbelt.

She looks at herself. MUSIC in memory. The

MAN IN SILHOUETTE reappears. Moves his hips to her. Beckons.

LATINA: He certainly didn't wear his either. (*turns away from the MAN*) I was always the smart girl. Straight A's and scholarships. Good girl. And I never slept around. At least that's what everybody thought. (*turns back to the MAN*) But that wasn't the problem. Everybody blames the sex. The sex was fine. We just weren't safe! We didn't take care of each other. He probably didn't even know. But that's no excuse. And now my life is changed. (*beat*) I owe it to everybody—to you—to be responsible. For as much time as I have left on this earth. I need to lead by example. I need to be safe.

She walks to the MAN. He stops dancing.

LATINO: (*not seeing the MAN*) What happened to him? The guy?

LATINA: I don't know. I tried to find him, to let him know, but it's like he disappeared. And he could be putting other partners in danger. Without even knowing he could be wrecking lives, even now. Or he could be sick himself.

The MAN sinks into himself; no longer supercool.

LATINA: He could be dead by now.

The MAN looks up in fear. She stares back unmoved.

No more MUSIC.

LATINO: I don't want that to happen to me.

LATINA: Then be smart.

LATINO: And lucky?

LATINA: You make your luck.

She watches as the MAN slinks off into darkness.

When she turns around, the BOY is in front of her.

LATINO: I—(*struggles*) I want to get lucky—with—

LATINA: Lucky with me? That is definitely not the way to talk to a lady.

LATINO: I don't mean like that! I mean—(*struggles*) Am I really handsome?

LATINA: You will be.

LATINO: Is it safe to --(*struggles*) Kiss you?

LATINA: Depends on the kiss. But, yes. It's safe.

LATINO: Then let me.

LATINA: I don't think your mom would approve.

LATINO: This isn't about mom. It's not even about me. I just want to kiss you!

LATINA: How's this? I'll kiss you. Okay?

LATINO: Okay.

LATINA: Close your eyes.

He does.

She strokes his face. Smiles.

She kisses his forehead.

LATINO: Hey!

LATINA: One kiss. Now go. Thank your mom for me. And tell her she doesn't have to worry!

LATINO: About what?

LATINA: About me. Or you either. Not as long as you stay smart.

LATINO: I will. (*smiles*) Smart is sexy.

LATINA: It is.

He goes. She is alone.

Removes prescription pills. Takes her daily dose.

Looks deep into the mirror.

END OF PLAY

rocio
A PESAR DE TODO
by Oliver Mayer
directed by Armando Molina

King King Nightclub
Hollywood, CA
Sundays & Mondays
8pm from June 5 to July 31

Original sketch for the King King Nightclub by
Guillermo Nericcio García

Marlene Forte as Rocio and Joe Quintero as Armando
Chuleta in _Rocio_ for the King King Nightclub, 2006.
Photography by Mario Melendez.

Rocio! In Spite of It All

a cabaret by Oliver Mayer
directed by Armando Molina
choreographed by Lesley Ann Machado
songs originally written by Manuel Alejandro, Julio Sejus, Honorio Herrero and Anna Magdalena, re-imagined by Oliver Mayer and Aaron Fischer.
Produced by Mario Melendez and Marlene Forte.
Performed for a two-month run beginning June 5, 2006 at King King Nightclub, Hollywood, CA.

CAST:

Rocio Del Rio	Marlene Forte
Inez Maduro	Lidia Ramirez
Man/Boy	Shalim
Announcer	Joe Quintero
Hortensio	Aaron Fischer
Dancer	Lesley Ann Machado
Dancer	Sean Dodder
Dancer	Michael Moshy

Dedicated to the loving memory of the divas come and gone in both Spanish and English.

King King Nightclub, Hollywood

In the dark—a Man-Boy sits in an easy chair. Somewhere, slightly raised, in the middle of the audience. Childlike, he hums to himself the tune to "SEÑORA" as he turns on the TV (onstage). The screen is snowy, boxy—definitely not a flatscreen. MUSIC.

ANNOUNCER: *EN VIVO Y EN DIRECTO . . . S-I-N Network, con Canal 34 presenta, el Show de las SUPER ESTRELLAS!!!!*

Onstage Lights RISE on a Live TV Broadcast, circa 1979, from decidedly south of the border. LIVE AUDIENCE claps approval. INTRO played live by the BANDA—schmaltzy! Johnny Carson, Latin style. DANCERS appear, very male and gay hot. They form patterns and smolder into the camera.

ANNOUNCER is revealed at the stand-up mic, wearing a bow tie. His accent is Ricardo Montalban. He does double duty because he's holding a baton for leading the band.

ANNOUNCER: *BIENVENIDOS, LATINO AMERICA*, whichever side of the border you may be. I am your host, Armando Chuleta! Tonight we bring you not so much a singer as an emotional experience. Tonight we bring you the life—*la vida de*—ROCIO DEL RIO. Up close and personal, *¡uno a uno, primer impacto!*, no holds barred. This is more than a true story. *Este es una vida en moción!* In front of the cameras, *viviendo, llorando, amando,* revealing ALL!!

The DANCERS smolder by in formation one more time. Suddenly the SCREEN above them comes to life as we the CONGAS beat out a heartbeat.

IMAGES come flooding, mostly of the still variety.

ANNOUNCER: FOTOS tell us the story of Rocio in pictures! Memories before the legend began.

BABY picture.

ANNOUNCER: Rocio was born on the island of Cuba to a Mexican Jew and a Czechoslovakian Gypsy in the year *(intentionally GARBLES the date)* These were performers, entertainers in the old style—

Picture of an ancient Gypsy caravan, of stone-age flamenco performers, blind street singers, maybe Laurel & Hardy.

ANNOUNCER: It was here that Rocio learned of her peculiar gift for the stage.

B/W picture of children, with Rocio's RED HAIR in color.

ANNOUNCER: She was a NATURAL.

Photos of her as ballet dancer, lindy-hopper, breakdancer. Also photos of her famous red hair in various hairstyles of the past.

ANNOUNCER: Her purpose in life was clear. She would be the voice of her generation, the voice of someone older— *(clears throat)* WISER than her years.

MUSIC CUE. A SCRATCHY RECORDING of a young Rocio emoting like Janis Joplin—perhaps the actual Janis.

The SCREEN shifts dramatically. Now ROCIO is HOT. Very early 60s, the young Rocio modeling with grown breasts and hips.

ANNOUNCER: *(affected)* Blessed with natural animal magnetism, Rocio could have been a great model, or the wife of an important man—

Images of Franco, Fidel, JFK.

ANNOUNCER: But no, her higher purpose called her and she came, and came again, over and over to the place she would call home . . . The TELEVISION *ESTUDIO*!!!

VIDEO of Rocio performing LIVE, dramatic, wild. Band strikes up a medley of HITS.

DANCERS make formations around the screen.

ANNOUNCER: Of course there were men . . .

Photos of Rocio with many many many men of all colors, ages.

ANNOUNCER: And scandals...

She always looks AMAZING while the men are often disheveled.

Among the photos, a recurring BULL FIGHTER.

ANNOUNCER: And there was loss . . .

Photo of a BULL goring a matador.

FOR THE FIRST TIME, we see a silhouette, standing to the side.

ANNOUNCER: But through it all, in spite of everything, Rocio sings on. Singing, living, loving for us. (*to the SILHOUETTE*) InCOMparable! (*coughs*) Except of course for her rival Inez Maduro—

FULL BODY IMAGE of IRIS CHACON.

At the mention of her name, the CROWD reacts in applause.

ANNOUNCER: The woman who has re-interpreted many Rocio songs in the tradition of the islands of the Caribe, and whose

mammary glandular graces have created quite a bit of attention—

DETAILED IMAGE of Inez's BOSOM.

CROWD reacts. The silhoutted woman reacts as well.

The SCREEN goes black.

ANNOUNCER: (*clears throat*) ¡Caramba! But back to Rocio! (*one more time*) InCOMparable!

MUSIC.

ANNOUNCER: And tonight, after so many many nights, performing, breathing, loving, crying, DYING for us—Tonight we give un homenaje to *La Única—La Divina—*ROCIO!!

Light on the silhouette reveals ROCIO, incomparable indeed.

To OUTDO the Iris Chacon image, she moves animal-like down the row of DANCERS like the mother of Madonna (and Madonnas everywhere). She goes to the Banda winking and slinking to each player. Then, finally, she addresses her audience.

ROCIO: *Mi público. Viva mi público! Viva Siempre en Domingo.* (*blows kisses*) I just want to give you EVERYTHING!

The song A PESAR DE TODO begins. DANCERS around her.

ROCIO: This is from the bottom of my *corazon.* (*dramatic hand gesture*)

IN SPITE OF ALL OF THAT

EVEN THOUGH YOU'VE TAKEN ALL MY HAPPINESS

I KNOW I'M ONLY HAPPY WHEN YOU SEE
ME
I BELONG TO YOU
IN SPITE OF ALL OF THE CRAP
EVEN THOUGH YOU'VE DONE ME WRONG
A BUNCHA TIMES
EVEN THOUGH IT'S TRUE YOU'VE CLEARLY
GROWN UNFAITHFUL
I COME BACK TO YOU
BECAUSE YOU
YOU HELPED MAKE ME WHAT I AM
YOU ARE FULL OF FAITH IN ALL THE STUFF
THAT MAKES ME CRAZY AS A JAYBIRD
ERES TÚ, A PESAR DE TODO TÚ
POR ENCIMA DEL AMOR
EL QUE RIE DE SÍ MISMO
POR EL BORDE DEL ABISMO
MEANWHILE I, IN SPITE OF ALL THAT, ME
PAST THE BOUNDARIES OF LOVE
KEEP ON COUNTING UP MY SPRINGTIMES
WAITING HOPING THAT YOU'LL LOVE ME
She flourishes to receive her applause, BUT—
Above her, in front of the screen, another silhou-
ette comes clear. With Iris Chacon moves, INEZ
MADURO appears. As she does, music changes to
a decidedly island sound, heavy on the congas.
With every move of the waist, the music SNAPS.
INEZ: Love ME!!!
ROCIO: *Sucia!*
INEZ: *Celosa!*
As ROCIO glares—
ANNOUNCER: This is AMAZING! *In-COM-*
parable times two! The one and only INEZ

MADURO has joined our *homenaje a* Rocio!
Which is pretty amazing since they hate
each other's guts!
ROCIO: I have nothing but love in my
heart!
INEZ: I got love in other places!
She WIGGLES to applause.
DANCERS leave Rocio and dance around INEZ.
INEZ picks up the song, salsa-izing it, to RO-
CIO's consternation.
INEZ: A PESAR DE TODO
EVEN THOUGH ROCIO'S DOMINATED TV
PROGRAMS
EVEN THOUGH THE BITCH IGNORES HER
SEXY YOUNGER RIVALS
YOU COME BACK TO ME
A PESAR DE TODO,
EVEN THOUGH I HAD TO CRASH ROCIO'S
PARTY
DESPITE MY SUPERIOR TV RATINGS
YOU KEEP WATCHING ME . . .
INEZ starts to dance, accentuating chest and
hips.
INEZ: PORQUE TÚ
ERES PARTE DE MI MISMA
ERES FERTIL Y FE DE PRISMA
QUE CULMINAN MIS LOCURAS—
Rocio, unable to take it anymore, jumps into the
song, turning it back into a torch-song. Banda
confused, tries to keep up. DANCERS go back to
her.
ROCIO: ERES TÚ, A PESAR DE TODO TÚ
POR ENCIMA DEL AMOR

EL QUE RIE DE SÍ MISMO
POR EL BORDE DEL ABISMO—
With an ass-shake, INEZ wrests the song back. Dancers stuck mid-way. Only the CONGUERO follows her every move.
INEZ: MEANWHILE I, IN SPITE OF ALL THAT ME
PAST THE BOUNDARIES OF LOVE
KEEP ON COUNTING UP MY SPRINGTIMES
WAITING HOPING THAT YOU'LL LOVE ME
Rocio grabs the stand-up mic from INEZ.
ROCIO: A PESAR DE TODO
Inez grabs it back.
INEZ: A PESAR DE TODO
They fight over it.
Rocio gets the stand between her legs. Partly to control it, partly out of pure passion, she HUMPS it.
ROCIO: A PESAR DE TODO!!!!
The Banda stops.
The audience goes silent.
She looks up at them with the mic stand between her legs.
ROCIO: WAITING, HOPING THAT YOU'LL LOVE ME . . .
Announcer signals the boom CAMERAMAN.
ANNOUNCER: Go to COMMERCIAL!!!
Man-Boy turns off the TV. He looks exactly like the MAXELL SPEAKER ADVERTISEMENT from the 1970s. Still sitting in the easy chair, his hair and clothes thrown back as if he were going sixty miles an hour. He rises. Feels his face. His body.

MAN/BOY: POR ENCIMA DEL AMOR,
In spite of all the love,
POR ENCIMA DEL DOLOR
In spite of all the pain . . . WAITING, HOPING THAT YOU'LL LOVE ME? Are you waiting? For me? Because I am waiting. In spite of everything I've been waiting . . . *para tí.*
No longer childlike, he walks away. Blackout, except for a single spot. Rocio pours a glass of champagne. We see her hand.
The music to A PESAR DE TODO plays softly behind her. The spot opens to reveal Rocio alone, crying. She has aged.
ROCIO: *A pesar de todo . . . (breathes deep)* In spite of everything—and that's a lot! You got to know who you are. I didn't know then. It's taken me this long to find out the truth. The sordid bitter beautiful truth. *(sings)* VUELVO A TÍ *(breathes)* I return to you. True! My mirror. The reflection of your eyes! *¡Tú!* Even if the glass gets a little foggy sometimes. All that heavy breathing. All that manly musk. All that misplaced sticky love juice. Ay. Ooooh. Aaaaah. Maybe it's me who gets a little over-steamed sometimes. *(fans herself)* It's just I need you to see me. All the years trying to get—trying to keep—your attentions. *(her tits)* My ladies. Their ups, their downs. Talk about a *telenovela. (squeezes)* Augmentation. Implants. Gel. Saline. Slit! Jamming 'em in. Slit! Yanking 'em out. Slit! In, out!

She reaches into her dress, pulls out two semi-transparent sacks.

ROCIO: I got so used to it I can do it myself. (*makes them talk to each other*) So squeeze-able! And they look just like chicken breasts! (*sticks them back in*) The nips, the tucks, surgeries to remove a rib here, a set of molars there—(*outlines her cheekbones*) *Rocio sees herself in the mirror of the audience.*

ROCIO: The fashions. The statements. The searching for a signature. (*adjusts her thong*) Accentuate the positive, eliminate the *pernil*! But that's hard on a La'in girl! The camera adds ten pounds, ha! I can add ten pounds at the local taco stand! But a good designer hides the *grasa* from the *masa*! The sin from the cinema! Or at least makes it look sexy. And firm. (*slaps her ass*) ESPERANDO QUE ME QUIERA . . . (*caresses herself*) And the men. ERES TÚ . . . Y TÚ, Y TÚ, Y TÚ. All the men—and a couple of women, for laughs. But that's all in the past. Men don't interest me anymore. What's left to see? I've done it all. Believe me, I've done it all. And it hurts. To give yourself away every time as if it were the first. To go with this man or that for love, and have it end up all about business. (*suddenly angry*) Turn it off. TURN IT OFF!!!
MUSIC STOPS.

ROCIO: It's because my heart was so BIG!!! Love does that—it exercises your heart muscle. (*to the audience*) You're mostly a bunch of 99 pound weaklings—(*sticks out her chest*) I'm Superwoman. That doesn't make me better—well, maybe it does. It's hard to love so much. I mean literally, your body gets tired. Why can't we all just be the way we were as children? Everything for the first time and no business to worry about? Just love.
She begins to sing to the tune of "Como yo te amo." MUSIC slowly backs her up.

Rocio: COMO YO TE AMO
COMO YO TE AMO
CONVÉNCETE
CONVÉNCETE
NADIE TE AMARA
OH HOW I LOVE YOU
OH WOW I LOVE YOU
FORGET ABOUT IT!
DON'T EVEN THINK ABOUT IT!
NO ONE CAN LOVE YOU LIKE ME
NO ONE CAN LOVE YOU LIKE ME
NADIE PORQUE
OH, I LOVE YOU WITH THE POWER OF THE OCEANS
OH, I LOVE YOU WITH THE WILDNESS OF THE SEABREEZE
OH, I LOVE YOU OVER DISTANCE AND THROUGH TIME ZONES
OH, I LOVE YOU WITH MY SPIRIT AND MY BODY
YO TE AMO COMO EL NIÑO A SU MAÑANA,
YO TE AMO COMO EL HOMBRE A SU RECUERDO,
YO TE AMO A PURO GRITO Y EN SILENCIO,

YO TE AMO DE UNA FORMA
SOBREHUMANA
YO TE AMO EN ALEGRIA Y EN EL LLANTO
YO TE AMO EN EL PELIGRO Y EN LA CALMA,
YO TE AMO CUANDO GRITAS CUANDO
CALLAS,
YO TE AMO TANTO YO TE AMO YO!!!
The song pours forth like a tidal wave.
She acts it out, grabbing her heart—and breasts.
When it's over, she smiles through tears.
ROCIO: A PESAR DE TODO. I remember as if
it were yesterday. The *homenaje* on *Siempre
en Domingo,* the camera zooming in on my
chest, of course, and the song just coming
out of me, like sweat, like, like the things
which must come out one way or another,
from me to you. (*sings*)
POR QUE TÚ

ERES PARTE DE MI MISMA!
*She does a pelvic thrust onto a nonexistent mic-
stand.*
ROCIO: And yes, I got a little excited, you
could say I forgot myself. But what really
happened is I remembered myself. I was
feeling the music. And the music felt me
back. And I'd do it again. *No importa* that the
networks won't let me perform live—not
even with a 5 second lag—because they're
afraid what I'll do. I was being myself. And
yes, there was a certain PERSON in the
room—(*wags a finger*) NO! We do not say her
name in this room. It colors the day and I
don't like that color. (*breathes*) Hey, it's ancient history. This was long before

Madonna slithered around in a wedding
dress, before Sinead O'Connor tore the
Pope's photo. I didn't mean to be sensa-
tional. I had sensations, and I let them out.
(*looks out into the audience*) And somewhere
out there there was a 12-year-old transfixed, watching me and dreaming. Well,
there's quite a few. I don't mean the gay
ones, bless their little hearts, who want to
be me. They can't! I mean a boy, nearly a
man—somewhere far from here, wishing
without knowing, hoping beyond his
imagination for something only dreamt of,
beyond J-Lo and Britney, and not his
Mama either, but another kind of *mama,* a
better kind of *mama . . .*
*She takes the imaginary mic stand and thrusts
again, but with love.*
ROCIO: REGRESO A TI. And he sees me. A
woman. He hears me. An enigma. And this
boy will never be the same.
The Man-Boy nods.
ROCIO: (*oblivious*) SOY DE TÍ
The bravest of these boys writes to me
from wherever the hell.
She reveals a stack of letters—a lot of them.
*The Man-Boy, blushing, holds a letter in his
hand.*
ROCIO: So much love. So much want. So
many obstacles. Such amazing secrets.
She opens one. A naked torso visible.
ROCIO: Such nice illustrations. I'm not a
stickler for beauty. But occasionally a cer-
tain boy comes to the fore and speaks to

me, the way my songs, my life, my self, my pain, speaks to him.

Man-Boy flings his letter towards her.

She picks it up.

ROCIO: *Corazón!*

A NAKED YOUNG MAN enters, a little zonked with bedhead. Refills her champagne. She pinches his ass as he goes back to the bedroom.

Man-Boy holds his heart, hurt.

ROCIO: *(shrugs)* It's hard to love so much. So deep. For so long. *(tugs at her thong)* Play it again.

MUSIC plays A PESAR DE TODO.

She hums, then sings, as she makes her way to the bedroom.

SPOTLIGHT on the Man-Boy.

The Man-Boy ever so slowly, ever so curiously, enters her space. Checks to see that he is indeed alone.

HE HUMS to himself. He touches the things Rocio left behind—stool, champagne flute, boa. He is part stalker, part lover. He caresses each thing with uncommon love. Not so much sickness as childlike wonder. Every so often, he experiences a FLASH of masculinity—something sexual. Otherwise he seems very shy.

He strokes the boa. Finally he wears it. Drinks from the flute. Then, for a moment, does a spot-on impersonation:

MAN/BOY: COMO YO TE AMO
COMO YO TE AMO
CONVÉNCETE, CONVÉNCETE
NADIE TE AMARA, --

When it comes to gesture, he's studied Rocio down to the most intricate beat.

But when he feels his breast, he suddenly falls out of the impersonation. He's pissed off, with himself.

He looks around the room. To his delight, he finds a dress discarded on a chair. Once again he tries:

MAN/BOY:
YO TE AMO CON LA FUERZA DE LOS MARES,
YO TE AMO CON IMPETU DEL VIENTO,
YO TE AMO EN LA DISTANCIA Y EN EL TIEMPO,
YO TE AMO CON MI ALMA Y CON MI CARNE—

Now he finds his REFLECTION in the mirror of the audience. Feels his chin stubble with distaste. As he scowls—

MUSIC begins, with an edge.

Man-Boy faces the mirror.

MAN/BOY: Rocio. Do I want to be with you? Or do I just want to be you?

He makes one last Rocio gesture.

MAN/BOY: If you could see me? Be me? Would you know my heart?

Then turns away to leave.

Rocio is there, drink in hand, sexily, dangerously staring straight at him, his new MIRROR.

ROCIO *(talk/sings to the tune of ESE HOMBRE):*
THE MAN YOU SEE BEFORE YOU OVER THERE
SEEMS SO ATTENTIVE AND GALLANT

SO ATTRACTIVELY ARROGANT
I KNOW HIM LIKE I KNOW MYSELF
THE DUDE YOU SEE BEFORE YOU OVER
THERE
SEEMS ALMOST DIVINE
SO EFFUSIVE AND SO FINE
ALL HE GIVES YOU IS SUFFERING!
HE'S A BIG ASSHOLE,
STUPID INGRATE, IGNORAMUS
EGOTISTIC AND CAPRICIOUS
CLOWNLIKE, EVIL, AVARICIOUS
INCONSISTENT, FULL OF RANCOR
FICKLE, DWARFLIKE, LACKING FEELING
'CAUSE HE DOESN'T HAVE A HEART
*MUSIC accompanies her effortlessly and edgily.
She approaches him like a panther.
He mouths the words as she sings:
She picks him apart, nearly touching him, as he
remains stock-still.
Every line she sings he translates quietly under
his breath.*
ROCIO: JEALOUSLY CRAZY
LACKING MOTIVE FOR HIS ENVY
A TORNADO OF EMOTION
SELDOM LOVING, LACKS DEVOTION
HAVING PROBLEMS WITH HIS SEX DRIVE
MAKING FUN OF FRIENDS AND LOVERS
AND IMPOSSIBLE TO LOVE
MAN/BOY(*simultaneous*): LLENO DE CELOS
SIN RAZONES NI MOTIVOS
COMO EL VIENTO IMPETUOSO
POCAS VECES CARINOSO
INSEGURO DE SI MISMO

INSUPORTABLE COMO AMIGO
INSUFRIBLE COMO AMOR
*She gestures with all her authority. Burns him
down. Walks away in victory. But before she
can leave—
Man-Boy mirrors her, every move, eye to eye.*
MAN/BOY: ESE HOMBRE
QUE TU VES ALLÍ
QUE PARECE TAN AMABLE
DAVIDOSO Y AGRADABLE
LO CONOZCO COMO A MI
*She translates under her breath as he picks her
apart:*
MAN/BOY: THE DUDE YOU SEE BEFORE
YOU OVER THERE
SEEMS ALMOST DIVINE
SO EFFUSIVE AND SO FINE
ALL HE GIVES YOU IS SUFFERING!
ROCIO (*simultaneous*):
ESE HOMBRE QUE TU VES ALLI
QUE PARECE TAN SEGURO
DE PISAR BIEN POR EL MUNDO
SOLO SABE HACER SUFRIR
*They circle each other. Then attack the audi-
ence with the song FULL-ON:*
BOTH: ES UN GRAN NECIO
UN ESTÚPIDO INGREIDO
EGOISTA Y CAPRICHOSO
UN PAYASO VANIDOSO
INCONCIENTE Y PRESUMIDO
FALSO
MAN/BOY: MALO

ROCIO:ENANO
BOTH: RENCOROSO
QUE NO TIENE CORAZÓN
LLENO DE CELOS
SIN RAZONES NI MOTIVOS
COMO EL VIENTO IMPETUOSO
POCAS VECES CARIÑOSO
INSEGURO DE SI MISMO
INSUPORTABLE COMO AMIGO
INSUFRIBLE COMO AMOR
As the music swirls around them—
Man-Boy tries to TOUCH her.
She reacts DRAMATICALLY—no way!
Raises a hand as if to hit him.
The hand's intent changes mid-air. She strokes his face.
Then she takes back the BOA from his neck.
Exits, putting it around her own.
Laughing.
ROCIO: I know him like I know myself.
Man-Boy stands defeated.
Takes off his shirt. Shoes, pants.
Nearly naked, he is about to leave.
When the SCREEN comes to life.
The Iris Chacon image of INEZ MADURO towers above him.
To himself, he begins to sing SENORA:
MAN/BOY: CUANDO SUPE TODA LA VERDAD, SEÑORA
YA ERA TARDE PARA ECHAR ATRÁS, SEÑORA
YO ERA PARTE DE TU VIDA Y TU MI SOMBRA, . . .

Man-Boy clothes himself—nice male clothes—as we for the first time in a long time see—
INEZ MADURO. She has also aged.
She sits in the easy chair. She sucks on a large drink. As the lights rise on her we see it's not a cocktail but a can of Slimfast.
Around her, rows and rows of STUFFED ANIMALS.
Man-Boy watches her. She continues oblivious.
INEZ: My Babies.
She kisses each stuffed animal within reach.
INEZ: I know how much you love me. I can see it in your eyes. (*holds one close*) No judgement. No lust. Well, a little. But your love is sweet. You don't see me as a piece of meat. I'm not your *mami*—I'm your Mommy!
For a second she sees herself in her earlier manifestation ON SCREEN. She snorts at the image.
INEZ: You don't compare me to HER! I'm just not that anymore! And unlike most of the male population in this world, you don't hold it against me. You think I'm BEAUTIFUL. And I think you're beautiful too.
As she kisses the animals—
Man-Boy appears.
MAN/BOY: Inez?
INEZ jumps into action. She apparently knows karate, capoeira, boxing and general bumrushing. She attacks!
Since Man-Boy either can't or won't fight, he's quickly on his back.

INEZ: Rapist! Kidnapper!

MAN/BOY: Help!

INEZ: Sneaking up on me—

MAN/BOY: The door was open!

INEZ: Staring at me—

MAN/BOY: I came to see you!

INEZ: You came to see the *Tetas*? The *Tetas* of your youth? Your dreams? Well here it is! Are you SATISFIED? Is your dream fulfilled, or is it broken into little pieces, shattered like my heart? Isn't that what you came here for?

She smothers him with her breasts.

INEZ: Well? This is what you wanted, isn't it? Isn't it what every man wanted, and what I was stupid enough to give away for free until— (*breaks off*)

MAN/BOY: Until what?

INEZ: Until you didn't want me anymore?

MAN/BOY: I still do.

INEZ: You want my *tetas*?

MAN/BOY: No. I mean yes. Not just the *tetas*.

INEZ: Are you gay?

MAN/BOY: Maybe. But that's not why I came.

By now they are more or less sitting normally, although he has to find a place to perch without disturbing the stuffed animal collection.

INEZ: Speak.

MAN/BOY: I love someone. So much I want to be . . . that person. But I can't. I want you to help me get closer.

INEZ: How?

MAN/BOY: Show me how to live every day as if it were *Sabado Gigante*, and every night as if it were *Siempre en Domingo*. Let me be Celia and Charytin and Ricky and Chayanne and even a little Vicente Fernandez! Give me Willie Colón and Lola Beltrán, show me Los Tigres del Norte and the Fania All Stars, and let me look like Robi Rosa while I'm at it. Breathe into me the spirit of all those shows, and all the shows to come, which confused the hell out of me as a child, and which tantalize my dreams!

INEZ: How am I supposed to do that?

MAN/BOY: Sing with me. On TV.

INEZ: I haven't performed in years.

MAN/BOY: It's time. Show us what we've been missing.

INEZ: But . . . I'm fat.

MAN/BOY: You're beautiful. (*beat*) Will you?

Silence.

INEZ: Let me see your chest.

Man/Boy shows Inez his chest.

INEZ: Nice.

MAN/BOY: Let's get started.

INEZ: What are we singing?

MAN/BOY: ESE HOMBRE, COMO YO TE AMO—

INEZ: Wait a sec—

MAN/BOY: A PESAR DE TODO—

INEZ: Hold on. This . . . person— ?

MAN/BOY: Rocio del Rio.

INEZ: She's my rival, my sworn enemy.

MAN/BOY: But why?

INEZ: I don't remember anymore. Who can remember such things?

MAN/BOY: Then make new memories!

INEZ: But the networks banned me when they banned her! I haven't been on Latin TV since the night she went porno on that micstand! Hey, I showed my *tetas* to the world, but I never did that! I'm a lady!

MAN/BOY: You are.

INEZ: She hates me.

MAN/BOY: Maybe. All I know is that ever since that fateful night, my life has never been the same. That *homenaje* needs to happen, if I'm going to move on in my life. And if you are going to get past stuffed animals to where you rightly belong. And even though you may not care—it needs to happen so Rocio can receive the love she deserves.

INEZ: From whom?

MAN/BOY: From me.

INEZ: What about my love?

Inez once again assumes a martial arts pose.

Man/Boy doesn't flinch.

Man/Boy extends his hand.

MAN/BOY: *Señora?*

She takes his hand.

They fall into an embrace. Stuffed animals go flying. ROCIO, once again in spotlight. Champagne bottle in hand.

A LETTER APPEARS.

She opens it, reads.

ROCIO: From the eternal twelve-year-old!

(*reads/sings to the tune of* Señora)

WHEN I FOUND OUT WHERE YOU LIVED SEÑORA

MY ENTIRE WORLD WAS ALREADY HERS SEÑORA

WITHIN MY VERY BEING I SMELLED HER AROMA

(*speaks*) The aroma of Inez?

(*read/SINGS*)

YOU SEE SHE TOLD ME SHE WAS FREE

LIKE THE AIR WE'RE BREATHING,

SHE WAS FREE

LIKE THE PIGEONS SHITTING SHE WAS FREE,

Y YO LO CREI . . .

(*speaks*) This isn't a love letter to me. This is war. An *homenaje* for Inez? After what she did to me? *Ahora es tarde, Señora . . .* It's late, but perhaps not too late. Vengeance is mine!

She walks off, with new purpose.

BLACKOUT, except for a spot on ANNOUNCER. He has also aged, but he still wears the same awful bow tie. His accent is less Montalban; now he tries to be cool with hip-hop mannerisms.

ANNOUNCER: What's up, Homies? Welcome to the concert no one would have believed could ever happen! I am your host, Armando Chuleta! After all these years, A PESAR DE TODO, we are here tonight to give *homenaje a*—the greatest butt to grace TV LAND—the one and only, the *inCOMParable*—INEZ MADURO!!!

Banda, muy salsera, plays ESE HOMBRE.

Spotlight moves to MAN/BOY, now sexily attired.

DANCERS surround him, moving suggestively.

Suddenly, without warning, from the CAMERA CRANE—

INEZ MADURO appears, looking AMAZING.

When she sings the song, it sounds entirely different, very La India.

She sings referring to Man/Boy.

INEZ: ESE HOMBRE QUE TU VES ALLI

QUE PARECE TAN GALANTE

TAN ATTENTO Y ARROGANTE

LO CONOZCO COMO A MI

ESE HOMBRE QUE TU VES ALLI

QUE APARENTE SER DIVINO

TAN AMABLE Y EFUSIVO

SOLO SABE HACER SUFRIR

Man/Boy begins to dance with one DANCER, then another.

INEZ: HE'S A BIG ASSHOLE,

STUPID INGRATE, IGNORAMUS

EGOTISTIC AND CAPRICIOUS

CLOWNLIKE, EVIL, AVARICIOUS

INCONSISTENT, FULL OF RANCOR

FICKLE, DWARFLIKE, LACKING FEELING

CAUSE HE DOESN'T HAVE A HEART

LLENO DE CELOS

SIN RAZONES NI MOTIVOS

COMO EL VIENTO IMPETUOSO

POCAS VECES CARINOSO

INSEGURO DE SI MISMO

INSOPORTABLE COMO AMIGO

INSUFRIBLE COMO AMOR

The crane deposits her onstage.

She pulls DANCERS away (with many of her martial arts moves) and grabs MAN/BOY. As they salsa—

Just then, by the spotlight, ROCIO appears, resplendent in plunging neckline and slit skirt.

MAN/BOY: SEÑORA!!!

ROCIO: I have returned.

BANDA changes to torch song.

The DANCERS stop.

Announcer grabs the microphone stand.

ANNOUNCER: This is AMAZING. The Battle of Angels has returned to our air waves! The reclusive Rocio has resurfaced here today! Which song reigns supreme?

Rocio sings to the audience, referring to INEZ.

ROCIO: ES UN GRAN NECIA

UN ESTUPIDA INGREIDA

EGOISTA Y CAPRICHOSA

UNA PAYASA VANIDOSA

INCONCIENTE Y PRESUMIDA

FALSA

Inez refers to ROCIO.

INEZ: MALA

ROCIO: ENANA

BOTH: RENCOROSA

QUE NO TIENE CORAZÓN

As the song ends—

Banda joins them as they change to "Muera el amor."

ROCIO: MURDER THE LOVE

THAT TELLS ME

DECEIVES ME

KISSES ME

SPIDERS ME

KILL THE LOVE

THAT STAYS WITH ME

RUNS FROM ME

CRUSHES ME

WEIGHS UPON

DIE THE LOVE

THAT LIES TO ME

PROMISES

PITIES ME

LAUGHS IN MY FACE!!!

Man/Boy responds the only way he can, by singing:

MAN/BOY:

MUERA EL AMOR, QUE ARROJA, QUE

ABRASA, QUE ROBA, QUE ARRASA,

QUE MUERA EL AMOR, QUE QUEMA QUE

HIELA QUE CORRE QUE VUELA

QUE MUERA EL AMOR, QUE DROGA, QUE

AGARRA DESGARRA Y QUE TE HACE FELIZ!

Now Inez grabs her chest:

INEZ: VENENO, VENENO

QUE ESTALLA POR MIS VENAS

COMO UN TRUEÑO.

ROCIO: EXPLODES IN MY VEINS LIKE

THUNDER,

OCEAN SURF AND SMELL OF SKIN

THAT BOILS IN ME WHEN I'M WITH HIM

BOTH: LOVE WITHOUT QUESTIONS,

WITHOUT LIMITS, WITHOUT END

Both ladies take back the song.

The sheer power of their emotion cuts through
Man/Boy with each note/word.

ROCIO: TÚ!!

YOU WHO KISS ME

YOU WHO CRUSH ME

WHO EMBRACE ME

WHO EMBRACE ME

YOU WHO PROMISE ME

YOU WHO LIE TO ME

AND I LOVE YOU

AND I WANT YOU!!!!

ANNOUNCER: Oh my God—

INEZ: TÚ

QUE ME BESAS

QUE ME PESAS

QUE ME ABRAZAS

QUE ME ABRAZAS

QUE PROMETES

QUE ME MIENTES

Y YO TE QUIERO

Y YO TE QUIERO!!!

As the music spirals to climax—
MAN/BOY leaps into the song himself.

ALL: MUERA EL AMOR

MUERA EL AMOR

MUERA EL AMOR!!!!!

All three go to their knees as, behind them—
DOVES fly—either real or on screen.
Dancers fling FLOWERS at them.
The ladies—INEZ first, then ROCIO, then both
take their bows. They have become sisters.
The LADIES EMBRACE!!!
But when they finally turn to MAN/BOY—he is
no longer there.
Everyone is surprised. Where is he?
As they look for him—he is revealed. He has re-
turned to his easy chair. No longer the Maxell
windblown image, he is a man in spiffy clothes,
more comfortable in his body, capable of many
many things.
He turns off the TV. Lights out on STAGE.
He straightens his clothes.

MAN/BOY: AHORA ES TARDE, SEÑORA
AHORA ES TARDE, SEÑORA
INEZ: AHORA NADIE PUEDE
APARTARTE DE MÍ
NOW NO ONE CAN TAKE YOU FROM ME
ROCIO:AHORA NADIE PUEDE
APARTARTE DE MÍ
NOW NO ONE CAN TAKE YOU FROM ME
MAN/BOY: AHORA NADIE PUEDE
APARTARTE DE MÍ
NOW NO ONE CAN TAKE YOU FROM ME
They see each other.
About to exit, he finds Rocio's BOA. Puts it on.
Man/Boy shakes ass Inez Maduro style.
They continue to SING.
As he leaves—

END OF PLAY |ENCORE POSSIBLE

Cast ensemble from the King King
Nightclub production of *Rocio!* 2006.
Photography by Mario Melendez.

Rocio! publicity poster by Guillermo Nericcio García.

Poetry

Blues

Institutions failing us,
armies away policing
strangers, now the rains
and winds of New Orleans
reveal our Union's poverty,
Third World squalor caddy-
corner to the French Quarter,
urban swampland anything
but Big or Easy, swollen,
cramped and pinched and old
as any ghetto in Calcutta,
Juarez or Port au Prince;
City of Marsalis and Bechet,
what music will you make today?

Little Big Poem

My feet are full—if they
Were eyes they'd cry, and not
For pain or sadness, but
For joy, even as they feel
Each second on the skin,
Each toe digging in,
Flying towards the next
Misstep, fearless—nearly.

A Poem

We need to ask ourselves
What's really going on?
We have to look outside
Beyond cliche, behind the media
Defining us without permission,
Without our even knowing . . .
Institutions failing us, not
Looking so not seeing, no vision
So no action, no love left
So no believing . . .
        Don't wait
For institutions, definitions,
Labels, chains that explain
Away our passion, keep us always
On the outside, suck the marrow
From our efforts till we question
What made us write, or act, or
Paint, or even ever want to . . .

What's really going on! ? Ask
Within. Don't speak. Release
The voice inside that knows,
The fingerprinted singularity
Beautiful and terrible, masterful
And rank, the generations
Of our blood, our cry of want
Our secrets buried then
Uncovered by the question

The visionary, bloody, joy-filled
question—what's really going on?

Putting Ana To Bed

The last night has come
and gone, the last lines
said, the last gunshot,
the last tears shed,
the last onstage hearkenings
to our offstage romance,
the last sexual pangs
of underwear and thigh revealed,
the last poetic monologues
as the play is put to bed.
Now, as friends disperse
on early morning planes,
you and Pops and I
stay up as we come down
from heights and depths, from
intoxicants passed beyond
the fourth wall, living,
loving on the skin through
this, and other plays
to come, and come again.

Portland, OR 11/28/04

LGA

The unanswerable questions—
   how long? how much?—
I let melt away.
            She comes
moving heaven, earth and
rehearsal schedules. I wait
unshaven, wild-eyebrowed,
feeling her before she's even here,
calm, but feeling every second
lost against my skin until
our actual inevitable bodies
truly meet, past clothes
and underclothes, beyond
beds and possibly past
the shudder of
 our simultaneous
coming—
            To what? To
the place with no language
other than the serendipities
of breath, my bear-like
grunt, content, my arm
around her waist, my eternal
hard-on against her unmatched
ass, my lips upon the secret
spot discovered the day
we fell, and were lifted, by
the great unanswerable—

And she? What today will
she bring me? What unspeakably
beautiful question? What sigh?
What golden gleam as she
glows by moonlight, attached to me?

To The Artistic Directors
    of SCR (among others)
Have we arrived?
Are we There yet?
(I don't remember
    That we ever left.)
The statement signifies we
somehow went away.
So we've arrived —
What does That mean?
Your mouths move but
are you saying anything?

To a point, I agree
We have arrived (I hope)
From ignorance, stupidity,
From racial generality,
From mainstream invisibility,
Having to apologize or shine
Our way onto your season

~~When all get to the class~~

~~A human life observed~~
~~A sense of humor, freed~~
~~A quirk of language / culture~~
food,

A human life, observed
A sense of humor, freed
A quirk of language
Crash of culture, mangled
melded, made, a
Drama without artifice
un manipulated, There
To be lived in each
latino piece of pop
or art or both

Ni modo —
No matter where we go
This is always here
This is always now
This is always us

We advanced the race —
    The human race —
About five hundred years
Ago, and every day a
little more —

So yes, we're here
We bought the ticket
and we're staying
for the show, to
witness who's arrived

For reals —
Not words but verbs
We're an active audience
We know the getting there
never ends, and
That's okay, 'cause
getting there means
we're alive; the answer
is
And we're very much alive

The question is,
Have you arrived?

Let's hope you're
not there yet.
(dad)

To the Artistic Directors of SCR
(among others)

Have we arrived?
Are we there yet?
   (I don't remember
   that we ever left.)
The statement signifies
we somehow went away.
So we've arrived—
What does that mean?
Your mouths move but
are you saying anything?

To a point, I agree
we have arrived (I hope)
from ignorance, stupidity,
from racial generality,
from mainstream invisibility,
having to apologize or shine
our way onto your season.

A human life observed.
A sense of humor, freed.
A quirk of language,
crash of culture, mangled
melded, made, a
Drama without artifice,
unmanipulated, there to
be lived in each latino
piece of pop or art
or both—

Ni modo—
No matter where we go
This is always HERE
This is always NOW
This is always US.

We advanced the race—
the human race—about
five hundred years ago,
and every day a little more.

So yes, we're here.
We bought a ticket and
we're staying for the show,
to witness who's arrived
for reals—

Not words but verbs—
we're an active audience—
we know the getting there
never ends, and that's
okay, 'cause getting there
means we're alive; the answer
is we're very much alive.

The question is,
   Have you arrived?

Feb 28, 2005

Oliver Mayer with his wife, the actress Marlene Forte, Los Angeles, CA. Janurary 2008.

Last Words/Smörgåsbord: The Odyssey of a Mexican American Playwright through L.A. Boxing Gyms, Cornell, Oxford, Columbia, U.S.C. and Bust

One Last Conversation with Oliver Mayer and William A. Nericcio

William A. Nericcio: You are a tad on the young side for a book of your collected works. Does this mean that the glory days are done and that OLIVER MAYER, whose collected papers are now housed at Stanford University Libraries, is ready to hang it up? Or is there still more fire in that belly, more blade for the heat?

Oliver Mayer: Actually, in my head, this is really Volume One of my collected works! I have a lot of fight left in me. I'm not as fast as I used to be, but I hit twice as hard. Plus I've learned some some pretty mean tricks from Pier-Six brawls along the way with both champs and chumps. As a writer and a person, I feel like I'm coming into my prime. So no hanging the gloves—or pen—up just yet. These are my "young" plays. The trial by fire, coming of age, testing the mettle of the metal type of plays. *Young Valiant* was written when I was about twenty-one. *Blade to the Heat* happened at 27-28 or so. *Joy of the Desolate* comes from my mid-30s. And *Bananas and Peachfuzz* and *Rocio* were written in my 39th year. It's an amazing cross-section, a rather blushingly staggering walk through my life, but the themes are unmistakable.

WN: *They sure are: mother love; father love, and loss; the brutality of physical conflict always married to the chance of sensual pleasure—I wonder, can you talk about this last thing: the fusion of violence (the test or quest) and pleasure in your works . . . let's start with YOUNG VALIANT.*

OM: Love matters. It's worth fighting for. It's also messy, unexpected, dangerous. If you don't get it right, people can get hurt. In YOUNG VALIANT I went to the source. It started, literally, as a Valentine to my mom. Just a scene I wrote for fun, a memory of my dad at the refrigerator. My dad loved my mom so much he couldn't stop talking or thinking about her. Theirs was a love connection you couldn't separate with a crowbar. Except that I was there—the product of their sexual and love union. Almost immediately, and completely without planning, the play began to get away from my personal memories and become mythic. The boy in question would have to challenge Mom and Dad in elemental ways, and the whole house would shake on its foundations. Names grew unimportant—they became larger than life MOM, DAD, and BOY. Their house would move away from photographic naturalism into a dramatic space with fabulous implications;

bed and kitchen and wall would take on meaning beyond themselves. The questions raised would become unanswerable but unrelentingly sought after.

I have always been highly dissatisfied with OEDIPUS as a play, inflential as it may be. I love the mistaken identity stuff, the incest, the transgression, the terrible conflicted feelings. But I hate the conclusions, the suicide and locusts and tearing out of eyes. Too easy! My retelling of the myth demanded that the players in question not give up on each other. Despite terrible emotional and, yes, physical violence, they had to stay in the game. That's the truth about families. You don't choose them—they choose you. Love is very much that way, too.

WN: *Speaking of Love and Choices, that gives us a perfect segue to the beautiful and painful dynamics found lurking on the page and on the stage with JOY OF THE DESOLATE—I wonder if you might want to talk with our readers about the similarities and differences between, say, the young boy, mother-loving MIXED-BLOODED CHICANO protagonist in YOUNG VALIANT and the young man NATIVE AMERICAN mother-loving, obsessed college student in JOY.*

OM: It's the dramatic education of a young man seen through the crisis points of sexual awakening. A man's relationship to his mother is pretty important—ask any woman or man who loves him if you don't believe me. If he screws up that seminal relationship, then what happens when he falls in love with someone? Both plays obsess a bit on Mom because the male lead is young; the deepest love he's yet experienced is mother love. Mom is an even deeper concept when you talk about Chicanos and Native Americans; there's a syncretism at play—one thing inside another. Mom is a goddess, a sorceress, and the big crime boss of the family, no matter who she might be in everyday reality. Mom is Mary, and Coatilicue too.

Chicanos and Native Americans live amongst such conundra. They (we) are tied generationally to our country's land, yet they are pushed culturally to the fringes. They live plurally—we all do, but it's even more richly dramatic and a little schizoid, too, for them. This cultural collision is eminently worthy of a play.

There's another imbedded reality at play. The ghost of the father inhabits both plays. This may sound weird in YOUNG VALIANT where DAD is such a vibrant character. But his mutability is the key. In JOY, the father's death is the first thing that happens - in essence the point of departure for D.C.'s coming of age. It's also the only purely non-fictional moment in the play. I got the same call on my third day at Cornell as a freshman. I guess that helped me come of age, too.

WN: And then, after YOUNG VALIANT and JOY OF THE DESOLATE, a funny thing happened on the way to the forum for an L.A. ex-pat: BLADE TO THE HEAT; it is 1994, right? And Oliver Mayer's play is opening up at the Public Theatre, directed by George C. Wolfe, and reviewed in the pages of Time (sweet) and Newsweek (savage) and movie rights bought up by Madonna— I wonder if you could take us back to those heady days of wine and roses and tell us how the impact of national recognition affected the trajectory of your career, and, perhaps, more importantly, how it altered your approach to writing for the theatre. Lastly, could you hazard a guess as to why it was BLADE that hit with the punch it did?

OM: BLADE was a gift from the sky. I felt like Willie Mays making that basket catch way out in center field. The play has always pumped with adrenal power unaided by steroids, fueled by fears and secrets and sexed up by hot music and boom bodies. When done right, it tends to take the roof off theaters and the top off people's heads.

Going into production, I toiled with the somewhat naïve belief that all I really had to do was write the play. I don't remember the reviews; this is a bit of a defense mechanism on my part, but also a policy derived from reading hatchet jobs and witnessing injustices done to innocent hard-working artists just trying to do the best they can. I don't write for reviewers; I write for me first, for those I love second, and for connection with curious theatre-goers locally and globally third.

National recognition is a funny thing, because at least for me nothing changed. It's just as hard to get a play done, maybe harder. I met some great people because of BLADE. It is a beautiful when someone comes up and lets me know what the play meant to them personally. The L.A. production was a real apotheosis—unforgettable moments onstage, galvanizing music by East L.A. Taiko, masterful direction by the late Ron Link. If I get hit by a bus tomorrow, at least I had that. Of course, I want more apotheoses!

WN: So give us a Hollywood story or two—name names, spill the beans; and then, tell us about what happens to Willie Mays AFTER the catch, after the hit, after the big-time; what did that kind of success so young do to Oliver Mayer?

OM: That's a Hollywood no-no! No kiss and tell! Deny deny deny! I know you want the dirt on Madonna, who bought the rights to make the film of BLADE. The reality is amazingly unromantic, really. I got a couple of gigs, met some famous folks. The best part of having done a show on the big stage(s) is that I now know for sure that it doesn't matter. I have had as good or better productions in 30-seat hole-in-the-walls. I didn't make a cent on those, but I've learned not to evaluate my theatre experiences in terms of money. It has to be about something else. I just got an email from a young man in São Paulo, who asked for permission to translate BLADE into Portuguese for production. I said yes on condition he invites me to the opening. That's gonna be fun! I recently talked to the great South African actor John Kani about a production of BLADE in the late 90s that never made it to opening night. He told me that the play was simply too hot for those revolutionary times. I promptly gave him the text. Maybe now it's just hot enough.

WN: All right, since you won't come clean with the goods, since you won't anoint your hungry readers without even an ounce of chisme, let's take it in a different direction, but don't think I won't circle back—this book is being published with HYPERBOLE Books, and you gotta know with a tagline "buy the hype" that we're gonna work you for the money shot, seduce you maybe for some sweet tasty dirt. For now, however, I will retain a quasi-academic guise (think Professor Kingston from the PAPER CHASE, with a Laredo accent) and ask you about actors and directors, maybe staying on the terrain of

BLADE TO THE HEAT—can you talk to us about different directions the play has taken in the voices, bodies and guises of different actors; the choices, cuts, and visions of different directors?

OM: I'm leading a workshop this month on rewriting, which is not an easy thing to do. I learned a great deal about revision from the BLADE experience. Robert Egan gave me initial support and encouraged me to write the Mantequilla monologue in Miami. George C. Wolfe and Morgan Jenness urged me to cut the fat, the meat, and some of the bone for the world premiere. That hurt; I needed time to recuperate. In the ensuing year, Ron Link urged me to find my original intentions for the Taper revised version, and I'll thank him forever for that. The play was originally called THE TEARS WILL TELL IT ALL (from a kickass Jackie Wilson song). Wolfe made me change the title, and somehow that affected the tone and mood of the whole piece. Link allowed me to replace THE TEARS back into BLADE. The version we're publishing hopefully brings it all back home, as Dylan might say.

As for actors, Paul Calderon won an Obie for a sparkling Mantequilla in New York. He boxed so well that a trainer asked him if he wanted to go pro. In L.A., I think about the mercurial Ray Cruz, whose Vinal changed nightly and who literally vaulted over the ring ropes. He gave me gray hairs, but I loved watching him work. I also think about a young Wayne Brady, new in town, understudying Garnet and blowing us away with the singing and improv skills he'd later use on WHOSE LINE IS IT ANYWAY? There's a reason why Madonna was so attracted to this piece in her day. It was ripe with hot R&B and Latin music, sex, violence, and extreme, exotic, one-of-a-kind moments, and it made no apologies for demanding the staggering talents of its players.

Let me take a moment to thank every actor who has attempted this play. It is a workout in more ways than one. The emotional gymnastics are as hard as the boxing. But that incredibly dangerous openness is what I'm driving at with BLADE, and with the other plays, too.

A successful director once said to me, "Oliver, your plays make me blush." She meant this to cut me, but I take it as one of the great compliments in my life. I do mean to make myself, my actors, my director, and the audience blush with self-recognition. The blood flows faster than the million defense mechanisms which pass for art and intelligence.

WN: So, what makes YOU blush?

OM: Fear. Whether it's the first day of school, the first time looking into the eyes of a beautiful girl, the first time getting work rejected, getting caught in a lie, running out of gas—literally on the freeway, or running out of breath in the ring—all these and a million more little and big fears that I will come up short. It's the fear of being revealed as less than wonderful, less than all-knowing—less than. In life, I blush a lot. I've learned on the page to push through the burning red ears of embarrassment and fear by seeing what happens next, by not cutting away but staying with whatever is being revealed and trying to reveal more. Thanks to my training (particularly with Howard Stein), I've come to trust blushing as a kind of diviner of the blood consciousness just beneath the surface. In essence, what's really going on. I strive to get out of my skin when I write for the stage; blushing reveals that can never happen, but strains at breaking through the membrane despite all.

I've been thinking a lot about what a play is—or better yet, what a play can be. My car didn't start the other day, and as I sat waiting for it to turn over I wrote in my little book that a play is a dramatic question, imperfect, raw. The striving for an answer is the art, the poetry, the insight. I like the plays that strive the hardest without achieving the full answer. I distrust the plays which proclaim to have the answers because I don't believe anything worth really asking can be answered satisfactorily except through living every moment, having sex, falling in love, shrugging at mortality, and not knowing. Still I'll try.

WN: *From the page to the stage, from paper to the body, an incredible metamorphosis takes place in the utter alienation (in the strict sense, transfer of property) of a piece of theater writing from the playwright through the director to the actors. I wonder if you might tell us of some of the surprises that have occurred to you and for you along the way—directors that revealed something you never knew, actors who showed you sites in your work unknown to you the writer.*

OM: Well, in the Mexico City production of BLADE, everybody got naked. The shower scene created buzz in several productions, but at the Teatro Lirico the director was not satisfied with one naked man. He had a working shower in which just about every male actor lathered up and washed the sweat off. That was a case of quantity over quality. In JOY OF THE DESOLATE, my friend Geraint Wyn Davies found time in his amazingly busy life to direct the play in Chicago. He found a yearning that is deeper than I realized. It lies in the music, and in his production approached a kind of rapture which he was able to tie to mother love and the terrible, sometimes suicidal desires of young people. I'm hoping for more director revelations. I'm planning a production of YOUNG VALIANT in Los Angeles this summer (2005) with the very talented and beautiful Marlene Forte as MAMA, and my U.S.C. colleague Jack Rowe directing. I'd love to see us really dig into the myth of this play, and if it's possible, outdistance OEDIPUS, which is a play that has always really pissed me off. I don't believe in gouging out eyes and bringing down locusts—except maybe for the current Bush presidency—and I'm positive that healing begins in the now, among adults. Jack is a man of great life experience, and I expect him to shed new light on all three journeys—but DAD's especially.

WN: I hate to ask this question, because it is always the question asked of writers; it is so damned cliché. But then I was reading a novel last summer, THE BIOGRAPHER'S TALE, by A. S. Byatt, and in the middle of a passage on natural selection, she segued into a prose riff on clichés being the semantic equivalent of a crocodile, sticking around because they had stood, through some odd version of linguistic determinism, the test of time; so brace for incoming.....your work is filled with absent and present, invisible and "pregnant" fathers, and, because I know you personally, I know what a deep role your father played in your life, so tell me, tell us, tell us about your father and your

work and your fathers and your work... and when you are done, how about some of the literary fathers AND mothers that populate Oliver Mayer's imagination . . . Saroyan's in there, right? and Tennessee Williams?

OM: My father died over twenty years ago, and I still think about him nearly every day. I idolized him on many levels; he was the very definition of a man: lover, fighter, artist, intellectual, laborer, connoisseur. He cried his eyes out every time he heard Rodolfo's aria from LA BOHEME—for a big strong guy, he cried a lot. It's hard to think about him without thinking about my mother, who I'm glad to say is alive and well. They had a union, not simply a marriage. As their child, I had this amazing vista into love, jealousy, sex, loyalty, and the million consequences of sharing a life with another body. I can't help but write about it. Since then, I've had a succession of art fathers. Saroyan is a biggie, as is Shakespeare. Valdez, Piñero, Peter Weiss. D.H. Lawrence, Robert Hayden. Bach to Donny Hathaway, Prokofiev to Jackie Wilson. I guess I'm a bit of an eternal son in that way. I like to sit at the old man's knee and pick up the old school moves.

WN: And, mothers, what of them? Can you whisper a bit about the role your mother played in your development as a man and as a writer—are their mother-diva writers whose pressure we should look for between the lines in your scripts?

OM: I've been a longtime follower of Robert Graves' THE WHITE GODDESS—except that my goddesses aren't always white. I started as a poet, and recently have been again writing poems to my very own personal goddess.

As for Mom, she's deep in my plays. I've written versions of her in BLADE, YOUNG VALIANT, and other plays—but not in JOY. That was a kind of anti-Mom at play. YOUNG VALIANT began as a valentine—a real Valentines Day valentine—to my mom, a memory of Dad and me at the refrigerator. It's a good way to write! I love the idea of plays as valentines to the ones you love and desire: dead, alive, or lost.

Oliver Mayer, 1996.

Mark Taper Forum Program
for *Blade to the Heat*

An Evening With
Oliver Mayer

Wednesday, November 11, 1998 7:00pm in Family Studies 108
A small reception with refreshments will be held briefly before the event

A 1998 public lecture poster promoting
Joy of the Desolate at SDSU.

Despedida: Some Brief, Scattered,
Last Ruminations on the Work of
Oliver Mayer

William A. Nericcio

In its beginnings, this collection would have been a labor of love, sweat, anger, angst, and jubilation by the would-be professor of an aspiring playwright; what it is in the here and now will be for you, gentle reader, to determine.

Back in 1986 I was the graduate teaching and research assistant to Carlos Fuentes, the greatest Mexican writer yet to be blessed by the Swedish French-kisses of Nobel and his prize.

One of my students was a tall, lanky kid with the face of an angel and the sass of a grifter—he turned out to be a Chicano mutt from L.A. (not East L.A. but from Studio City in the Valley), and, eventually, he turned out to be a pretty damned good playwright, writer, and U.S.C. professor by the name of Oliver Mayer.

The pages of this volume house the fruits of our surreal, improvised collaborations over the years—from the time I left Ithaca for my first gig at Storrs, Connecticut, at the University of Connecticut, to my present incarnation as a film studies scholar and chair of an English and Comparative Literature department at San Diego State University.

Since 1988 I have been bringing Oliver Mayer in to meet and hang out with my students—teaching his plays, sharing his West Coast visions, and immersing my literature students in the ins and outs of life in the American theater.

In the early years, there were no published scripts of his works to distribute for the students to prepare. Mayer and I concocted a shadowy publication company by the name of *La Prensa de la Vanidad* (Vanity Press, natch) so that we could distribute his works to the students with some vestige of legitimacy. Mayer visited U.Conn. to the delights of my students then, and I still remember the after-class parties we used to stage at Ted's Pub, a Storrs fixture, where students and playwright and professor alike would delight to the age-old charms of ale, lies, literature, gossip, flirtation, and outrage.

"Glory Days," Bruce Springsteen calls them, and they were in a way—I was a 26-year-old professor with a Ph.D. from Cornell; Oliver was 23, a Columbia University M.F.A. student in playwrighting. Somehow a Mexican-American kid from Laredo, Texas, and his Chicano *carnal/* undergraduate from Los Angeles had stumbled onto a lifelong collaboration that would change each of our lives forever. We owe Carlos Fuentes big *besos y abrazos* for bringing our destinies together.

"OH, MOTHER, I FEEL TERRIBLE. THE DRUG THAT DRIVES MEN TO MADNESS HAS BEEN GIVEN ME AND I DON'T KNOW WHAT AWFUL THINGS I'VE DONE UNDER ITS SPELL."

Here, Foster's illustration from *Prince Valiant* takes on added significance in light of Mayer's dramatic recasting of related issues in *Young Valiant*.

Harold Foster, *Prince Valiant*, Sunday November 12, 1967 (single panel) © King Features Sydicate. The Swann Collection of Caricature & Cartoon, New York. This panel is cited in Judith O'Sullivan's *The Art of the Comic Strip: Catalog of An Exhibit at the University of Maryland Art Gallery, April 1-May 9, 1971*, p.45.

One of the xeroxed resource file pages from the *Prensa de la Vanidad* edition of *Young Valiant*.

I remembered how it worked—and it worked for close to two decades: Oliver would mail and then, later (high-tech Aztecs), email me his working scripts; I would lay these out and format and typeset them (or just xerox them) and take them to a copyshop. I would add a couple a bucks a copy to cover Mayer's honorarium or travel expenses and sell them to my students. After his readings and the ensuing discussions in my classes, we would retire to some campus-area pub where Mayer would inculcate theater into my young charges (we were young then, too, of course), and my students would get to hang out with a writer whom Madonna (believe me, she was *big* at the time) wanted to direct.

And the rest, as they say, is showbiz.

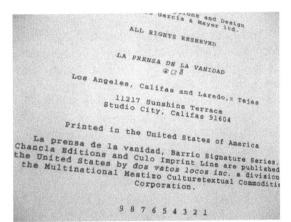

A copywright page from a *Prensa de la Vanidad* Mayer/Nericcio project in literary larceny.

But don't let the informality, would-be larceny, and Dionysian-laced excess of the scene confuse you: this was the University at its best—its most exciting, collaborative, inventive, and compelling.

Years later when Mayer was selected to teach at U.S.C., I used to laugh to myself that the wily Angeleno owed me tons of bucks for his decades-long paid appren-

ticeship—those years of lecturing S.D.S.U. and U.Conn. undergraduates, semester after semester, year after year, had given this maven of the typewriter, an insider's education, the run of the house, and he, of course, had made the best of it.

ii.

But the years pass. Now Mayer's a legitimate force in American theater, and I am a reasonably legitimate professor and chair of English and Comparative Literature, with plausibly stable sidelines in film and cultural studies scholarship and book editing and designing with SDSU Press. We had to grow up, and in this volume I think you hold the product of that maturation.

Mayer's *oeuvre* reveals a top-shelf imagination—a knowing eye for culture and gender, a savvy wit, a Freud-laced comedic sensibility, and one of the first American writers in the theater to simultaneously deal with issues of ethnicity, gender, sexuality, and aesthetics. Mayer's plays have the inventive irony of Quentin Tarantino's screenplays, but *with* the righteous (not self-righteous) vision of a Spike Lee, the sublime ear-to-the-pulse instincts for Latina/o cultural metamorphosis of a Luis Valdez, but with an earthy all-American lustiness of a Charles Bukowski. But where the debauchery of Bukowski grew tedious and predictable at times toward the end of his tenure as our American poet-laureate of the bowery, Mayer's plays are more provocative, less resolved, more prone to oscillation—we see that the Man/Boy of *Rocio* is like some odd, next-generation revision of Boy from *Young Valiant*, still hungering for the Mother figure(s) or the Mother herself (no writer does better spins on Jocasta than Oliver Mayer). But this "Boy" is more like the boys or the men, or, for that matter, the butterflies, one finds in the writings of Cuban *escritor* Severo Sarduy—illusory beings between sexes, between sex, who willingly leap into the throes of life with a passion for costume, camouflage, dissembling and simulation.[16] Mayer emerges in his later writing as an inheritor of Sarduy's mantle with plays that defy any essentialist vision of America.

Oliver Mayer could have easily emerged as American Theater's Chicano boy wonder—and in plays like *Young Valiant* and *The Road to Los Angeles* he has made good on that promise. But that may, in the end, be *the least* of his achievements, for in his work and in this volume one encounters a sensual *Mayerian* universe of peoples and sexes that remains true to the *omniracial, hermaphrosexual* panoply of the Americas: from the Afro-Carribean characters in *Blade to the Heat* to the Native American lead in *Joy of the Desolate*; from the Irish pater familias in *Young Valiant* to the Pan-Latina/o hybrids in *Bananas and Peachfuzz*, Mayer's readers and audiences experience the fertile cornucopia of our Americas.[17]

---

[16] For more on this, see César Augusto Salgado's "Hybridity in New World Baroque Theory," *Journal of American Folklore* 445 (1999), 316-31 or the passages indexed on Sarduy in *Tex[t]-Mex: Seductive Hallucination of the "Mexican" in America* cited above.

---

[17] The hermeneutic legacy of dramatic studies focused on Latina/o authorship is being written as you read this footnote. For book-length studies in this field don't miss Yolanda Broyles-Gonzaléz's *El Teatro Campesino: Theater in the Chicano Movement* (Austin: University of Texas Press, 1994); Jorge Huerta's *Chicano Drama: Performance, Society Myth* (Cambridge: Cambridge University Press, 2000); and Diana Taylor's & Juan Villegas's *Negotiating Performance: Gender, Sexuality, and Theatricality in Latin/o America* (Durham: Duke University Press, 1994). Articles of note in this area over the years include: Anne Cruz's "Postmodern and Cultural Criticism: Chicano, Latin American, Luso-Brazilian, Spanish, and U. S. Latino Theaters," *Gestos: Teoria y Practica del Teatro Hispanico*, (1994) 9 (17); Bradley J. Nelson's "Pedro Monge-Rafuls and the Mapping of the (Postmodern?) Subject in Latino Theater," *Gestos: Teoria y Practica del Teatro Hispánico*, (1997), 12:24, 135-48; Melissa Fitch Lockhart's "Queer Representations in Latino Theatre," *Latin American Theatre Review* (1998) 31(2): 4, 67-78; María Teresa Marrero's "Out of the Fringe: Desire and Homosexuality in

One magic night stays in my memory—opening night for *Blade to the Heat* at the Mark Taper Forum in downtown Los Angeles. It is that most uncanny of theater nights—uncanny in the deepest Freudian sense where everything is familiar and, simultaneously, everything is strange. I am outside the Forum caught up in the circus-like atmosphere. And I am surrounded by an unusual "mob" for a theater opening: in front of me is a large boxing ring, with amateur boxers sparring in real time—the blood, the sweat, the bell, the heat is all very real. Boxers are here, as are their fans, watching duels with gloves and blows with sweat like some old-school Madison Square Garden scene—there amongst the throngs of theater-goers are agents, fighters, trainers, managers, and producers from the West Coast elite of boxing. This is not theater—or, better said, this is not *the* theater as I came to know it in the United States, where seas of retired blue-haired subscribers set the tone and pace for the American stage. But get this—these lovely ladies, Taper-subscribers all, are there, too, standing there laughing and reveling in the cultural bacchanal alongside the boxing fans.

There's a third constituency present for the opening of *Blade to the Heat*, as large and representative cohorts from the *crème de la crème* of Los Angeles's gay and lesbian coalitions are out in force, too—Pedro Quinn's sexual, existential odyssey a lure to a community in L.A. still at times forced to find their entertainments off the main stages of SoCal's finest venues. Boxers, bluehairs, and the LGBT elite all together—

the '90s Latino Theatre," *Latin American Theatre Review* (1999) 32:2, 87-103; Michelle Habell-Pallán's "'Don't Call Us Hispanic': Popular Latino Theater in Vancouver (174-89) in *Latino/a Popular Culture*. Michelle Habell-Pallán & Mary Romero, editors (New York: New York University Press, 2002); Teresa M. Marrero's "Teresa Out of the Fringe: Desire and Homosexuality in the 1990s Latino Theater" (283-94) in Alicia Gaspar de Alba's *Velvet Barrios: Popular Culture & Chicana/o Sexualities* (New York, NY: Palgrave Macmillan, 2003); Claudia Villegas-Silva's "Chicano/Latino Theater Today" (III: 427-33) in *Literary Cultures of Latin America: A Comparative History, I: Configurations of Literary Culture; II: Institutional Modes and Cultural Modalities; III: Latin American Literary Culture: Subject to History*. Valdés, Mario J. & Kadir, Djelal eds. (Oxford, England: Oxford UP, 2004); and, last but not least, both Caridad Svich's "U.S. Polyglot Latino Theatre and Its Link to the Americas," *Contemporary Theatre Review: An International Journal* (2006) 16 (2): 189-97 and her "Re-Mapping Latino Theatre: American Playwrights on the Edge of the Edge," *Theatre Forum* (2005) 27: 94-96. Critics, please understand that this short catalogue is a mere truncated prolegomena to a bibliography of contemporary studies of Latinas and Latinos in American theater and drama criticism.

blacks, Chicanas/os, Latinas/os, whites, Asian-Americans, and more sprinkled throughout any and all of the three clusters of humanity here together and digging the *scene* of Oliver Mayer's play.

Retelling the tale of that opening night feels a bit apocryphal, but it nonetheless happened that magic night in downtown Los Angeles, a night when the scribblings of a talented American of Mexican descent, and the ensemble talents of the Mark Taper Forum, under the steady hand of Ron Link, *Blade to the Heat's* late, fine West Coast director, brought together constituencies that very often ignore each other at best, and actively seek to avoid each other at worst.

This edited volume of *hurt*, then, reveals a pretty serious *business*—the emergence in American arts and letters, the surfacing in American theater, of a red, white, and blue original whose soul bleeds brown, and whose blood is as hot as the Latino stereotype would have it, but whose imagination has the precision and elegance of a very *Euro* Swiss watch channeled through the intellectual cauldron of a formidable Mexican of American descent. In the end, we are the recipients of a gift—a set of works that allow us to rethink the future of theater in a volatile, dynamic, and unpredictable 21st-century—a gift very much like Frida Kahlo's "ribbon wrapped around a bomb," from Oliver Mayer, *my* friend, *our* very American playwright.

The first draft of the cover of *The Hurt Business* by Guillermo Nericcio García, 2005.

Contributors' Notes

Geraint Wyn Davies

Geraint Wyn Davies was 12 when he was first bitten by the acting bug, appearing in a school production of "Lord of the Flies." His professional stage debut was made in 1976 in Quebec City when at 19 he appeared in "The Fantasticks", "Red Emma," and "A Midsummer's Night Dream." After Quebec, Geraint moved on England where he played the lead in "The Last Englishman." He then spent 2 seasons with Wales' leading theatre company, Theatre Clwyd, touring the United Kingdom in "Enemy of the People" and "Hamlet". It was his performance in "Hamlet" that led to the Regional Theatre Best Actor Award. Most recently Geraint appeared at Washington DC's "Shakespeare Theater in "Cyrano (a Helen Hayes Award winner), "Love's Labor's Lost," and "Richard III." Geraint's directorial accomplishments include multiple episodes of "Forever Knight," "Black Harbour," "Pit Pony," "Power Play," and "North of 60." In June 2000, Geraint took on the challenge of directing Oliver Mayer's "Joy of the Desolate" in Highland Park, Illinois. A "back-burner" project for Geraint is "Horatio Salt", a collection of four short films that he is producing and directing.

Jorge Huerta

Dr. Jorge Huerta holds the Chancellor's Associates Endowed Chair III as Professor of Theatre at the University of California, San Diego. In January of 2005 Huerta was appointed Associate Chancellor and Chief Diversity Officer by Chancellor Marye Anne Fox. He is also a professional director and a leading authority on contemporary Chicano and U.S. Latino theatre. Dr. Huerta has published many articles and reviews in journals and anthologies. He has edited three anthologies of plays: *El Teatro de la Esperanza: An Anthology of Chicano Drama* (1973); *Nuevos Pasos: Chicano and Puerto Rican Drama* (1979, 1989), with Nicolas Kanellos); and *Necessary Theatre: Six Plays About the Chicano Experience* (1987, 2005). Huerta published the first book about Chicano theatre, *Chicano Theatre: Themes and Forms* (1982) now in its second edition. Huerta's latest book, *Chicano Drama: Society, Performance, and Myth*, was published by Cambridge University Press in late 2000.

Natsuko Ohama

Natsuko Ohama is one of the premier voice teachers in the country. Trained under legendary Master Kristin Linklater at the Working Theatre, she is a founding member and permanent faculty of Shakespeare and Company Lenox, Mass., and senior artist at Pan Asian Rep New York. Natsuko is currently a lecturer in performance at USC School of Theatre; she has taught at numerous institutions all over the country including the NYU Experimental Theater Wing, Cal Arts, Columbia University, the Sundance Institute, New Actors Workshop, the Stratford Festival, and was the Director of Training at the National Arts Center of Canada. She also has an extensive workshop and private teaching practice. A Drama Desk nominated actress, she has portrayed roles ranging from Juliet to Lady Macbeth from Hamlet to Prospero (Los Angeles Women's Shakespeare Company) from action films to the cult series "Forever Knight" and *American Playhouse* on PBS. She has been seen on screen in *Pirates of the Caribbean 2* , and on stage at the Kirk Douglas Theatre in *Dogeaters* as Imelda Marcos.

Tommy Tompkins

As an emancipated minor he left the East Coast and Ivy League for California where he fought the law, with predictable results. He worked as a letter carrier, autoworker, cabbie, and songwriter, and spent two decades working in the alternative press, the last 13 years as arts editor at *The San Francisco Bay Guardian.* In August, he traded that position for a loft in Los Angeles. He won a Sundance Arts Writing Fellowship and is about to enter the Antioch University's M.F.A. program in creative non-fiction. He loves the work of José Rivera, Rappin' 4-Tay, Campo Santo, Søren Kierkegaard, Philip Gotanda, Suzan-Lori Parks, Esther Phillips, Denis Johnson, Tony Kushner, Hisaye Yamamoto, Alvin Lu, Naomi Iizuka, Paris, William Maxwell, John Coltrane, Walter Mosley, Too Short, Prince, and Exene Cervenka. And—work or no work—he loves Karen Amano, his seven Abyssinian cats, Michael Tompkins, and certain controlled substances. He was born without mid-range responses, and has led his life accordingly.

Raymond Salcedo

Raymond Salcedo is a graduate student in the Ph.D. program in literature at the University of California, San Diego. He presently is living and teaching in Europe.

Howard Stein

After 38 years of university teaching and administrating, Howard Stein retired from Columbia University in 1992. His career included 11 years at the Yale School of Drama, where he was Associate Dean and Supervisor of the Playwriting Program; seven years at the University of Iowa, where he supervised the Playwriting Program; and 10 years at Columbia University where he was appointed the first permanent Chairman of the Oscar Hammerstein II Center for Theatre Studies and Supervisor of the Playwriting Program. Stein's plays have appeared in *The Best One-Act Plays of 1951-52* and *The Best Short Plays of 1959-60*. Harcourt Brace published his book, *A Time to Speak* in 1974 and Scribner's recently published his essay on James M. Barry in their British Writers series. Dr. Stein's essays on dramatic criticism, dramatic literature, theatre history, and dramaturgy have appeared in a host of journals since the 1950's. He has directed National Endowment Summer Seminars for College Teachers 10 times since 1979. Although he is currently retired, until 1997 he recently visited the USC School of Theatre to work with their MFA playwrights. Howard presently lives the good life in Connecticut with his lovely and vivacious wife, Marianne.

Caridad Svich

Caridad Svich is a playwright-songwriter-translator and editor of Cuban-Spanish, Argentine, and Croatian descent. She is the recipient of a Harvard/Radcliffe Institute for Advanced Study Bunting fellowship, and a TCG/Pew National Theatre Artist Grant. Recently premiered: her play *Iphigenia...a rave fable*,7 Stages (Atlanta); *Antigone Arkhe*,The Women's Project (NY); her multimedia collaboration (with T. Cerveris & N. Philipppou) *The Booth Variations* at 59 East 59th Street Theatre (NY); and her version of Lorca's *The House of Bernarda Alba* at the Pearl Theatre (NY). Other plays include *Alchemy of Desire/Dead-Man's Blues, Any Place But Here, Fugitive Pieces, and Twelve Ophelias)*. She is editor of *Trans-global Readings: Crossing Theatrical Boundaries*, (Manchester Univ. Press/Palgrave). She is co-editor of *Conducting a Life: Reflections on the Theatre of Maria Irene Fornes* (Smith & Kraus), *Out of the Fringe* (TCG), and *Theatre in Crisis?* (MUP/Palgrave). Some of her translations are collected in *Federico García Lorca: Impossible Theater* (Smith & Kraus). She holds an M.F.A. from U.C.S.D., and is resident playwright of New Dramatists. She is on the advisory committee of *Contemporary Theatre Review* (Routledge/UK), and contributing editor of *TheatreForum*.

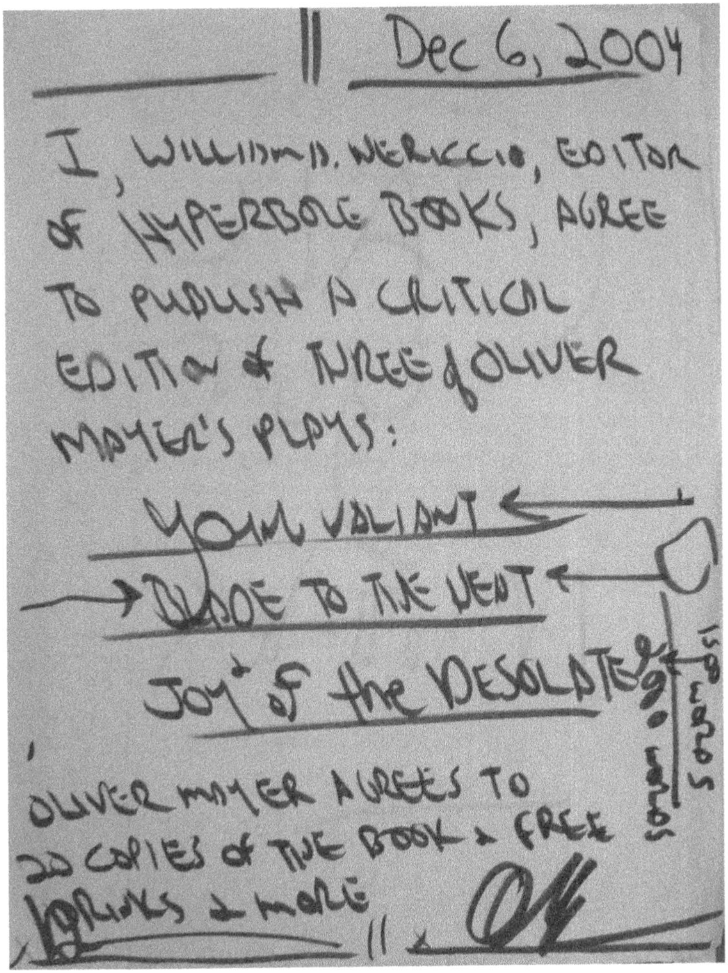

Dec 6, 2004

I, WILLIAM A. NERICCIO, EDITOR OF HYPERBOLE BOOKS, AGREE TO PUBLISH A CRITICAL EDITION OF THREE OF OLIVER MAYER'S PLAYS:

YOUNG VALIANT

BLADE TO THE HEAT

JOY of the DESOLATE

OLIVER MAYER AGREES TO 20 COPIES OF THE BOOK & FREE DRINKS & MORE

This book was dutifully typeset in Gentium, Tuesday, April 1, 2008 by Guillermo Nericcio García in
San Diego, California. "Gentium is a typeface family designed to enable the diverse ethnic
groups around the world who use the Latin and Greek scripts to produce readable,
high-quality publications. It supports a wide range of Latin-based alphabets and
includes glyphs that correspond to all the Latin ranges of Unicode. The design
is crafted so as to be highly readable, reasonably compact, and visually
attractive. The additional 'extended' Latin letters are designed to
naturally harmonize with the traditional 26 ones. Diacritics are
treated with careful thought and attention to their use.
Expansion of the character set to include more
extended Latin glyphs, archaic Greek
symbols, and full Cyrillic script
support is underway."

textmex.blogspot.com

memo@sdsu.edu

scripts.sil.org